BUILDING OUR FUTURE....

First Grade Religious Education class.

The Nativity Youth Ministry Group at The Munster Center for the Performing Arts

Marian Shrine

2005 Watermelon Mess at Nativity School

Working together to become the
Body of Christ in Portage....
Our part in His Story continues....

In the Presence of Angels

A History of

The Diocese of Gary

By Dominic V. Bertino

I thank you, Lord, with all my heart,
you have heard the words of my mouth,
In the presence of angels I will bless you.
I will adore before your holy temple.
(Ps. 138:1)

Commemorative window in the sacristy of Bishop Grutka's residence.

PUBLISHER
Éditions du Signe
B.P. 94
67038 Strasbourg - France
Tel: 011 333 88 78 91 91
Fax: 011 333 88 78 91 99
Email: info@editionsdusigne.fr

PUBLISHING DIRECTOR
Christian Riehl

DIRECTOR OF PUBLICATION
Joëlle Bernhard

PUBLISHING ASSISTANT
Audrey Gilger

DESIGN AND LAYOUT
Juliette Roussel
Sylvie Tusinski

PHOTOGRAPHY
John Glover

PHOTOENGRAVING
Atelier du Signe - 106601

ISBN-10: 2-7468-1415-3
ISBN-13: 978-2-7468-1415-8

Printed in China

Bishop of Gary

DIOCESE OF GARY

9292 BROADWAY
MERRILLVILLE, IN 46410-7088

219-769-9292
FAX: 219-769-2066

January 2007

Dear Brothers and Sisters in Christ,

Fifty years ago, Pope Pius XII signed a decree establishing the Diocese of Gary by separating Lake, LaPorte, Porter, and Starke Counties from the Diocese of Fort Wayne. Since a diocese is "that portion of God's people which is entrusted for pastoral care to a bishop," the Diocese of Gary officially began on February 25, 1957, when Bishop Andrew G. Grutka was consecrated in Holy Angels Cathedral.

In this history, Father Dominic Bertino recounts stories of the original missionaries who came to our region and the various bishops, priests, parishes, and institutions that were founded to spread the Good News of God's love and healing care. While we now give thanks to God for the blessings of the past, our Golden Anniversary is the appropriate occasion for us to recommit ourselves to be the holy people God desires us to be and to fulfill the mission that Jesus has entrusted to each one of us through His Holy Spirit.

Together, we are the one, holy, Catholic, and apostolic Church founded by Jesus. Through Baptism, we have all been given an incredible dignity as God's children and, together, we have been entrusted with the mission to continue the saving, healing, and reconciling work of Jesus.

The same Holy Spirit, who has empowered the Church of Gary over the past 50 years, will empower us to grow in unity and charity and to witness to the Gospel of Jesus in word and in action in the decades to come.

As you read the pages of this book, you will identify with women and men, clergy, religious, and laity who have made a significant contribution to our parishes and institutions, as well as to our society in Northwest Indiana. For all of them, we give thanks to God.

Trusting in God's grace and continued presence to us and in us, we look forward to "A Future Full of Hope." May we, also, one day be counted as good and generous stewards who have helped make our parishes and institutions, as well as our society in Northwest Indiana, more holy, just, loving, and peaceful.

Grace to you and peace from God our Father!

Sincerely yours in the Lord Jesus,

+Dale J. Melczek

Most Reverend Dale J. Melczek
Bishop of Gary

Acknowledgments

I am grateful to the many members of the diocese who were so kind and patient in taking the time to assist me in gathering the information for this book. In particular, I am grateful to Bishop Melczek for his confidence and his permission for me to undertake the project; to Father Jon Plavcan and his staff at the Pastoral Center who enabled me to navigate through the diocesan archives; to Reverend Monsignor Ferdinand Melevage, Reverend Monsignor Joseph Semancik and Miss Rose Lepara for their many kindnesses and suggestions in preparing the text; to Fathers Charles Niblick, Martin Dobrzynski, Walter Rakoczy, and Michael Yadron for their assistance, particularly in their comments and suggestions in emending the text; to Mrs. Anne Verbecke of the Pastoral Center for her help regarding Pastoral Councils and the Lay Ecclesial Ministry Program; and to Mr. Steve Euvino and Ms. Karen Callaway of the Northwest Indiana Catholic for their assistance particularly in the gathering of the photographs for first section of the book.

At Saint Bridget Parish, the parishioners have been most understanding in allowing me the time to write the text with few interruptions (even the funerals were few in number these past few months). I am grateful to members of the parish staff, particularly Mrs. Brenda Bondi for her help with preparation of the photographs and graphics; to Mrs. Mary Anne Shaw for a "brutal" and thankless job of proof reading; to Mrs. Lynda Bodie-Fernandez who checked facts and transcribed my talks; and to Mrs. Miriam Thompson who had the thankless job of keeping me on schedule as well as organizing the parish visits for the publisher.

Lastly, to the staff at Éditions du Signe, particularly to Ms. Audrey Gilger, we wish to thank you for your patience and co-operation as well as for the beautiful design and layout of this work.

Table of Contents

Sacred Heart Church, Whiting

Introduction

The Second Vatican Council revealed a model of the Church that was new to the minds of many of the faithful; "the Pilgrim People of God." Yet, as the Fathers of the Council would remind us, it is an ancient idea based on our spiritual ancestors, the people of the Old Covenant. Being set free by Divine Providence, and being formed into a nation, they spend their time wandering in the desert on their way to the Promised Land. The story of their deliverance and freedom is the story of a family.

Reflecting on this, all families have such a story; perhaps not as dramatic, but still all families have that hazy prehistory which tell of their beginnings and their patriarchs as in Genesis. They can tell of their establishment as recognized by others that they are truly a family as in Exodus. Then there is the development of their customs, a regrouping and a recommitment as in Leviticus, Numbers and Deuteronomy.

Keeping to this theme, we members of the Body of Christ in the Diocese of Gary have our family story. We have been formed and established, and as the People of God wander, not aimlessly, but with a purpose, toward the Promise Land of eternal life.

The first section of this book is the result of a number of talks given in the diocese between the fall of 2004 and the spring of 2005. As such, for the purpose of our jubilee, it is anecdotal in nature and, I believe, reveals those elements found in the stories of every family: our patriarchs in a hazy past, our development, establishment, a regrouping of sorts, and a commitment toward our promised future.

I have been preparing this book for almost fifty years. Born and raised in Holy Angels Parish, I witnessed many of the important events in the early history of the diocese, sometimes from the choir loft, and sometimes as an acolyte in the sanctuary. While too young to be present for Bishop Grutka's consecration, I vividly remember watching it on the television that February day. As the parish prepared for the event, the excitement was palpable, and I can still see in my mind's eye the scaffolding that was built over the entrances to the cathedral transepts for WTTW's television cameras.

Since those early days, I have paid attention to the stories told by priests and their parishioners and carefully stored them away for the future. I have tried to give a balanced and accurate account of our diocesan history and while I admit to omissions in our story, some have been because of space and others are inadvertent.

As pastor of Saint Bridget in Hobart, I am the ninth successor to the young Francis Thomas Jansen, the first resident pastor who would go from here to found the Church in the city of Gary. When the cornerstone was laid for the present church in 1953, Father Schaeffer invited Father Andrew Grutka to preach the sermon. He told the assembled crowd that Saint Bridget Parish was the mother of all the parishes in Gary, a fact he would reiterate as Bishop at the celebration of the silver jubilee in 1982. In the one hundred years since Father Jansen's arrival in what would become Gary, and in the fifty years of our collective past as a diocese, we give thanks to God for those dedicated members of the Body of Christ who established the faith in our hearts which enable us to move forward to our promised inheritance.

Dominic V. Bertino
Saint Bridget of Kildare Parish
Hobart, "the cradle of the diocese"

Line of Apostolic Succession

Prospero Lorenzo Lambertini 1724
(Pope Benedict XIV)

Carlo della Torre Rezzonico
1743 (Pope Cement XIII)

Marcantonio Cardinal Colonna
1762

Hyacinthe-Sigismond
Cardinal Gerdil
1777

Giulo Maria
Cardinal della Somaglia
1788

Carlo Cardinal
Odescalchi, S.J.
1823

Constantino
Cardinal Patrizi Naro
1828

Lucido Maria
Cardinal Parocchi
1871

Giuseppe Melchiore Sarto
1884 (St. Pius X)

Gaetano Cardinal De Lai
1911

Raffaele Carlo
Cardinal Rossi, O.C.D.
1920

Amleto Giovanni
Cardinal Cicognani
1933

John Francis
Cardinal Dearden
1948

Edmund Casimir
Cardinal Szoka
1971

Dale Joseph Melczek
1983

Andrew Gregory Grutka
1957

Enrique Cardinal Enríquez
1743

Manuel Quintano Bonifaz
1749

Buenaventura
Cardinal Córdoba Espinosa
de la Cerda 1761

Giuseppe Maria
Cardinal Doria Pamphilj
1773

Francesco Saverio
Maria Felice Castiglioni
(Pope Pius VIII) 1800

Giovanni Maria
Mastai-Ferretti
(Bl. Pius IX) 1827

Alessandro Cardinal Franchi
1856

Giovanni Cardinal Simeoni
1875

Antonio Cardinal Agliardi
1884

Basilio Cardinal Pompilj
1913

Adeodato Giovanni
Cardinal Piazza O.C.D.
1930

Egidio Cardinal Vagnozzi
1949

Willliam Graham Connare
1960

Norbert Felix Gaughan
1975

Today's bishops, as successors of the apostles, place great importance on the unbroken line of succession that traces back to apostolic times. This "family tree" of our three bishops traces back to their "common ancestor" Prospero Lambertini who was consecrated a bishop in 1724 and would later become Pope Benedict XIV.

25 February 1957: Clergy of the new Diocese of Gary by the year of their ordination

1898

Francis J. Jansen

1906

John Woods

1907

Julian Skrzypinski

1909

Peter A. Biegel

1910

Richard Grunenberg
Augustine VanRie

1911

Michael Abraham
John A. Sullivan
Edward Vurpillat

1913

Casimir Bikauskas
John Costello
Paul J. Roederer

1917

John Biernacki
Michael Gadacz
Paul J. Schmid

1918

Julian F. Doktor
Michael Petzold

1920

Robert Emmons

1922

Theodore V. Fettig
John J. Lach
Joseph S. Wonderly

1923

Louis Michalski

1924

H. James Conway
Leo P. Hildebrandt

1925

Louis Bozik
Raymond G. Derrick
Wencel Karp
Ladislaus Krause
Herman J. Miller
Charles Seeberger

1926

Joseph Hammes
Valerian Karcz

1927

Carl Holsinger
Alfred W. Reinig
John B. Schaeffer

1928

Michael A. Campagna
Wilfred Mannion
Stanley Zjawinski

1929

Joseph Sipos
W. Edward Sweigart

1930

Joseph Smith
Anthony Quinlisk

1931

John F. Bart(kowski)
Clemons L. Koors

1932

Walter Pawlicki

1933

John N. Beckmann
Alfred J. Junk
Michael Kelner
Andrew Topor
Frederick Westendorf

1934

Joseph P. Casey
George Masley

1935

Theodore Janicki
Eugeniusz Pogorzelski
Ignatius Urbonas

1936

Joseph Buczyna
John J. Frawley
Everard N. Klein
Louis Madejczyk
Robert B. Weis

1937

Louis G. Duray
Lawence Grothouse
Ralph G. Hoffmann
Alvin J. Jasinski
James A. Stapleton
Ambrose E. Switzer

1938

Leonard J. Cross
Ignatius C. Vichuras
Gilbert Wirtz

1939

Roman Wojcicki
Chester P. Zurawiec

1940

Louis A. Jeziorski
Walter S. Mastey
Dominic A. Pallone
Eric A. Schaff

1941

Paul P. Bogovich
John P. Zubak

1942

Timothy Doody
Ferdinand J. Melevage
Bernard Shank
Anthony J. Suelzer
Albert H. VanNevel

1943

Leo Armbruster
Matthew J. Kish

1944

Henry J. Ameling
Milan F. Bach
Stanley J. Milewski
Casimir E. Senderak

1945

John Bargielski
Cornelius Bergan
Ambrose McGinnity
Henry Smartz
John C. Witte
Albert Zimmerman

1946

John Daniels
Philip N. Fusco
Frank A. Seimetz
Joseph E. Till
William E. Vogt

1947

Edward Litot
Matthew Spebar
Stephen V. Varga

1948

Vincent L. Lengerich
Stephen J. Vrabely

1949

Paul S. Haney
Patrick A. Meehan
William Peil
Louis Wozniak

1950

Anthony A. Balczun
Julian A. Jercha
Henry I. Krysinski

1951

Benjamin Domsich
John Minnich

1952

John J. Strebig

1953

Charles E. Doyle
Joseph Semancik
George M. Vrabely

1954

John J. Charlebois
Louis M. Letko
Leonard Lukaszewski

1955

Raymond Fowerbaugh
Eugene Hoffman
Thaddeus Plawecki
Alphonse Skerl
Richard F. Zollinger

1956

Emil E. Bloch
Anthony Ficko
William Martin
William Spranger

Roster of Priesthood Ordinations during Bishop Grutka's Episcopate

25 May 1957

Robert L. Charlebois
Lawrence M. Heeg
Carl F. Mengeling
Aloysius J. Nondorf

15 December 1957

James A. Coriden*

31 May 1958

Dennis J. Blaney
Stanley J. Dominik
George B. Kashmer
Joseph Sedlak
Michael Tomaszewski

30 May 1959

Joseph A. LaMere
John A. Murzyn

28 May 1960

Robert Barry Evers
James Fisko
Francis M. Lazar
John F. Morales
Edward Ramesh

13 August 1960

Michael A. Kenney
Gerald A. Sroka

18 December 1960

Henry J. Govert*

7 May 1961

Edward J. Misch

20 December 1961

Don C. Grass*

23 December 1961

Joseph J. Viater*

26 May 1962

Robert J. Mantel

22 December 1962

Dana Achor
Joseph R. Niezgoda
Joseph Zajdel

18 December 1963

Clare J. Hendricks*

30 May 1964

James P. McGrogan

16 December 1964

Michael P. Ruggaber*

29 May 1965

David H. Gosnell
Robert Mayhew
Dennis J. Teles

28 May 1966

Richard H. Ameling
Timothy A. Benante
Robert Gumienny
Lawrence J. Kew
Joseph E. Vamos

31 August 1966

Robert P. Gehring

17 December 1966

David E. Hauskins*

27 May 1967

Ronald Bartnicki
James Mazepa
Theodore J. Mens
Joseph V. Murphy
John J. Savio
John J. Siekierski

21 December 1967

Patrick J. Connolly*

25 May 1968

Paul Jackura
Joseph Smrt
Anthony L. Spanley
Michael Zych

20 December 1968

J. Patrick Gaza*
John R. Winterlin*

16 May 1969

John V. Scott

15 May 1970

Joseph Mosko

30 May 1970

Paul Wehner

27 June 1970

John Zivich^

28 August 1971

Edward J. Moszur
Gerald H. Schweitzer
Paul D. Tomasula

4 December 1971

Michael G. Heimer

17 December 1971

John R. Blonski*
Gregory P. Holicky*

29 September 1973

Edward F. Webb

30 September 1973

Joseph M. Pawlowski
Richard A. Orlinski

21 September 1974

Roy T. Beeching
Derrick F. Dudash
Charles W. Niblick
Thomas T. Tibbs

29 June 1975

Dennis M. Hand*

4 October 1975

John T. Ambre
Dominic V. Bertino
Henry A. Lazarek
Mark S .Pavlina
Raymond C. Schulte

30 October 1976

Walter R. Verbish

28 January 1978

Walter J. Rakoczy

1 July 1978

Richard A. Emerson

30 June 1979

J. Anthony Valtierra

18 August 1979

Stephen J. Titko
Robert J. Tokarz

15 August 1980

Sammie Malletta
Theodore Nordquist

2 October 1980

Mark G. Mazza

11 July 1981

John B. Barasinski
Walter M. Ciesla
Clarence E. Danforth
Stephen G. Gibson
Stephen D. Kosinski
Thomas E. Mischler

21 August 1982

Terrence J. Steffens

28 May 1983

Michael J. Yadron

2 July 1983

Michael L. Maginot

19 May 1984

Terrence R. Chase
Martin J. Dobrzynski

*Ordained in Rome
^Ordained in Louvain

Roster of Priesthood Ordinations during Bishop Gaughan's Episcopate

4 May 1985

Charles A. Mosley
David G. Nowak

3 August 1985

Joseph J. Gazarkiewicz

17 May 1986

Mark Toth

6 September 1986

Douglas J. Mayer
James W. Meade

3 October 1987

John Zemelko

10 September 1988

Peter J. Muha
David A. Schena

10 June 1989

Kevin P. McCarthy

1 June 1991

Joseph Angotti
Kevin R. Huber

30 May 1992

Andrew Malarz
Joseph Montoro

Roster of Priesthood Ordinations during Bishop Melczek's Episcopate

5 June 1993

Andrew Corona
Edward Kennedy
Keith M. Virus

4 June 1994

Thomas D. Howell
Patrick J. Kalich
Jon J. Plavcan
Frank Torres

1 June 1996

William F. O'Toole
Ian J. Williams

7 June 1997

David W. Kime
James Wozniak

23 October 1999

Lee Purcell

3 June 2000

Eduardo Malagon

23 June 2001

Brian D. Chadwick

25 June 2004

Terrence Bennis

4 June 2005

Michael J. Hoffman

3 June 2006

Leonardo J. Gajardo

Roster of Permanent Deacon Ordinations during Bishop Grutka's Episcopate

9 May 1971

John Beda

8 December 1972

Walter Stone

22 February 1981

David Brown
Robert Bucheit
Melvin Clark
Joseph Codespoti
Rafael Godinez
Dennis Hawkins
James Keough
John McGuckin
Robert O'Donnell
Joel Paulson
Joseph Rapal
Michael Richardson
John Roscoe
Arthur Weeks

20 June 1982

Raymond Dec
Martin Denkhoff
Richard Duszynzki
James Etter
Gregory Fabian
Robert Fischer
Robert Gill
Leonard Holland
William Jones
Alexander Saims
Joseph Zemelko

17 June 1984

Robert Bonta
Daniel Bowmar
Sherman Brown
Juan Delgado
Robert DeVore
Martin Gomez
David Hajduch
Rufus Harris
Nicholas Jurasevich
Joseph Manchak
George Modrak
Vincent Neely
Gilberto Perez
Frederick Romanski
Joseph Sobek
John Townsend
Leslie Vendl

Roster of Permanent Deacon Ordinations during Bishop Melczek's Episcopate

10 June 2000

John A. Bacon
Michael D. Foster
James C. Haugh
Richard W. Huber
Melvin J. Jefferson
Edward A. Kozub
Joseph E. Kwitko
Malcolm A. Lunsford
Charles S. Patrick
Michael J. Prendergast
Dale C. Walsh

7 June 2003

Robert Angelich
Edwin Gatons
Thomas Gryzbek
Jack Krol
Brian Nosbusch
Mark Plaiss
Joseph Stodola
Napoleon Tabion
Steven Zubel

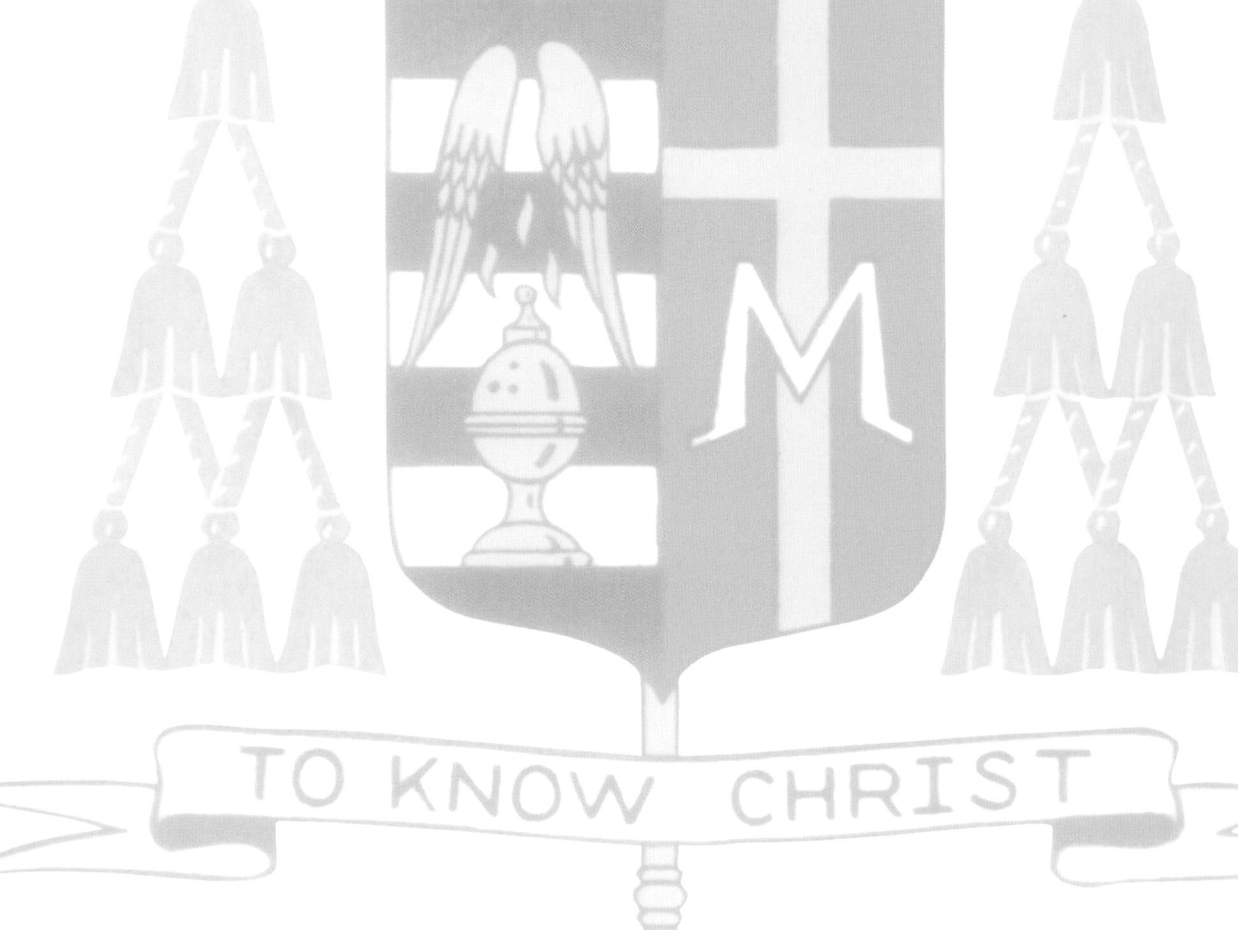

CHAPTER 1
Explorations and Development

It is hard to imagine that the area in which we live was once part of the kingdom of France. Yet, in the seventeenth century much of the continent stretching from Canada down to the mouth of the Mississippi River was exactly that. Individuals such as De La Salle, Joliet, Marquette and others would explore that vast area to enrich their country and bring the faith to the natives. With the explorers came adventurers who would settle these areas and would establish trade with the natives. In Indiana and neighboring regions, the main occupation was fur trapping. As part of the settlement of the land, the French government established outposts in order to protect its citizens and hold the land. In Indiana, three such outposts were established along the Wabash River. In 1717 the French established Fort Ouiatenon which would later develop into the city of Lafayette; in 1721 Fort Philippe, which would eventually become Fort Wayne; and in 1732, Fort Vincennes. As a result of the French and Indian War (1754-1763), the land was lost to the British; from then on it would be referred to as the Northwest Territory. Although the government may have changed hands, those Catholic settlers, French in nationality, were still cared for by the French missionaries under the jurisdiction of the Bishop of Quebec. Men such as Pierre Gibault, Benedict Flaget, and John Rivet ministered to those settlers in far-flung areas of American wilderness.

After the American War for Independence, the Northwest Territory was part of the new nation. The thirteen states as well as the Northwest Territory now comprised the Prefecture Apostolic of the United States of America with John Carroll, S.J. the Prefect Apostolic, a priest with jurisdiction over the entire area to serve the needs of Catholics and develop the prefecture to diocesan status. This occurred in 1789 when the Church erected the Diocese of Baltimore, with John Carroll as the first bishop for the United States. The only diocese in the country now stretched from the Atlantic Ocean to the Mississippi River and from Canada to Florida.

Stephen Badin, V. G.: *Protosacerdos Baltimorensis*

Stephen Badin has the distinction of being the first priest ordained in the United States. He was born in Orléans, France in 1768. As a student in the Sulpician seminary he left France during the Revolution and came to America. He entered Saint Mary Seminary in Baltimore also administered by the Sulpician Fathers. Bishop John Carroll ordained him on 25 May 1793 and made him his Vicar General in the West. He spent the next twenty-six years covering an area that would eventually comprise the states of Indiana, Illinois, Kentucky, Michigan, Ohio, and Tennessee. In 1819 he returned to France recruiting missionaries for the bishops of America.

When he returned to the United States in 1826 he joined the diocese of Cincinnati and was sent to work among the Pottawatomie Indians in Northern Indiana. In 1831 he bought a piece of property and built a chapel on St. Mary's Lake near the St. Joseph River. This would later become the property of the Holy Cross Fathers and Brothers and be the beginning of Notre Dame University. Father

Badin died in Cincinnati in 1853 and was buried in the crypt of the cathedral. In 1904 he was removed to a replica of his chapel (the original having been destroyed by fire in 1856) on the grounds of Notre Dame University.

On 8 April 1808 the Holy See promoted the Diocese of Baltimore to the status of an archdiocese. The new province of Baltimore headed by Archbishop Carroll would have four new dioceses: Boston, New York, Philadelphia, and Bardstown, Kentucky; the choice of Bardstown being chiefly the recommendation of Father Badin. The first bishop of Bardstown was Benedict Joseph Flaget, a member of the Society of Saint Sulpice. He was born in Contournat, France in 1763 and ordained in 1788. As a missionary he worked in the Northwest Territory, often from Fort Vincennes. While he was bishop of Bardstown, Indiana was admitted to the Union as a State in 1816.

Badin Chapel

The Diocese of Vincennes

The Diocese of Vincennes was erected on 6 May 1834 and comprised the entire state of Indiana and part of eastern Illinois. The first bishop of the diocese was Simon William Gabriel Bruté de Rémur who was born in Rennes, France on 20 March 1779. Always devout, he was something of a modern day Saint Tarcisius, a ten year old smuggling the Holy Eucharist to the imprisoned during the French Revolution. He originally studied medicine but entered the Sulpician seminary in Paris where he was ordained in 1808 as a member of the Sulpician Congregation. He taught in the seminary until 1810, when a chance meeting with Benedict Flaget, the bishop-elect of Bardstown, caused him to come to America. He taught in the Sulpician seminary at Baltimore and also did missionary work. On 28 October 1834 he was consecrated bishop by Bishop Flaget. His diocese had one church, Saint Francis Xavier in Vincennes and about twenty-five priests. It was during his episcopate the government began relocating the Native American Indians in the north of the state opening the way for pioneer settlement. Many who came were farmers from eastern and southern states. Also, the building of canals aided the development of the area, encouraging commerce and travel. The building of these canals brought Irish and German immigrants to the area for the first time. Bishop Bruté found himself constantly on the move throughout the state, visiting the faithful, encouraging the priests, preaching, teaching, and writing. The first parish in Northern Indiana was that of Saint John the Evangelist in St. John, Lake County. A community of German farmers was visited by

Bishop Simon Bruté
Courtesy of the Archdiocese of Indianapolis

missionaries as early as 1837. Worn out from his labors Bishop Bruté died in 1839 at sixty years of age.

The second bishop of Vincennes was Célestine René Laurent Guynemer de la Hailandière, born in Triandin, France on 2 May 1798. Originally trained as a lawyer, he then studied for the priesthood and was ordained for the diocese of Rennes in 1825. He came to America at the suggestion of his bishop, who favored a request from Bishop Bruté, asking for a priest that could be of use to him as his Vicar General. Father de la Hailandière returned to France in 1838 on a recruiting mission for the diocese. He was able to prevail upon the Eudist Fathers and also a new congregation, the Holy Cross Fathers and Brothers, to come to America to establish foundations in the diocese. While in France, he was informed by Rome of his nomination as coadjutor bishop of Vincennes on 17 May 1839. Barely one month later, on 26 June, Bishop Bruté was dead. Bishop de la Hailandière was consecrated in France on 18 August 1839 by the Bishop of Nancy.

In Vincennes, the Eudists established a school. When the Holy Cross brothers arrived in 1841 with their superior Father Edward Sorin, they settled at Black Oak Ridge approximately twenty-five miles east of Vincennes. By 1842 a conflict arose between the two religious congregations. The Eudists were upset because the bishop had promised them that if they would establish a school, he would not allow another foundation in proximity that would vie for students. A compromise was reached late in the year. Father Badin had deeded his land in the north of the state to the bishop of Vincennes, provided the debt would be paid and an orphanage established there. If Holy Cross would move to the north, they could have the land, provided the orphanage was established. They accepted and arrived at South Bend on 26 November 1842. They immediately set themselves up to the task, and with the arrival of more priests from France, began to evangelize the area. Many of the early foundations in LaPorte, Porter and Lake Counties are the fruits of their labor. In 1844 the Diocese of Chicago was established restricting Vincennes to Indiana only. Still, it was the entire state and the difficult life of a missionary bishop was too much for Bishop de la Hailandière. He prevailed upon the Holy See to allow him to retire, and permission was granted in 1847. He died in France in 1881.

Bishop Célestine de La Hailandière
Courtesy of the Archdiocese of Indianapolis

Bishop John Stephen Bazin

Courtesy of the Archdiocese of Indianapolis

Bishop Jaques-Maurice des Landes d'Aussac De Saint Palais

Courtesy of the Archdiocese of Indianapolis

His successor was John Stephen Bazin. He too was born in France in 1796 and became a missionary priest, ordained on 22 July 1822 for what would become the diocese of Mobile, Alabama. He succeeded as bishop and was consecrated at Vincennes on 24 October 1847 and died five months later, 23 April 1848.

The fourth bishop, Jaques-Maurice des Landes d'Aussac De Saint Palais was born in La Salvetat, France on 15 November 1811 and ordained a priest for the diocese of Vincennes by Bishop Bruté on 28 June 1836. He was named Vicar General by Bishop Bazin and became the Apostolic Administrator to care for the diocese owing to the death of the bishop. He was appointed to the see in October and consecrated on 14 January 1849. During his tenure as bishop the parishes of Saint Ambrose in Michigan City, The Nativity of the Blessed Virgin Mary in LaPorte, and Saint John the Baptist in Turkey Creek would be established due to the work of the Holy Cross Fathers. Bishop de St. Palais celebrated the sacrament of confirmation at St. John in 1846, the first such event in Lake County. In 1857 the Holy See informed him of the intention to create a new diocese in the north of the state. On 22 September 1857 forty-two counties would form the new Diocese of Fort Wayne and John Henry Luers, a priest of Cincinnati would be its first bishop.

Saint John the Evangelist Church

First parish church in the Lake County

CHAPTER 2
The Development of our Corner of the Diocese of Fort Wayne

FOR ALMOST EXACTLY NINETY-NINE YEARS, our four counties were part of the Diocese of Fort Wayne. During that time, five bishops ministered and encouraged the development of communities throughout the diocese. Of course, for our purposes we will concentrate on the communities established in Lake, LaPorte, Porter, and Starke counties.

The municipal growth of today belies the fact that these counties were rural in nature, and communities found themselves surrounded by acres of open land that was either wetlands in the north or fertile land suitable for farming in the south.

LaPorte County

The county of LaPorte was incorporated in 1832. It is bounded by the Lake and the Michigan state line to the north, the Starke county line to the south, the Porter County line to the west, and the St. Joseph county line to the east. The county seat is the city of LaPorte established in the same year. Michigan City was intended to be the port of Indiana; but as the railroads were being built, that plan never came to fruition.

Porter County

Porter County was established in 1836 and named for Commodore David Porter who fought in the War of 1812. It is bounded by the Lake to the north, the Kankakee River to the south, the Lake County line to the west, and the LaPorte county line to the east. The County seat was established in the middle of the territory as Portersville but renamed Valparaiso the next year. The Church established parishes in both Valparaiso and Coffee Creek. Other small communities were established mainly to the south and east, but no other city existed in the county until the villages of Crisman, Garyton, and McCool incorporated as the city of Portage. With its growth of industry and commercial ventures, it is now the largest city in the county.

Lake County

The territory of Lake County was designated a county in 1837 having been divided into three townships the year before. It is bounded by the Lake to the north, the Kankakee River to the south, the state line to the west, and the Porter county line to the east. Originally the county seat was at Liverpool but its unsuitability caused a move to Lake County Courthouse which would later be renamed Crown Point.

The settlement of the county was primarily German immigrant farmers. The main settlements were in the south of the county: St. John, Turkey Creek (also called Lottaville), Crown Point, and Hobart. The undeveloped land in the north of the county was wetlands and dunes as one moved closer to the lake, good for hunting, but not much else. It was not until the U. S. Steel Corporation laid out plans for its new industrial city that the land would be cleared and new settlements arise around it. At the time of its establishment, Lake County was in the diocese of Vincennes and one Catholic community existed, that of Saint John the Evangelist in St. John on the western border of the county.

Starke County

The county was organized in 1844 and named for John Stark, a hero of the Revolutionary War. It is bounded on the north by the Kankakee River and LaPorte County, on the south by the Pulaski County line, on the west by the Porter County and Jasper County lines, and on the east by the Marshall County line. The area in the middle of the county was determined in 1850 to be the county seat. The city of Knox would eventually be established there. The oldest Catholic settlement in the county is at San Pierre.

The Congregation of Holy Cross

We owe a debt of thanks to those early missionaries who traveled from their foundation at *Notre Dame du Lac* to minister to the settlers. Covering a radius of eighty miles they would visit settlements.

Names of such Holy Cross priests as Christian Schilling, Francis Cointet, Bernard Force, Paul Gillen, Edmund Kilroy, Michael Rooney, and others will be found in earliest volumes of the sacramental records of these early parishes.

While our area was still the diocese of Vincennes, Saint John the Evangelist parish was established. There doesn't seem to be any agreement as to a date of foundation. Father

Francis Fisher who was assigned to Chicago would visit the John Hack family and minister to their needs as early as 1837. Afterward, came the Holy Cross Fathers. Bishop Alerding places the date of the parish as 1840s with the building of the church and calls the parish the mother church of all the churches in Lake County. From there the priest would also visit the community of Turkey Creek. It was in 1850 that a parish was established there under the patronage of Saint John the Baptist. It was situated at what would today be Delaware Street at 56th Avenue in Merrillville. This is the present site of the parish cemetery of Saints Peter and Paul. In 1860 it was decided to move the parish approximately one mile west on farmland donated by Peter Fox. As Father M. Paul Wehrle was the pastor, the parish was renamed to honor the patrons of both men. Today, in the cemetery, a stone marker will be found commemorating the site of the original church.

The missionaries visit Baillytown, the homestead of Honore Gratien Joseph Bailly de Messein (1774-1835), who was an independent fur trader. He set up his fur trading post in 1822 on the Sauk Trail. It became a stopping point for those traveling between Detroit and Chicago. It is said that he held title to approximately two-thousand acres of land that is today in Porter County.

Much closer to Notre Dame, the Fathers ministered to the two developing communities in LaPorte County. In Michigan City, the parish of Saint Ambrose (1849) at 2nd and Washington Streets was established for the Irish. In 1851 the Parish of the Nativity of the Blessed Virgin Mary was established in LaPorte on the eighth of September.

When the diocese of Fort Wayne was established, we find a change in the ethnic makeup of the region. The land had been evangelized by French missionaries; but now with the infusion of Irish and German settlers, the Church in Fort Wayne takes on a predominantly German character. The first Bishop of Fort Wayne was John Henry Luers, born in Lutten, Germany in 1819. He was

Saint Mary Church, Michigan City

ordained a priest for the archdiocese of Cincinnati, a predominantly German settlement, in 1846 and worked there until he was appointed to Fort Wayne in 1857. He was consecrated in Cincinnati by Archbishop Purcell on 10 January 1858 and made his way to his new see city. During his tenure as bishop, twelve parishes would be established in our corner of the state. In 1858, All Saints would be established in San Pierre, the first parish in Starke County; Saint Joseph parish would be established for the Germans in LaPorte; and in Porter County, Saint Paul in Valparaiso and Saint Patrick in Coffee Creek

Bishop John Henry Luers
Courtesy of the Diocese of Fort Wayne-South Bend

(known today as Chesterton). These places were visited by the Holy Cross Fathers with the exception of All Saints which was established by priests from Lafayette.

In 1859, Saint Mary Parish was established in Michigan City for the Germans; and the community at Hanover Centre (present day Cedar Lake) would found the parish of Saint Matthias. Later when the church was destroyed by fire it would be moved to Cook and renamed Saint Martin and finally in 1940, a third church building would be erected and dedicated to the Holy Name of Jesus.

In 1860, Saint Martin of Tours was founded in LaPorte County at Schimmels. Later when this church would burn down, the parishioners would move two miles to the south and rebuild at LaCrosse. Saint Anthony was founded at Klaasville. This community, basically the property of the Klaas brothers, was a farming community south of St. John. It was in

Saint Joseph, Dyer

existence until 1912 when it was suppressed by Bishop Alerding. Today you will still find the St. Anthony Cemetery just west of U.S. Highway 41 west of Cedar Lake.

In 1865, Saint Mary Parish in Crown Point would be established, having been visited by priests from Turkey Creek until that time. Saint Joseph Parish in Dyer would appear two years later, and Saint Edward in Lowell in 1870.

It was determined that the parishes in Michigan City could not afford to support two priests. In 1867, land was procured on the outskirts of the city (today 10th and Buffalo) and both parishes merged to form the parish of Saint Mary, the Immaculate Conception.

Bishop Luers died in 1871 and was succeeded by Joseph Gregory Dwenger, C.PP.S. a member of the Society of the Most Precious Blood. He was born in Saint John's, Ohio in 1837 and is therefore the first native born American citizen to be named bishop in Indiana. He was ordained for the Precious Blood Fathers in 1859 and worked in there various foundations until appointed bishop. He was consecrated by Archbishop Purcell of Cincinnati on 14 April 1872. During his episcopacy eleven parishes were established in our area.

Bishop Joseph Gregory Dwenger, C.P.P.S.
Courtesy of the Diocese of Fort Wayne-South Bend

In 1873 Saint Bridget Parish was founded in Hobart as well as Saint Mary Parish in Otis. Saint Mary's was the first parish in the state for Polish immigrants. The next year, Saint Michael the Archangel Parish would be established in Schererville. In 1879 the city of Hammond on the Illinois state line was large enough to support the foundation of Saint Joseph Church.

Saint Mary in Otis

Saint Michael the Archangel, Schererville

In 1881, the parish of Saints Cyril and Methodius was founded in North Judson, the second parish in Starke County. Bishop Dwenger invited the Society of the Precious Blood to establish their community in his diocese. They came to Rensselaer, Jasper County, to land that was purchased by Bishop Luers for an orphanage. It was here that they established Saint Joseph College. Members of the congregation would serve the surrounding communities. It 1887 the Church of the Most Precious Blood was founded in Wanatah. It would later be renamed Sacred Heart Church in 1911. Holy Cross Parish was founded in Hamlet, Starke County in 1888, as well as Saint John Kanty for the Polish in Rolling Prairie the same year. In 1889 Sacred Heart Church was established in Whiting. In 1890, Saint Casimir parish was founded for the Polish by the community in Otis. The very next year they would do the same for the Poles in Michigan City with the establishment of Saint Stanislaus Kostka.

Saints Cyril and Methodius, North Judson

Saints Cyril and Methodius, Cornerstone laying by Bishop Alerding

Bishop Joseph Rademacher became the third bishop of Fort Wayne when he was consecrated by Archbishop Patrick Feehan of Chicago on 24 June 1893. Born in Westphalia, Michigan in 1840, he would be ordained as a priest for the Fort Wayne diocese by Bishop Luers on 2 August 1863. During his brief tenure as bishop, there would be four parish communities established in our area. All four were in a burgeoning section of Lake County: All Saints, Hammond in 1896; Saint John the Baptist, Robertsdale in 1897; Saint Mary in East Chicago in 1898; and Saint Stanislaus in East Chicago in 1900.

Bishop Joseph James Rademacher,
Courtesy of the Diocese of Fort Wayne-South Bend

Bishop Herman Joseph Alerding
Courtesy of the Diocese of Fort Wayne-South Bend

Bishop Herman Joseph Alerding, a native of Westphalia, Germany was born in 1845 and ordained to the priesthood on 22 September 1868. He was consecrated the fourth bishop of Fort Wayne by Archbishop Henry Elder on 30 November 1900 and would serve the diocese until his death twenty-four years later, 6 December 1924.

Of the twenty-six parishes formed in this area, twenty-two would be in Lake County. There was a population explosion which would one day lead to a new diocese.

In LaPorte County two parishes would be formed honoring the Sacred Heart of Jesus. In 1912 at LaPorte for Poles and in 1915 at Michigan City for Maronite Syrian Catholics of Lebanese nationality who would follow the Roman Rite.

In Porter County, Saint Mary in Kouts was established in 1921. And the last parish to be founded in Starke County would be Saint Thomas Aquinas at Knox, the county seat, in 1923.

But Lake County had the most activity in the twenty years beginning in 1902. Saint Adalbert Parish was founded for the Polish in Whiting and Saint Patrick Parish for the Irish in Indiana Harbor.

Also in 1902, Father Charles Stetter was the resident pastor of Saints Peter and Paul at

Saint Mary in Kouts

Saints Peter and Paul

Turkey Creek. The place was also referred to as Lottaville. Still a parish in the country, the pastor was also required to care for the faithful who lived in the city of Hobart about six miles to the northeast of the parish. Saint Bridget parish had been founded by Father O'Reilly of Valparaiso in 1873 and had never had a resident pastor. At first Hobart was cared for by the Valparaiso priests but then it fell to the pastor of Turkey Creek.

Bishop Alerding had ordered Father Stetter to build a parish school; the parishioners were balking at the idea. The dispute had been in existence since the previous fall; letters had been exchanged between pastor and bishop, and the congregation and bishop. In letters that were exchanged in 1902, the pastor explains to the bishop why he hadn't started the pledge drive. He was having trouble in securing a group of sisters to take charge of the school and it had been a wet spring and the farmers "felt very gloomy and discouraged, expecting very poor crops;" perhaps when the crops start to flourish and the congregation is in a better mood, the pledges will reflect that.

A delegation of the parish writes the bishop telling him that the public school is adequate enough, as the pastor is given leave to catechize their children; and besides they're too poor to build a school.

In August Father Stetter again writes the bishop:

Lottaville, Lake Co. Ind. Aug 12, 1902
The Rt. Rev. Herman J. Alerding D.D.

Rt. Rev. dear Bishop,

Just now I received a written notice signed by almost all the men of this congregation in which they do most emphatically oppose and strictly refuse to pay for the proposed parochial school, or any debts accumulating there from. The school will cost about $1000. The contract is made, the contractor has some material on the ground, and other material ordered, but he is afraid to go ahead because Mr. Fred Krieter and Mr. Frank Halfman who are the principal [sic] agitators against the school have threatened that they would take out an injunction against him, if he would dare to start to build the school.

I write you this information, because I think that perhaps you would like to write something to the people about this matter, before we go to the retreat. Your letter ought to leave Fort Wayne Friday morning if it is expected to get here by Saturday.

With kind regards I remain Your Lordship's
Most obedient servant in Christ,
Chas. V. Stetter.

The bishop orders a halt to construction in August and the pastor writes the Chancellor giving an accounting of the current loan:

Hobart, Lake Co. Ind. Sept. 9. 1902
The Rev. John H. Bathe, Chancellor
Bishop's House, Fort Wayne, Ind.

Rev. dear Father,
When, by your letter of Aug 14th, I was directed to stop all work on the proposed Turkey Creek school-house, I did so at once. I had borrowed from John Thyen of Hobart $700.00 for which I had given him a note, approved by the Rt. Rev. Bishop, dated July 26. 1902.
The expenses for the school already incurred, when all work for the building was stopped, are as follows:
1. $45.00 for school desks, which are stored in the teacher's house;
2. 40.00 for service to Chas. W. Kallal, Architect
3. 77.00 to the Contractor for work done, and time lost etc.
162.00 All this I paid from the money loaned for the erection of the school. The balance, $538. is deposited in the Hobart Bank.

With kind regards I remain
Yours fraternally, Chas. V. Stetter

The congregation also appealed to the archbishop. At this time the Fort Wayne diocese was in the Cincinnati province and Archbishop William Henry Elder replied in a letter dated 25 November 1902:

"Since then, your Pastor and your Bishop judge that it is time for you to have schools entirely your own, it is your duty to accept their judgement and apply yourselves earnestly to accomplish it. Your present arrangement may work fairly enough for a congregation that cannot do better; but it is not what the Church desires. The Pastor ought to have entire control of teachers, studies, books etc. without having to obtain consent of trustees or a school board. So, my dear Friends, as you want your children to obey you and to have confidence in your guidance, give them the example of obeying Our Lord Himself in the Pastor and Bishop to whom He has given the direction of you and your children. I give you my affectionate blessing. +William Henry Elder"

At one time Father Stetter suggested to the bishop that he go to live in Hobart, until the dust settled. But Bishop Alerding had another idea in mind. Father Stetter was to be transferred to Saint Joseph in Kentland, Newton County, and Father Francis Thomas Jansen, ordained in 1900 and currently assistant in Michigan City would become Saint Bridget's first resident pastor. Unfortunately the bishop did not have anyone else available for Turkey Creek, so Father Jansen would have to care for the congregation there also. He does this until 1906, when after the community at Lottaville decided it was ready to build its parish school, Father Frederick Koenig was assigned as pastor. It was a good thing too, because Father Jansen was about to become very busy.

With the advent of the United States Steel Corporation's new mills on the shores of Lake Michigan, the new city planned by that corporation and named for Judge Gary had every indication of becoming a boom town; and the Church would be there at the very beginning serving the needs of the new city's residents. During a pastoral visit to Saint Bridget in Hobart in the spring of 1906, Bishop Alerding consulted with Father Jansen about his plans to care for the spiritual needs of the new community in the dunes seven miles to the Northwest of Hobart.

Father Francis Thomas Jansen

Father Jansen eagerly concurred with the Bishop. The new parish was placed under the patronage of the Holy Guardian Angels; by September of 1906, the first mass was celebrated in Gary by Father Jansen, who would care for the community as a mission, coming on horseback from Hobart, until he took up residence as the city's first pastor in July, 1908. Father Jansen lost no time in establishing a permanent foundation. By November 1908 the cornerstone was laid for a building that would accommodate a school on the first floor and the church on the second; the building was dedicated on 24 May 1909. Under Father Jansen's leadership the growth of the parish paralleled the city's development. Eventually other parishes would be formed from this community by priests who were his assistants. Father Jansen served as pastor from its foundation till his sudden death in 1942 at the age of sixty-nine.

While during most of the nineteenth century the ethnic make up of the area was predominantly German and Irish, a shift was about to occur. U. S. Steel also advertised its new mill overseas and soon hundreds of new immigrants particularly from central and Eastern Europe would be flocking to Northwest Indiana in search of a better life.

Saint Hedwig Parish was established in 1908 and with a generous donation of fifty-thousand dollars from U. S. Steel, five more "national" parishes were erected for these immigrants: in 1911 Holy Trinity for the Slovaks; in 1912 Holy Trinity for the Croatians (this parish would be renamed Saint Joseph the Worker when it moved to Glen Park); in 1913 Saint Emeric for the Hungarians, and Sacred Heart in Tolleston for the Polish; and in 1916, Saint Casimir for the Lithuanians. In 1940, Bishop Noll stated in his history of the Fort Wayne diocese that "unfortunately they were located in the same area, so that when the third generation will need no more than one large church and school there will be several." And indeed there would be. In 1957, there would be sixteen parishes within the city, nine of which would be national parishes.

As the city expanded, there would soon be a need for other communities not ethnic in nature. In 1917, Father Jansen sent his assistant, Father Frank Gnibba to found Saint Luke Parish on the east side of Gary, and in 1923 Father Joseph Ryder would become the first resident pastor of Saint Mark in the Glen Park district.

Original church of Saint Hedwing

As the city and its industry developed, the surrounding areas also grew as a byproduct. East Chicago, Indiana Harbor, and Whiting found themselves with growing populations even before Gary was founded; in 1902 Saint Adalbert in Whiting was established as well as Saint Patrick in Indiana Harbor; in 1905, Saint John Cantius in Indiana Harbor.

Saint Luke Church and School

Original Saint Luke Church

Afterward more parish communities would develop, all "national" in makeup. In 1907, Holy Trinity for the Hungarians in East Chicago; in 1910, Saints Peter and Paul in Whiting for the Croatians; in 1913, Assumption of the Blessed Virgin Mary for the Slovaks and Saint Francis for the Lithuanians, both in Indiana Harbor; in 1915 Assumption of the Blessed Virgin Mary for the Polish in New Chicago; in 1916 Holy Trinity for the Croatians and Saint Joseph for the Polish both in East Chicago.

Although in that area in the north of Hammond called Robertsdale (and often referred to as Whiting as it is on the western border of that community), Saint John the Baptist Parish was formed for the Slovaks; a disagreement arose among the community and their pastor. It seemed by some that because he had invited the Sisters of Providence to staff the parish school, he was trying to deemphasize (and some might say destroy) the cultural heritage of the people, by not allowing their children to be taught in Slovak. A compromise could not be reached, and a new Slovak parish dedicated to the Immaculate Conception was formed on the Eastern edge of Whiting in 1923.

In Gary, the church organized the Catholic Instruction League in 1913 which involved volunteers who taught the children of the Catholic immigrants aiding in their growth as citizens of a new land. This would later develop in 1923 into the Judge Gary-Bishop Alerding Settlement House. Again with the help of U. S. Steel, a building was erected that housed an auditorium, recreation rooms, living quarters for teachers and Saint Anthony Chapel that eventually served the needs of both Italian and Mexican immigrants, hence it would often be referred to as "Saint Anthony for the Latins." But for most Gary natives it was just the "Settlement House."

Bishop Alerding was succeeded by John Francis Noll, a native of Fort Wayne, born in 1875. He was ordained by Bishop Rademacher in 1898 and served in various parishes until 1910 when he became pastor of Saint Mary in Huntington. He would serve there until his nomination as

Archbishop John Francis Noll
Courtesy of the Diocese of Fort Wayne-South Bend

bishop of Fort Wayne. As a pastor he also distinguished himself as a writer, a journalist, and an editor, founding *Our Sunday Visitor* in 1912 and in 1925 the publication entitled *The Acolyte* that would eventually be renamed Priest magazine. Bishop Noll was consecrated on 30 June 1924 by George Cardinal Mundelein. Pope Pius XII named him an assistant to the papal throne in 1941 and gave him the personal title of Archbishop in 1953. During his episcopacy, he invited a number of religious congregations to work in the diocese. The Capuchin Franciscans of the Detroit province would be invited to build their new novitiate in Huntington in 1928, but later also a house for their college seminarians in the country between Crown Point and Schererville in 1957. Slovak Franciscans who established their provincial house in Pennsylvania would arrive in 1929 and build Seven Dolors Shrine in South Haven, Porter County. This foundation would later become Our Lady of Sorrows Parish.

The Oblates of Mary Immaculate arrived in 1934 to work among the African Americans at Saint Monica parish. The Priests of the Sacred Heart were invited in 1935 to work with the Hispanic Catholics in East Chicago at Our Lady of Guadalupe and later at Saint Jude parish for African Americans. In 1937 Bishop Noll would place Holy Trinity (future Saint Joseph the Worker) Parish in the hands of the Conventual Franciscan Fathers from Croatia, who care for the parish to the present day. In 1938 Franciscan Fathers from the Polish Province headquartered in Pulaski, Wisconsin would buy the former Einsele Estate in Cedar Lake and establish two houses on the one-hundred seventy acre property: The Immaculate Conception House of Theological Studies for their seminarians which Bishop Noll dedicated in 1938, and the Stella Maris Retreat House for the laity which was blessed in 1941 by Bishop Noll. The Salvatorian Fathers from the Province of Krakow, Poland arrived in the United States in 1938 to do mission work among Polish-Americans. They were invited into the diocese and established a house in Gary in 1941. Their current foundation in Merrillville houses a Shrine to Our Lady of Fatima which has become a place of pilgrimage for the faithful. A group of Polish Carmelites, refugees from the Second World War, would be given aid by the bishop to establish a foundation in the diocese. They first came to Hammond in 1949. In 1951 the opportunity arose to purchase the former Mount Mercy Sanitarium in Munster. They would establish their friary there and erect a number of shrines which also has become a popular place of pilgrimage particularly among Polish-American Catholics from the diocese as well as the Chicago area. The Salesians of Don Bosco would arrive in Cedar Lake in 1956 to establish a day school and minor seminary. While bishop, he established twenty-six parishes in what would become our diocese: four in LaPorte County in the 1950s, two in Porter County, and twenty in Lake County as the population continued to grow and spread throughout the northern region of the county.

Saint Monica School Children

Seven Dolors Shrine

In 1926, Holy Family Parish in Gary was established for the Polish, while in East Chicago, Sacred Heart Parish was founded for the Slovaks. The parish would not receive a resident pastor until 1944 when Father Andrew Grutka would arrive from Elkhart. In 1927, Our Lady of Guadalupe Parish was established for Hispanic Catholics in East Chicago and Saint Monica Parish was organized by Father H. James Conway for African Americans.

The city of Griffith began its development around the year 1891. The Catholics there worshipped at Saint Michael in Schererville. In 1928, because of the development of the community, it was felt that there was an adequate amount of people to have its own parish.

Model of the New Saint Mary Church in Griffith

Saint Mary was established in that year under the direction of Father Joseph Suelzer who was the pastor at Kouts. He remained there until 1932 when he was replaced by Father Leo Hildebrandt, an assistant of Father Francis Jansen at Saint Joseph in Hammond. Father Hildebrandt remained as pastor until his retirement in 1972 and continued to serve the community as Pastor Emeritus until his death in 1979.

The town of Miller, which was considered a resort area on Lake Michigan was eventually annexed by Gary. In 1929, it was deemed necessary to found a parish. Saint Mary of the Lake was founded by Father Francis X. Guerre, another assistant from Holy Angels. One year later in 1930, he would organize another parish just to the South, at East Gary (currently Lake Station), Saint Francis Xavier. Gary was also growing on its western border, and by 1931 Holy Rosary Parish would be established.

Hammond too, was developing southward. In 1934, due to the work of Father Schmid and the priests at Catholic Central High School, Saint John Bosco was established. In 1935, Father Michael Campagna, a native of Italy, organized a parish for the Italians in East Chicago named for the Immaculate Conception. The settlement of Hessville, south of Hammond would eventually be annexed by that city. Our Lady of Perpetual Help was organized by Father Alfred Reinig in 1937.

To the far south, the community of Shelby, on the Kankakee River had been without a priest since the parish in Lake Village south of the river closed. In 1938, Father John Wood, who had been ordained as Vincentian priest, was given permission to start a parish there. It was given the name Saint Theresa. In the past two decades, it had been administered alternately by the pastors at Cedar Lake and Lowell. It was closed in January of 2005.

When the original parish church of Our Lady of Guadalupe was damaged by fire, it was hoped that a new church would be built closer to the community's homes. When this was done in 1941, the original church became the parish

Saint Ann, Black Oak

Blessing of the cornerston by Msgr Mungovan at Saint Thomas More, Munster

of Saint Jude for use by African Americans. It was likewise staffed by the Sacred Heart Fathers and remained in existence until January, 1973. Also in 1941, Bishop Noll instructed Father Theodore Fettig, the newly appointed pastor of Saint Peter's in LaPorte to also care for the people who worked at the Kingsbury Ordinance Plant at Kingsford Heights nine miles south of the city. After the war, the plant closed and the population shrunk, yet the remaining community petitioned the bishop for a pastor. The parish was named in honor of the Immaculate Heart of Mary and would continue in existence until May of 1999.

Black Oak on the southwestern edge of Gary is just north of Griffith. That small community would travel for the sacraments to either city until Saint Ann Parish was organized for them in 1942.

The Village of Independence Hill was in the area of Lake County that is today around 73rd Avenue and Cleveland Streets in Merrillville. Father Alvin Jasinski organized the parish of the Immaculate Heart of Mary in 1947. When new property south of U. S. Highway 30 was acquired in 1966, it was renamed Our Lady of Consolation.

In 1945, the onion fields of the town of Munster were vanishing because of the new housing developments after World War II. The community had been served by Saint Mary in Griffith. Father Hildebrandt informed Bishop Noll that the time was ripe: "A Munster Catholic has property the size of a city block and is willing to sell the church about half of it, three acres for $8,000. The property is worth it and the location is as good as can be found. So the time has come to make a definite decision about Munster. . . Father Weis has on hand some 150 names of Catholic families living there. All signs point to a building boom in all the towns that skirt other larger cities of the Calumet Region." (Letter of 12 September 1945) Bishop Noll decided in a letter to Father Weis: "I am herewith appointing you to direct the formation of a new parish in the Munster area. You are free, even while you serve as assistant to Father Hildebrandt, to gather a census and funds from the Munster people, and to regard them as all under your jurisdiction from the date of this appointment." (Letter of 2 October 1945).

In 1947, as the city of Gary continued to grow, Father Louis Madeczyk, an assistant at Saint Hedwig in Gary, would move to the south of Glen Park to found Blessed Sacrament Parish.

Another parish would be formed from Father Hildebrandt's parish at Griffith. Our Lady of Grace would be established at Highland in 1949.

Also in 1949, because of the generosity of Bishop Noll to Catholic Central High School, the administration, with the building of the new wing, would rename the school Bishop Noll High School. Almost forty years later, then Monsignor Schmid who as a young priest founded the school in 1921 was living in retirement at the convent of the Albertine Sisters at Saint Joseph Parish in Hammond. He was in his mid eighties and understandably hard of hearing, but his mind was still sharp at that time. He was told by one of the priests on the Noll faculty that he had seen his picture in the *Northwest Indiana Catholic* with the school football team from 1927. "Forty-seven?" was his reply. "No Monsignor, twenty-seven" the priest said a little louder. Then there was a moment of silence. And finally, "Yep, a fella gives the place a little money, and they go and name it after him!" In 1952, the priest faculty developed the community around the school to form Saint Margaret Mary Parish.

LaPorte County in those years found development in Michigan City taking place. As the east side of the city grew, Queen of All Saints would be founded in 1950 and a little further east in the town of Long Beach, Notre Dame Parish would be organized in 1953. On the other side of Michigan City just over the county line in Porter County, the tiny community of Beverly Shores would organize themselves into Saint Ann of the Dunes in 1956. Before this time people attended either Saint Patrick in Chesterton or Saint Mary in Michigan City.

The Building of Holy Angels in 1948

Holy Angels Dedication Day January 29, 1950

Other small communities were also being developed. Saint Helen Parish would be founded in Hebron in 1946 and Saint Anthony of Padua in Fish Lake in 1948. The final community to be established before the establishment of the Gary diocese was the Church of Saint Catherine of Siena in the Hessville section of Hammond in 1956.

The Ridge Road Runners

One could say that it started out as an act of charity. In days past when parishes all had housekeepers, it was not unusual to follow what was almost a national custom, doing the laundry on Monday. For those of us who lived in the middle third of the twentieth century, we will remember laundry day as an all day affair. And so it was also in the parish rectory. A group of pastors in south Lake County would take turns hosting lunch in their rectories to allow the housekeepers the opportunity to get the laundry done without interruption. It was a great opportunity for the housekeepers until it was their turn to make the lunch for the priests. Then they were twice as busy.

Eventually (perhaps because of a revolt?), the pastors decided to meet at a restaurant on Monday. For many years it was not unusual for as many as thirty priests to gather at Teibel's Restaurant in Schererville. A private dining room was set aside for that purpose. Priests would start to gather around noon to visit and by twelve thirty when it was determined that whoever was attending had arrived, the waitress would take the luncheon order. The "patriarchs" of the area would preside. Those notables such as Monsignor Hildebrandt, Father Hammes, and Father Wonderly who by the mid seventies were retired were always on hand with a story or two that would reduce the younger priests to tears of laughter. The older generation of pastors who were the assistants of these men in the thirties and forties made up the bulk of the group, followed by a smaller group of younger men. It was a fine tradition of fraternity that began to fade in the eighties as the older generation died. By 1992, the group had dwindled to less than a handful. Younger priests these days having heard of the tradition have often tried to rekindle it in other areas of the diocese, yet for one reason or another, it has never caught on.

January 29, 1950 at Holy Angels, Msgr John Sullivan, Archbishop Noll, Msgr Charles Charles Feltes

Andrew Gregory Grutka, D. D.

Born:	17 November 1908 Joliet, Illinois
Ordained a Priest:	North American College, Rome, Italy 5 December 1933
Consecrated a Bishop:	Holy Angels Cathedral 25 February 1957 Consecrator: Archbishop Amleto Cicognani Co-Consecrators: Bishop John P. Cody Bishop Leo A. Pursley
Motto:	*Ubi Caritas Ibi Deus* (Where there is Charity, there is God)
First Bishop of Gary:	25 December 1957 – 9 July 1984
Died:	11 November 1993 Valparaiso, Indiana
Entombed:	15 November 1993 Holy Angels Cathedral

CHAPTER 3

The Diocese of Gary is Established

Like his predecessor Bishop Leo Aloysius Pursley was born in Fort Wayne and ordained a priest for that diocese. In 1950 he was named auxiliary bishop for the diocese to assist its seventy-five year old bishop. As Bishop Noll's health continued to decline, Bishop Pursley was named Apostolic Administrator of the diocese in 1955.

Twenty years later, when because of scheduling difficulties with confirmations, Bishop Grutka would sometimes have to schedule more than one parish at the same time. When this was the case, he would ask Bishop Pursley to assist him. The Bishop would stay at the cottage at Camp Lawrence. A Master of Ceremonies would be sent to escort him to the parish where the confirmation would be celebrated and then return him to the camp afterward. On these trips to and from the parish, he would often regale the emcee with stories of his early days as a bishop and his experiences with Bishop Noll.

On one such occasion he remarked that Bishop Noll's last words to him were, "Don't let them make Gary a diocese." One could imagine the old bishop's thinking. The diocese, which stretched across the width of the state, was mostly rural. The city of Gary, while only fifty years old had already achieved prominence as one of the important industrial centers in the nation. Its population was heavily Catholic and the loss of this asset to the diocese would be, in his opinion, severe. Bishop Pursley continued his story: "But what could I do? Five months later it was a fact." It would have done no good to protest as he would not be named bishop of Fort Wayne until December twenty-ninth, two weeks after the announcement of the new diocese.

And so it was announced. 17 December 1956 the new diocese would comprise the four counties of Northwest Indiana: Lake, Porter, LaPorte, and Starke. The decree was signed by Adeodato Cardinal Piazza, O.C.D., former Patriarch of Venice and current secretary of the Sacred Consistorial Congregation. He would later have a personal link to the diocese in the person of his grandnephew and namesake, the Italian poet Adeodato Piazza Nicolai whose family immigrated to Hammond and where he would later raise his own family as members of Our Lady of Perpetual Help parish.

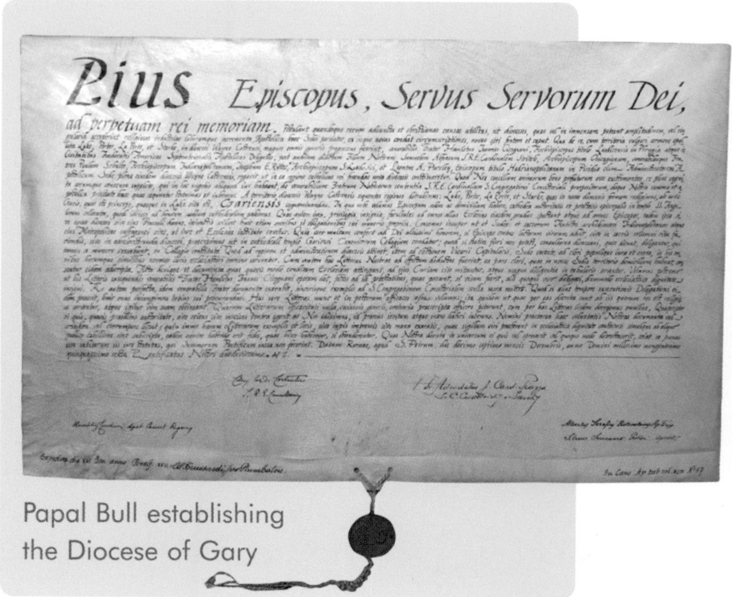

Pius Episcopus, Servus Servorum Dei,
ad perpetuam rei memoriam.

Papal Bull establishing the Diocese of Gary

Another interesting aside, when the diocese was formed, five sets of priestly brothers found themselves separated by diocesan boundaries: Fathers Ralph & Leo Hoffman, Louis and Anthony Letko, Ignatius and Michael Vichuras, twins George and John Vrabely and older brother Stephen, and William and Daniel Peil.

+Andrew Gregory Grutka, D. D.
1908 – 1993
Nemo dat quod non habet

The motto for the new bishop would be *Ubi Caritas ibi Deus:* loosely translated "where there is charity God is there." Yet among those who heard him preach and especially in his talks to the priests of the diocese they would often hear the phrase: *Nemo dat quod non habet:* "No one gives what he doesn't have". For Bishop Grutka this was an important attitude that he wished to instill particularly among the priests. We have the opportunity to share divine life and to share that life with the faithful. But it cannot be done if it isn't in the person himself. His attitude came from his experience.

Commemorating his first Solemn Mass at home in Joliet

And as such, he saw himself as pastor first, last, and always. This could be understood particularly by the way the diocese was developed. His experience was his teacher.

Andrew Grutka was born in Joliet, Illinois (Archdiocese of Chicago) on 17 November 1908. His parents were Slovak immigrants who raised their children in an atmosphere of piety and devotion to family, faith, and community. He attended the parish grade school of Saints Cyril & Methodius and then Saint Procopius in Lisle for high school and college. At the time, it was the attitude of the Chicago archdiocese not to accept anyone to study for the priesthood that did not attend their own diocesan institutions. And so, young Andrew Grutka was accepted by the neighboring diocese of Fort Wayne to study for the priesthood. Bishop Noll sent him to the North American College in Rome where he completed his studies. He was ordained in Rome on 5 December 1933 by Francesco Cardinal Marchetti Selvaggiani, an auxiliary bishop of Rome.

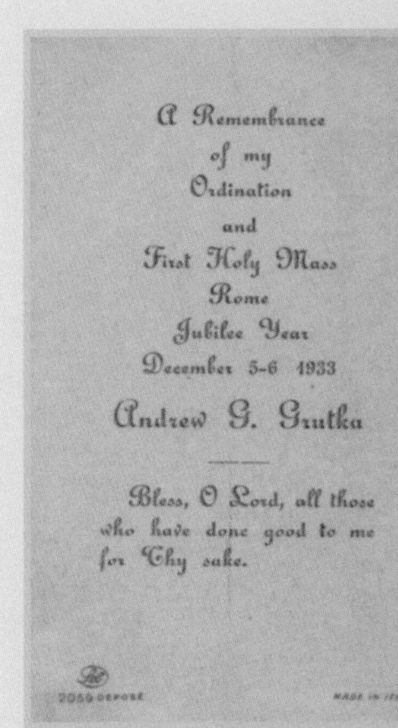

First Mass Holy Card

Back at home, he was assigned as assistant pastor of Saint Vincent Parish in Elkhart where he distinguished himself as a successful developer of youth programs. In 1942 he was given his first pastorate, the Church of the Sacred Heart in East Chicago, a small Slovak parish, where he stayed for two years. He would later describe it as a difficult time, not because of the people but, because there seemed to be little to do, and he was often alone. He spent two years there and was transferred to another Slovak parish, Holy Trinity in Gary in 1944.

Here there was plenty of work; the parish was a vibrant community with a parish school and all sorts of activities. He would also set upon himself the task of building the new parish church

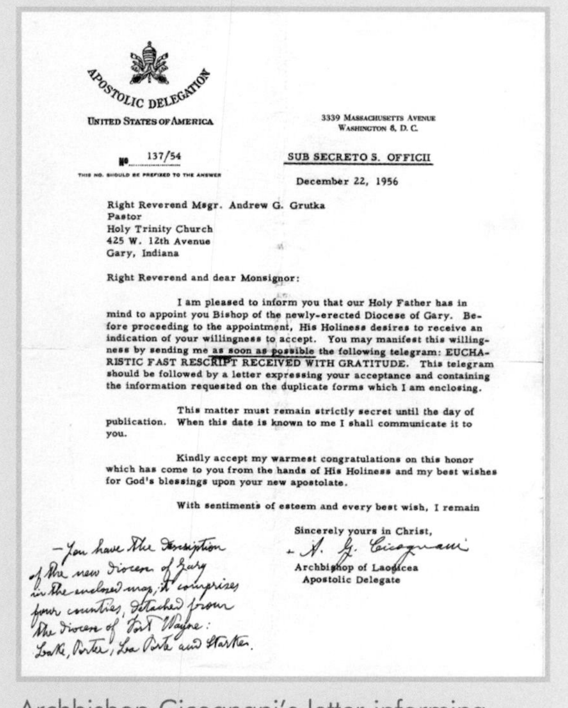

APOSTOLIC DELEGATION
UNITED STATES OF AMERICA

3339 MASSACHUSETTS AVENUE
WASHINGTON 8, D. C.

No. 137/54
THIS NO. SHOULD BE PREFIXED TO THE ANSWER

SUB SECRETO S. OFFICII

December 22, 1956

Right Reverend Msgr. Andrew G. Grutka
Pastor
Holy Trinity Church
425 W. 12th Avenue
Gary, Indiana

Right Reverend and dear Monsignor:

I am pleased to inform you that our Holy Father has in mind to appoint you Bishop of the newly-erected Diocese of Gary. Before proceeding to the appointment, His Holiness desires to receive an indication of your willingness to accept. You may manifest this willingness by sending me as soon as possible the following telegram: EUCHARISTIC FAST RESCRIPT RECEIVED WITH GRATITUDE. This telegram should be followed by a letter expressing your acceptance and containing the information requested on the duplicate forms which I am enclosing.

This matter must remain strictly secret until the day of publication. When this date is known to me I shall communicate it to you.

Kindly accept my warmest congratulations on this honor which has come to you from the hands of His Holiness and my best wishes for God's blessings upon your new apostolate.

With sentiments of esteem and every best wish, I remain

Sincerely yours in Christ,
+ A. G. Cicognani
Archbishop of Laodicea
Apostolic Delegate

— You have the description of the new diocese of Gary in the enclosed map; it comprises four counties, detached from the diocese of Fort Wayne: Lake, Porter, La Porte and Starke.

Archbishop Cicognani's letter informing Bishop Grutka of his nomination.

which was completed in 1954. On 2 June 1956 he was raised to the rank of Domestic Prelate.

On Christmas Eve, he received a letter in the evening mail nominating him as the first bishop of Gary. He had to think it over and reply very soon. He responded on 26 December:

The above letter was found, written in long hand with pencil as a rough draft on yellow legal paper, on 3 September 1995, almost two years after the bishop's death. His secretary of so many years, Miss Rose M. Lepara, found the letter while sorting through his papers for storage in the diocesan archives. This original was stored with a typewritten copy which she did that day. As she would report, "…copied from the handwritten work papers which Bishop Grutka used to compose his acceptance of the Episcopacy. Because it was so nervously scribbled on yellow tablet paper, we thought it best to type it before it cannot be read anymore."

The circumstances regarding the response would be reported by the Benedictine Father Philip Bajo, from Saint Procopius, who had come to stay at the parish during the Christmas holidays to offer help and give the assistant a chance to spend time with his family. On 2 January 1957, after the announcement was released, he would report his experience of 26 December: The Bishop-elect pondered over his desk in the office across from the living room where Father Philip

Most Reverend and Archbishop Cicognani:

This is a feeble and extremely nervous attempt to answer Your Excellency's letter, dated December 22, and received by me at about 8:30 in the evening of the Eve of Christmas.

Humbly prostrate at the feet of His Holiness, this unworthy person in a state of profound, utter amazement, completely and unreservedly submissive to the wishes of the Holy See is sincerely reluctant---albeit willing to accept the appointment as Bishop of the newly erected Diocese of Gary.

This is only further proof of how inscrutable are the ways of God and His Church, that one from such humble circumstances should be considered for the indescribable dignity of the Episcopacy – the fullness of the priesthood and succession to the Apostles of Christ the Lord.

From the early days of seminarian life to this very day, my evening prayers always [included] the petition to be a holy priest. I sincerely do not understand this turn of events. May God's Holy Will be Done.

Enclosed, Your Excellency will [also] find the questionnaire filled as requested.

Wishing your Excellency a New Year blest with robust health and the all-permeating warmth of Jesus Christ's love.

Most sincerely and devotedly, *(signed)* Andrew G. Grutka

was watching television. He had earlier informed Father Philip that he would be busy in his office writing some thoughts and letters.

Much later he came to Father Philip and wanted the assurance that he had an expression translated correctly into Latin. The words that he had translated were: "May God's holy will be done." Finally the Bishop-elect informed Father Philip that he was taking some letters to the post office. Father offered to take them there, but he kindly refused the offer saying he needed to do it himself.

And so, his attitude as bishop would be no different than that of a pastor. His flock would now be larger. His experiences as pastor of two ethnic parishes (and indeed the experience of growing up in one) would set his attitude of what parish life should ideally be like: a magnet for the community where not only would one worship and receive the sacraments, but also be a place to educate your children and occupy the family in activities that you shared with your neighbors. This was all presided over by the pastor who knew you by name because he was your "father." He often remarked that a pastor must know his people. The worst thing he was ever known to say about a priest was "he doesn't know his people."

He kept this attitude with him in regard to the priests of the diocese. He considered himself a good judge of character. During the summer, he would often come out to Camp Lawrence. He enjoyed spending time there especially when the children were present. But he seemed to have other motives. He would pay close attention to the seminarians working at camp. One would often notice him looking out from a window of the cabin where he stayed not only watching the activities, but also noticing how the seminarians interacted with the children and each other. Many a decision as to the future of those men was made from those observances.

Others were from his personal interviews with the seminarians. The winning smile that often looked at you from the pages of Our Sunday Visitor would be there, but there was also a serious side that was often unnerving, especially in the form of the "pregnant pause." In his conversations with you, that pause would often occur, sometimes after you asked him a question. While he was formulating an answer, which seemed like an eternity, you had to wonder what was going on. Was he looking into the future (yours), trying to figure you out, or just making you nervous?

And still there was that solicitude for his flock. He was concerned for the good of the whole diocese, but that concern was often manifested toward the individual person. He wanted only the good for the individual and would do what he could to accomplish it.

Once he called a young priest to his office to inform him of his transfer to a new assignment. The news took him completely off guard since he considered himself to be doing a successful job where he was and was loathe going to the new place. He was informed that he was being moved on account of the person he was replacing. Father was having some personal difficulties and, as the Bishop said, "We have to save his vocation." "What about my vocation?" was the priest's response. To which the Bishop replied: "Oh Father, you'll never leave!" The priest left the office not sure if he was complimented, but the bishop was completely convinced that one vocation was strong enough to bear the experience, while the other needed special ministrations.

On a Sunday visit to a parish to confer the Sacrament of Confirmation, he lingered at the dinner table afterward. It was obvious he had nothing more for the day and was in no hurry to leave. At one point in the conversation with the pastor and other dinner guests he looked at his master of ceremonies and asked, "And what are your plans for today?" The priest responded, "I believe my mother was expecting to see me today" (it was Mothers' Day). Some minutes later it was time to go. When he was returned to his residence the Bishop asked the priest to stop in for a minute. He took a prayer book

Bishop's Residence and first chancery

from his desk and wrote an inscription, asking the priest to please give this to his mother; a small gesture in his mind, but certainly his way of saying sorry for keeping you from filial duties.

He emphasized good preaching and often said all you needed was the "scriptures in one hand and the newspaper in the other." A preacher well grounded in the gospel and aware of the world around him would be able to better share the good news of the kingdom with his flock. *Nemo dat quod non habet.*

He would organize his chancery simply. The bishop's new residence at 668 Pierce Street, just two blocks from the cathedral was a commodious place (to which a chapel would be added) to where he would transfer his current household. His assistant, Father John J. Charlebois, would be the first Chancellor of the Diocese, and Miss Rose Lepara, parish secretary and housekeeper would add comptroller to her duties. The Tribunal would also operate from the Bishop's residence, but the business of all other diocesan offices would be conducted by the priests chosen for the job from their own rectories. This continued until the mid 1970s when the bishop was prevailed upon to consolidate the chancery offices at what was then known as the Cathedral Center.

It seemed that the bishop would not have a chance to settle into a comfortable pattern of ministry. The early days were taken up with organization as well as his new sacramental duties. And then there was the announcement by the new pope that he would convoke an ecumenical council.

Vatican II, procession to the Basilica

Vatican II attendance

The Bishop attended all four sessions of the Council (1962-1965). In a speech he gave to the assembled bishops on racial discrimination in which he gained some national prominence, this was the quote that appeared for publication: “It is a scandal to see parishes deserted whenever Negro families move in. The Council must proclaim the absolute opposition of the Church to all forms of racial discrimination.” His pastoral letter How Good a Neighbor Am I? published in 1968 at the height of the country’s civil unrest over racial equality was a call for understanding and charity; a challenge to live the gospel.

Another passion was the freedom for the Slovak people from the tyranny of Communism. He was one of the founders of the Institute of Saints Cyril & Methodius in Rome, a seminary for Slovak refugees who would one day return to their country to serve the Church.

He had always wanted to have his own seminary one day. He prepared for this by choosing seminarians and priests for graduate degrees in Rome. The day seminary at Bishop Noll Institute was to be the forerunner for the future, but sadly, with the societal upheaval of the hedonistic sixties, coupled with a decline in vocations and even clerical departures it did not come to pass.

During his tenure as bishop, ninety-five men were ordained for service in the diocese. He ordained eighty-four while the others were ordained in Rome. He established ten parishes and two schools.

He welcomed the Albertine Sisters to the diocese and built the retirement home for priests that they staff.

Before his retirement he announced the creation of fourteen new Honorary Prelates (Monsignori) which he had not done since the close of the Vatican Council. For many, this was seen as an opportunity for him to show his gratitude for the diligent work accomplished in the diocese for so many years.

He was able to celebrate the silver jubilee of the diocese (1982) and his own golden sacerdotal jubilee the next year. He retired in 1984 to Camp Lawrence and remained active at the pleasure of the new bishop. Bishop Grutka died 11 November 1993 and is entombed in the east transept of the Cathedral.

Consecration and Installation

Preparations were set in motion. He first informed Monsignor John Sullivan, the dean of Fort Wayne’s Gary Deanery and pastor of Holy Angels parish, that his church would become the cathedral of the new diocese as it was the mother church of the city.

The parish was founded in 1906 with establishment of the city. The original building built by Monsignor Jansen, the founding pastor was still in use as the parish school, but next to it was the magnificent new edifice completed just six years earlier in the gothic style and faced with Wisconsin Lannon stone and trimmed with Indiana limestone. Monsignor Sullivan would remain as the Rector, but after all, the new bishop would be the pastor. During the month of January 1957 the church was readied. A

Consecration, Litany of Saints

Prayer of Consecration

Consecration Grouping

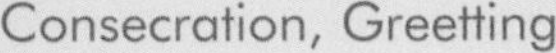

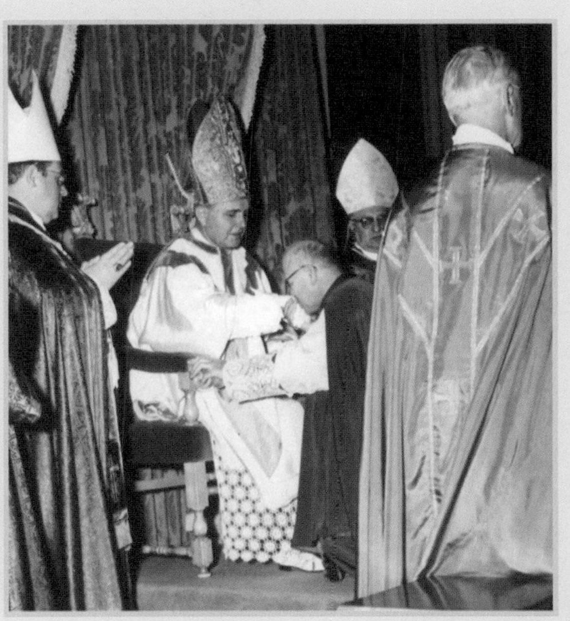

Consecration, Greetting

temporary cathedra (the bishop's throne) would be installed and the ambo was moved to the opposite side of the sanctuary to make room for it.

The Apostolic Delegate to the United States, Archbishop Amleto Giovanni Cicognani would be the principal consecrator, assisted by Bishops John Cody and Leo Pursley, friends of the new bishop. The Archbishop of Indianapolis, Paul Schulte would preach:

"Now as a duly consecrated prelate of the Church, Bishop Grutka takes his place at the head of a new Diocese. It is a beautiful and a happy marriage that we are witnessing this morning –the nuptials of a young bishop and his maiden diocese. But these are not strangers that are meeting before the altar of the Gary cathedral in this ceremony of Episcopal consecration and installation. This portion of the Lord's vineyard that is now the Diocese of Gary has long known

Bishop Grutka. It has known him as a youth, as a young priest and as a pastor, always zealous, always capable, but above all, always kind.

"...the need for a multiplication of languages here is fast passing away. Immigration is being drastically curtailed, while the young people are forgetting the language of their fathers. From what was once a melting pot of diverse nationals has come forth a community of the most loyal Americans in the land with but one flag, one Church and one language.

Yes the need for the National Church is passing. With the younger generation moving to new territorial parishes, we see the marks of decline already showing in many of the old mother churches. The eventual unscrambling of overlapping parochial jurisdictions will present its problem. We doubt however, that it is so imminent as to become the new Bishop's main worry."

Crisis: Steel Strike—1959

As the developing diocese entered its third year, talk of a strike in the steel industry became more pronounced. Such an event would be devastating to a city so dependent on the industry for the success of its economy and the well-being of its citizens. In the spring of 1959, Bishop Grutka issued the following order, hoping that the prayers of the diocese would help both sides of the dispute do the right thing:

"In case a steel strike takes place all the Churches in Lake County will observe the following program: Exposition of the Blessed Sacrament each day except Sunday for a period of eight hours from 11:00 a.m. to 7:00 p.m. In parishes with more than one priest the exposition is to begin with Holy Mass at 11:00 a.m. A mandatory oration, no. 13 –*Pro quacumque Tribulatione*, for any trouble, is to be added in every Mass. The evening devotions are to consist of a Rosary, Litany of the Saints and Benediction of the Most Blessed Sacrament."

The union did strike and carried the dispute through a summer of blistering heat into the fall. In a letter of 27 September 1959 the bishop informs the diocese of his obligation to report on the state of the diocese to the Holy See. But the strike was ever on his mind: "As you read these lines I will be aboard a ship sailing for Rome and my first AD LIMINA VISIT. I leave with some sadness in my heart due to the prolonged and still existing strike in the steel industry.

"The physical growth of our infant diocese is being stunted. Much as we deplore the damage to the material side of the diocese we are heartened by the opportunities for spiritual progress which the strike presents and of which many of our people are taking good advantage. The special devotions each day in many of our churches, though not too well attended, will build up spiritual resources for individuals, for parishes and for the whole diocese and will pay big dividends in time and eternity.

"Since devout prayer is an infallible means for obtaining Divine Assistance I urge all the people of the diocese most sincerely to lift up their hearts and minds in confident, resigned, persevering and child-like prayer. May these prayers bring about an abrupt but just settlement of the difference between management and labor in the steel industry now debilitating the strength of our nation in a wasteful strike."

As an agreement was finally reached, the strike ended in November 1959 and the Bishop was pleased to call upon the people to offer prayers of "gratitude to Almighty God and devoutly beseech Him to pour out on the deep wounds created by this strike a healing balm of heavenly blessings to quickly restore the friendliest relations between management and labor for the common good of all."

Camp Lawrence

One of the jewels of the diocese is a parcel of one-hundred fifty acres in north central Porter County known as Camp Lawrence. After World War II, the country found itself in the grip of a different kind of war: the Cold War. A war of philosophies and nerves that pitted our country against Communism; and with such quotes from Khrushchev as "we will bury you" the nation found itself in an atmosphere of preparedness against attack in this nuclear age. Throughout our counties there were a string of Nike Bases, which were manned for our defense, and Camp Lawrence was developed into a rest and recreation site for the soldiers who manned the bases. The property was purchased by Father Lawrence Grothouse, who was the district moderator for the Catholic Youth Organization. He envisioned the property as a summer camp for children, a place for fresh air and wholesome activities under supervision.

With the help of the army, the land was developed for that purpose. Those campers from the early years will still remember the Quonset huts erected by the soldiers for use as cabins.

Bishop Grutka formally dedicated the camp in 1958. The camp began to flourish especially under the direction of Father William Martin, who served as the executive director of the CYO from 1970 to 1984. The camp operated from June to mid-August with separate sessions for boys and girls. The girls' sessions was staffed by college women, while major seminarians staffed the boys' session and manned the maintenance department. This was a particular directive from Bishop Grutka. He felt it important to keep them busy and under supervision. For the seminarians, many of whom were hoping for other (more lucrative) employment, it actually turned out to be a good experience. Since the bishop had men at different seminaries throughout the mid-west, the summer work at the camp became a way for the seminarians to get to know each other and learn to work together. With the declining number of those entering the seminary, it was necessary to find others to staff the camp. By the mid 1980s the seminarians were no longer required to work as counselors. The camp continues to flourish as it changes with the times. New cabins and a dining hall were built in 1982 and the boys' and girls' sessions were merged that year.

Bishop Grutka with Father Martin and Monsignor Grothouse, Directors of the C.Y.O.

Camp Lawrence

Andrean High School

Andrean groundbreaking

Blessing Andrean High School

One of the first projects of the new diocese was the founding of a new Catholic high school for the Gary area. Bishop Noll High School in Hammond was at the western edge of the diocese, and Saint Mary Parish High School (which would later become Marquette) in Michigan City was at the eastern edge. A new high school would be situated in a central location south of Gary and accessible for surrounding communities such as Crown Point. The diocese acquired thirty acres of land in what was still called Turkey Creek at Fifty-ninth Avenue on Broadway. Bishop Grutka secured the services of the Congregation of Saint Basil, primarily a teaching order of priests headquartered in Canada and the Sisters of Saints Cyril and Methodius, a teaching order of Sisters who staffed many of the Slovak parish schools in the area; the school would be co-institutional. The school was given the name Andrean High School under the patronage of Saint Andrew the Apostle, Bishop Grutka's patron. Ground was broken for the new building on 12 August 1958. The building was built in the shape of the Capital letter "A" with one wing reserved for the boys' classrooms and the other for the girls'.

The school opened in the fall of 1959 with a freshmen class only. The school population increased by the admission of a new freshmen class each year; the first matriculants of 1959, also being the first graduating class in 1963. Under the supervision of these two teaching orders, the school quickly gained a reputation of academic excellence which continues to this day. With the declining number of vocations, particularly among groups of women religious, the Sisters of Cyril and Methodius currently have only two sisters on the faculty. The Basilian Fathers formally ended their agreement to staff the school with priests in June of 2000, but have allowed the current principal, Father Paul Quanz, to remain in the job until his term expires.

New Parishes

After World War II, newer communities began to develop as suburbs. The Hessville section of Hammond was growing in population; Saint Catherine of Siena being the last parish formed in 1956 before the diocese of Fort Wayne split. It was now up to the new bishop to determine if the time was ripe for new parishes. The first parish to be established in the diocese was in the new city of Portage in Porter County. The villages of Crisman, Garyton, and McCool incorporated as Portage in 1964. The Catholic faithful who had up to this time attended either, Saint Bridget, Saint Francis Xavier, or Saint Patrick petitioned the Bishop for a parish of their own. It began as a project of the chancery. The parish was given the title Nativity of Our Savior in commemoration of the date (Christmas Eve) when Bishop Grutka was informed of his nomination as bishop. Father John Charlebois, the diocesan chancellor was commissioned to organize the community. The first resident pastor was Father Joseph Till. Until land could be obtained and developed, a portable trailer was placed at one end of the Portage Mall. Mass would be celebrated there while the faithful participated from their cars in the parking lot.

The area known as Turkey Creek would incorporate into the Town of Merrillville in 1972. By that time there would be five parishes in the town all carved from Saints Peter and Paul: Saint Andrew the Apostle in 1965 organized by Father William Vogt; Saint Joan of Arc organized initially by Father Michael Kenney in 1968; and Saint Stephen the Martyr organized by Father Lawrence Heeg in 1969. The fifth parish, Immaculate Heart of Mary, founded in 1947 by Father Alvin Jasinski, would move south of U.S. 30, where Father Herman Schoudel would build a new church in honor of Our Lady of Consolation in 1966.

The first pastor of Saint Joan of Arc was transferred to Michigan City, the second left the priesthood and the third would also be transferred before joining the Navy. The parish having no developed property on the east side of Broadway, merged with Saint Andrew on the west side of Broadway, worshipping together on Sunday, yet keeping their collections separate until the community would find themselves financially strong enough to be independent. This occurred in 1978 when Father Sroka built the church.

Chapel on the Mall in Portage

Chapel on the Mall, Nativity

Perhaps it was because Bishop Grutka came from the experience of small ethnic parishes or the prevailing attitude after the Vatican Council that parishes should be "small faith communities" they remained small for the most part. Certainly in the 1960s, even with defections, the diocese had plenty of priests and it seemed like this was the way things would·go.

In other areas of the diocese more parishes would be organized. In 1967, Father Eugene Hoffman would develop Saint James the Less from Our Lady of Grace, Saint Matthias (the diocese's secondary patron) would be established on the south side of Crown Point by Father John Strebig, splitting off from the hundred year old Saint Mary Parish, and Seven Dolors Shrine in South Haven, the countryside of Porter County, and under the care of the Franciscans of the Slovak Custody in Pennsylvania would be raised to·the status of a parish calling itself Our Lady of Sorrows.

Bishop Noll Institute

In the early hours of 10 January 1962 a fire broke out at Bishop Noll High School. The Gymnasium and some classrooms were destroyed by the fire. Because of the severe weather, the school was closed for the day so that a more devastating tragedy was averted and no one was injured. Plans began immediately for the rebuilding effort. There were those who wanted to rebuild as before. Others thought that a smaller school would suffice for the area with another school to be built farther south in Lake County. Monsignor Hildebrandt had purchased a parcel of land at 45th and Kennedy Avenue in Highland for such a purpose. Would the time be right to consider two new high schools? Bishop Grutka had his own thoughts on the matter and would provide a grand plan for its rebuilding. A magnificent new structure, state of the art, would be built that would include an auditorium, a field house, a swimming pool, a cafeteria and a classroom wing with sixty new classrooms added to the wing not touched by the fire. A new convent would be built for the Holy Cross Sisters who staffed the school and a new residence for the Christian Brothers who would take over the school's administration.

Since the Christian Brothers were founded in the seventeenth century by St. John Baptist de la Salle only to instruct boys, the co-educational school would now become co-institutional for the first time in forty years. It would also receive a new name: Bishop Noll Institute. Bishop Grutka envisioned the place as a place of learning and activity almost around the clock; after the normal academic day, there would not only be sports and other activities, but the school would also become a center for adult education. Although this did not exactly come to fruition as planned, still the new edifice became a magnet for the community and was used for various diocesan functions. During the sixties, the enrollment peaked at twenty-seven hundred students. The Christian Brothers

Fire at Bishop Noll High School

ended their association with the school in 1972 and the new administration returned to the co-educational tradition. From the very beginning of the school's history, diocesan priests had always played a major role in the life of the school; teaching as members of the faculty as well as forming the administration. Bishop Grutka kept and fostered this tradition. It was not unusual for him to assign a dozen diocesan priests to teach at Bishop Noll. Many spent their early years in the priesthood in this ministry and later as pastors of area parishes would have many former students as members of their flocks. With declining vocations, Bishop Gaughan felt it necessary to curtail this ministry. This last priest on the faculty was Father Charles Mosley who remained at Noll from 1986 until becoming the pastor of Our Lady of Perpetual Help in 2005.

Groudbreaking for Bishop Noll Institute

Calumet College of Saint Joseph

The Missionary Fathers of the Precious Blood have had a relationship with the community since first coming to the diocese of Fort Wayne. With the establishment of their college at Rensselaer, Saint Joseph College served as a hub for priests to serve surrounding communities. In 1925, Father Racajny invited them to assist at Saint John the Baptist which they would later take under their administration up to the present day. They also established in East Chicago, in 1951, an extension to their college. It become known as the Calumet Campus and was sprinkled among the business district, using various storefronts as offices and classrooms.

In 1976 they received as a gift Standard Oil's research and development building in Whiting which allowed the institution to consolidate their efforts and give them a recognizable identity. The Precious Blood Fathers retained the administration of the college until 1987 when Doctor Dennis Rittenmeyer became president. Also that year, the name was changed to Calumet College of Saint Joseph to reflect their historical and geographical history.

Marquette High School

The history of Marquette High School is linked with Saint Mary the Immaculate Conception Parish. The parish school was opened in 1886 under the supervision of the Sisters of Holy Cross. A secondary course of study was offered for the students, and the school would graduate its first class of high school students in 1894. With the exception of the parishes that would be established for ethnic groups (Saint Stanislaus in 1891 and Sacred Heart in 1914) Saint Mary was the only territorial parish in the north of the county and by the end of the Second World War, one of the largest in the state. The fact that it supported its own high school made it in effect the Catholic high school for the city. While the folklore of the area will tell of rivalry between the pastors in the city, students of the other parishes would matriculate at Saint Mary High School. In 1897, the pastor invited the School Sisters of Notre Dame to take charge of his schools. They would do so until 1934, when the Holy Cross Sisters would return. The parish built Marquette Hall for parish functions in 1914; by 1925 the high school department which was growing in numbers would be moved into this building. In 1954 it would be enlarged with the addition of a modern building on the corner of Tenth and Wabash Streets. By 1966 there was talk of building a new school for the entire city across from the new Rogers High School in

Marquette High School

which students would have use of both the public and parochial facilities with the target date of 1971. As the school would be the responsibility of all the parishes in the city, a change of name would also be discussed; and it was decided that the school would open the 1968 school year as Marquette High School. The student body reached its highest enrollment in the late 1970s with over three-hundred fifty students. While this would be considered small in comparison to the other high schools, Marquette has had a rich heritage of academic excellence. The cramped quarters that the student body have endured for so many years have been marvelously alleviated with the addition of the Scholl Student Center, dedicated on 19 November 2001.

Second Crisis

The nineteen sixties was a turbulent time for both Church and Country. A time of change and upheaval, the diocese found itself in the center of these difficulties as indeed did many of the industrial cities in the country. The *aggiornamento* of the Second Vatican Council, while sorely needed, was disturbing for many Catholics who did not understand the reason for all the "changes." They were told how important it was to follow their consciences and not be blindly obedient. But some found this difficult to do since they saw their spiritual lives as a pattern of doing what their pastors told them. Coupled by the fact that some of the older priests were not in agreement and some of the younger priests found themselves questioning their vocations and mystifying their pastors with a lack of co-operation or even obedience made it difficult for the faithful. Among both clergy and laity some of the older would resist (passively) and some of the younger would defect. Uniformity both in the practice of the liturgy and in the understanding of one's beliefs would seemingly disappear.

In society, the conflict in which the nation found itself mired in Viet Nam led the citizens to question authority all the more. A new era was dawning in which young people no longer saw the need to trust the older generation. It was a time for doing as you pleased. Everything was questioned; age old rules of etiquette and dress were breaking down or disappearing altogether. It was also a time for racial unrest. The diocese found itself at the forefront of the civil rights movement. A city the size of Gary with a diverse population would not be unaffected. Parish communities often organized on ethnic lines would form their own enclaves within the city. They may have all worked together in the steel mills, but they had their own neighborhoods; and many liked it this way. Open housing for all was something difficult to accept. And many fled the city for the south of the county. Turkey Creek had been developing new subdivisions since the fifties and they would soon incorporate as the Town of Merrillville so that they would not be annexed by Gary. This exodus dubbed "white flight" appalled Bishop Grutka. He was a constant voice of reason for justice, working with his own clergy and on an ecumenical level to do anything to promote racial justice. He became a good friend of the Reverend Robert Lowery, Pastor of the Saint Timothy Community Church in Gary. Together they worked on various commissions in the city to promote harmony. During the Vatican Council, Reverend Lowery traveled to Rome as a guest of the Bishop. One major achievement of the bishop at this time was his pastoral letter *How Good a Neighbor Am I?*, published in 1968 and subtitled *Racial Justice and Charity*.

He wrote: "The most precious pieces in the divine mosaic of the world are human beings. Although each differs from the other in color, shape, size and brilliance, together they give tone, quality and character to the mosaic. Because God is a flawless Artisan, each piece fits perfectly and contributes faultlessly to the harmonious unity of the divine masterpiece. Hateful spite can make even the most beautiful mosaic an object of brutal defacement. Of the many attempts at disfigurement which persistently plague the divine mosaic of mankind, none are more annoying and none more in need of prevention than those stemming from racial tension. These tensions exist in all parts of the world, in many cities of our own country, and right here around us. It is to the elimination of racial injustice that this letter is addressed. The purpose of this pastoral message is to focus attention as sharply as possible on the divine mosaic with the hope that the blotches and scars on it will be recognized for what they really are—heinous crimes against God and man. The intellectual conviction that racial segregation and discrimination are not Christian—is sterile without the total commitment of our souls and hearts to this fact."

Visible Changes

With the liturgical reform of the Second Vatican Council, the parish churches of the diocese found themselves in need of remodeling. Often portable altars would be placed in sanctuaries barely large enough in which to move about. Sometimes the removal of the communion rail gave more space. But as time passed, and the needs of the revised liturgy were understood, more permanent renovations took place in later years. This was also true of the cathedral.

When Holy Angels was given the status of a cathedral in January of 1957, the ambo had been moved to the right side of the sanctuary to make room for the bishop's throne on the left side. This first cathedra was a temporary affair, a high back chair on a platform backed by green drapery and a canopy. Soon a new cathedra would be installed. Twenty-one feet in height, it resembled a gothic spire which formed a natural canopy as the seat was in the base. Four archangels framed the opening of the seating area. The upholstery was of green leather with the bishop's coat of arms above the bishop's head. In 1972, Bishop Grutka decided it was time to make permanent renovations. The plans actually show something of how the church looks today. The Blessed Sacrament Chapel was to be formed out of the sacristy to the right of the sanctuary, the cathedra would remain in its place and the seating for the celebrant would be at the back of the sanctuary under the crucifix where the high altar once was, the altar itself would be fashioned from the mensa and pillars that supported it as part of the original high altar. This new altar would be placed on an apron built out just a few feet into the main aisle. The communion rail would of course be removed to accomplish this. For whatever reasons, the plan was scaled back.

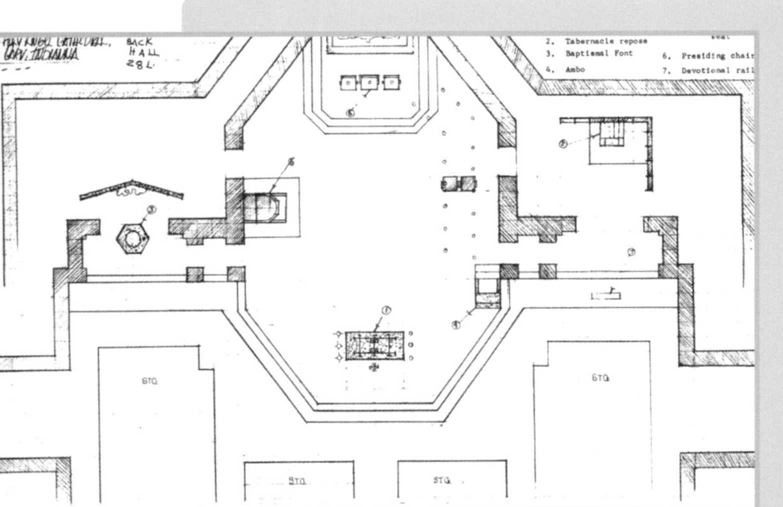

1973: Plans for Cathedral

1959-1973 Cathedra

Cathedra remade

The tabernacle would remain in the position of the original altar; the new altar would be positioned at the edge of the sanctuary still removing the communion rail. The cathedra was removed. In the booklet written for the dedication of the newly renovated cathedral in January 1998 the following was written: "By 1973, these plans were considerably scaled down; the rail was removed, the sanctuary carpeted, the altar was not moved as far forward, the tabernacle remained in its original place, and inexplicably, the cathedra was removed."

Some weeks after the cathedral's dedication, Father Greg Holicky met at a Forty Hours Devotion celebration the author of those words. "I see you didn't know why the cathedra was removed from the cathedral. I can tell you that story." At the time in question Father Holicky was assistant to Father John Morales at Saint Mark in Glen Park. Originally the woodwork in the cathedral was of a blonde oak finish. The new cathedra would match that finish when it was installed. During the cathedral's renovation it was decided to stain the woodwork a darker color, and the company that fashioned the cathedra was contacted for that purpose. As they replied it would be too difficult to take it apart and thus too costly to stain it, the bishop decided to get rid of it. As Saint Mark's was also undergoing renovation, they took the chair off the bishop's hands and fashioned it into a table for the tabernacle. Father Holicky's listener was confused. "But it's stained a dark maple," he said. "That's the irony of the situation," replied Father Holicky, "when we took it to Saint Mark's it had to be taken apart. And once that happened we found we could easily stain it."

New Plans for Catechesis

At the inception of the diocese the Bishop appointed Father Edward Litot as director of the Confraternity of Christian Doctrine. This office would oversee primarily the catechetical instruction of children not enrolled in parish schools. Known as CCD to many, the program was staffed by sisters from the parish schools and dedicated members of the laity. In the early days, some would have considered it a somewhat simple task. After all it was just making sure that the children learned the answers to the Baltimore Catechism. Answers are one thing, but instilling an attitude of devotion is something else; a tall order that many parishes wrestled with. Father Litot was succeeded in 1968 by Father Michael Kenney who remained in the office until his departure from the priesthood in 1970. After that Bishop Grutka reserved the supervision of the program to himself until 1978 when Father J. Patrick Gaza was named to the post. But it was in the early seventies that the bishop began to work on a plan that would improve the catechesis in a post-Vatican II world. The plan developed in 1973 as the Institute of Religion which would be under the direction of Father Carl Mengeling, who was then pastor of Nativity Parish in Portage. Catechists would be formally trained in theology and educational methods and would receive college credit for their work. In collaboration with Saint Joseph College, Calumet Campus students would be awarded credits for their work that could be used toward a Bachelor of Arts degree. The courses would be taught at satellite sites in the evenings throughout the diocese so that students would not have to travel to the college. The faculty would be priests of the diocese whose degrees were in the area of study of the courses offered. Courses were offered in Scripture, Liturgy, Theology, Methods, and History and would rotate around the different sites so that a student could finish the entire program at the same place. Throughout the program's history, sites were often at Marquette in Michigan City, Saint Peter in LaPorte, Saint Paul in Valparaiso, Saints Peter & Paul in Merrillville, Saint Mary in Crown Point, Our Lady of Grace in Highland, and Bishop Noll Institute in Hammond. The areas had different nights during the week so that if a student wanted to take more than one course a semester, it could be done. The program was a great success and flourished until the early nineties, when the Clock Hours Program meant to serve as post graduate enrichment supplanted it.

Thunderhouse

What was originally a doctor's clinic owned by Porter Memorial Hospital has become a busy Catholic community formed by Catholic undergraduates attending Valparaiso University. The idea was formulated in 1973 by the pastor of Saint Paul Parish, Monsignor John Charlebois and his assistant, Father Joseph Murphy. The parish church was not close to the campus and students, particularly those without transportation found it difficult to attend mass on Sundays. The hospital had announced their plans for expansion, and as the clinic was in the way it was to be razed and bids for the project were solicited.

As Monsignor's bid was the only one offered, the building was his for one-hundred dollars. Knowing that the building would have to be close to the campus for the program to be a success, parishioners and friends of the project got together to raise the necessary funds to move the building to its present site down the street from the hospital and across from the campus; a mere walking distance from new dormitories. The resituated and remodeled building would include a lounge, study rooms, a counseling area, Chaplain's quarters, kitchen facilities, and chapel.

Thunderhouse (named for the apostles James and John, "the Sons of Thunder") was dedicated on 25 April 1974 by Bishop Grutka. Father Murphy was the first chaplain. He was succeeded by Father Michael Ruggaber (1975-1977), Father Timothy Benante (1977), Father John Savio (1978-1982), Father Roy Beeching (1982-1984), Father Thomas Mischler (1984-1986), Father Terrence Chase (1986-1988), Father Douglas Mayer (1988-1996), and the current chaplain Father Kevin McCarthy since December of 1996.

The apostolate has been a great success, and though in 1987 Bishop Gaughan had toyed with the idea of terminating the program, he instead initiated a change of name: Saint Teresa of Avila Catholic Student Center to give the place a more recognizable Catholic identity. It had been argued that Catholic students, not knowing what Thunderhouse meant, did not realize that it was a Catholic Center.

The advisory board in 2000, realizing more space was needed, was able with the approval of Bishop Melczek, to secure title to the building next door, a former pharmacy. This building has become the worship space not only for students but of friends of the program. The center has unofficially developed into a University Parish and has been quite successful in its apostolate.

Disappointments

Catechesis would come to the forefront of attention at this particular time, as parish schools were beginning to close. Costs were beginning to rise particularly in heating oil, insurance, and salaries. Many of the congregations of Sisters who staffed these schools were experiencing a shortage of vocations; so as older teachers retired or died, there was no one to replace them. Pastors were forced to consider whether or not to continue with faculties comprised of lay teachers only. Some places were happy to do this; others found it to be cost prohibitive and so they eventually closed. Orders of religious men also were finding it difficult to keep there own institutions. The Capuchin Franciscans, who were invited to Fort Wayne by Bishop Noll in 1928 to establish their novitiate, eventually built a house of study as their college department in the countryside of Crown Point in 1959 which Bishop Grutka would dedicate on 22 August. From there they would be appointed to Marathon, Wisconsin to study theology. The Fathers and seminarians were of great help to the diocese, as the priests would help local pastors on Sundays. The seminarians would often be on hand at the Cathedral as the choir for Holy Week Services. In 1974, the provincial consultors decided to consolidate their property. Their foundation at Crown Point would be sold and the students moved to Marathon. Bishop Grutka was offered the property, which was extensive. Many said it would have been ideal for the seminary he had always wanted. It could have also served as a retirement home for priests, which he was planning at the time, and also a retreat house. It was big enough for all those opportunities. For whatever reason, he passed on the offer. The property eventually went to the First Baptist Church in Hammond who established Hyles-Anderson College on the property. The Salesians of Don Bosco, who operated a minor seminary in Cedar Lake, closed their property in 1979 also to consolidate their manpower. The seminary had opened in January of 1956 and was popular in the diocese for their weekend vocation retreats that were offered to junior high school age boys in the area. It was estimated that 700 hundred boys annually made the vocation retreats.

The A.F.T. and fear of the loss of Catholic Identity

What started as a question of fairness, snowballed into a struggle that caused hurt feelings, the exile of priests, embarrassment to the diocese, legal suits, and the original question forgotten.

In 1974, some of the women teaching at Bishop Noll Institute were concerned about the pension program which was restricted to ten consecutive years of service. This would exclude anyone who took time from teaching to raise their children.

Hoping to be able to change the policy, a letter was planned to the Superintendent for redress. Instead, during discussion of the draft, the aims were broadened to consider organizing for collective bargaining.

With the advent of 1975 the group approached diocesan officials by letter and in public meetings, stating their intentions based on the social teachings of the Church, particularly in the writings of Popes Leo XIII and Pius XI as well as the documents of the Second Vatican Council. At first the group intended to form an independent union, but instead some teachers suggested affiliation with the American Federation of Teachers (AFT). Some of the priests on the faculty, consulted on these social teachings, were seen as giving aid to the group.

The Superintendent of Schools would reply in May stating that a teachers' union in a Catholic school would be "incompatible with the faith community effort."

With the beginning of the school year 1975-1976, Bishop Grutka attended the opening faculty meeting at Bishop Noll Institute in the company of a new principal. He attested to his support for Catholic education and the fact that he would always take care of the teachers. He also mentioned, as something of an afterthought, that two of the priests on the faculty the previous year had been transferred to special assignments. Privately he would tell the priests on the faculty that they were to make no public statements on the issue. Talk among the laity, however, was that there would be a vote to unionize.

Some months later, the Superintendent of Schools wrote to all the teachers of the diocese:

"Either we as Catholics are in the field of education together, or there is no human or Faith reason for Catholic Schools to exist. He who wants to choose up sides forgets that the Catholic Faith is unifying in its concept, not divisive or adversarial in nature."

The National Labor Relations Board (NLRB) accused the diocese of unfair labor practices; the diocese sued in Federal Court, and the disagreement was played out in the newspapers. The "union" was still unofficial having no formal recognition other than support from the AFT. The recognized "president" was fired for insubordination in February of 1976 for publishing an open letter stating that Bishop Grutka's reputation as a friend of labor needed to be "exposed as the sham it is."

The next month in a letter dated 14 March 1976 to the people of the diocese, the bishop would state:

"The right to govern our schools according to the mind of the Church and in them –to teach as Jesus did—is being threatened. This is the real reason why we are struggling to prevent anyone from interfering with ecclesiastical jurisdiction over our schools. …

"Most reluctantly we had to resort to a Court of Justice in order to question as firmly as possible the propriety of an agency of the United States Government entangling itself with our schools in response to a demand by some of our lay teachers. …

"The United States Government – through repeated decisions by its Supreme

Court – has consistently ruled that our schools are religious institutions and therefore ineligible for supporting funds from the Government. This means that our schools are denied the financial aids which would enable them to pay their teachers salaries equal to teachers in the public schools. ...

"Problems of whatever kind involving the Church should be solved within the Church community. Entanglement with the governmental and other secular agencies should be scrupulously avoided. We shall resist with all our strength any interference from outside sources in the conduct of our schools. ...

"This letter is being written in response to considerable pressure directed at the office of the Bishop to reveal his mind in this situation. There has been an awareness on my part of the unrest in one or another of our schools for some time. My very strong belief in the principle that one who governs best is one who governs the least, kept delaying my intervention. The tension has now reached the point where decisive action on my part becomes absolutely unavoidable."

In October 1976, the courts ruled in favor of the diocese concerning the unfair labor practice suit, but allowed the vote to continue. The NLRB counted the votes which revealed the decision of the diocesan lay teachers not to unionize by a vote of 260 to 172. The diocesan chancellor when asked to comment on the decision stated, "I think it indicates that our teachers see the wisdom of noninterference by the government in our schools." Some of the organizers were convinced that the AFT was their downfall; if they had stayed independent within the social teachings of the Church, they felt that even the hierarchy within the diocese would have supported them.

Saint Hedwig Church, Gary

Losses suffered

On 6 May 1971, some members of the faculty at Bishop Noll Institute participated in an outing by attending the dinner theater at the Candlelight Playhouse in Summit, Illinois. Upon leaving the theater, the group was struck by a car that careened out of control onto the pavement. A number of teachers were seriously injured, and thirty-year-old Father David Hauskins was killed. Father Hauskins was ordained in Rome on 17 December 1966 and assigned to the faculty at Bishop Noll Institute with residence at Saint Joseph Parish the following July. Very popular with students and parishioners, his funeral mass at Saint Joseph on 10 May was one of the largest the city had ever experienced; mourners, unable to get into the crowded church were forced to stand in the street. A native of Michigan City, he was buried in the Priests' section of Saint Stanislaus Cemetery.

Mark Furman

In May of 1973, Father Martin, the executive director of the CYO announced that Mark Furman would become the new director, replacing the retiring Robert Begin. A graduate of Bishop Noll Institute and Lewis College, he was well-suited to the task, full of fresh ideas and energy. Not only Camp Lawrence, but all areas of the CYO: the music program, the volunteer program, day camp, summer field trips, sports and academic programs were infused with new energy. Father Martin as well as others who worked closely with the youth of the diocese was hopeful that this would be a long and successful partnership. And so, it was with great shock that on the morning of 18 January 1978 it was announced on the radio that a couple returning from Milwaukee to their home in Schererville were involved in an auto accident on the Calumet Expressway. In later broadcasts

CYO Awards

CYO band

their names were released. Mark and Claudia Furman were hit from behind, and when they pulled over to the shoulder of the road, the driver and passenger of the other car approached their car and shot them. Passersby summoned for help; Mrs. Furman survived her injuries and was taken to Saint Margaret Hospital in Hammond. Mark Furman did not survive. The funeral mass was concelebrated by Bishop Grutka and priests of the diocese at Our Lady of Grace Church in Highland on 23 January. A crowd of mourners filled the church listening to Father Martin as he preached the homily of the mass: "We simply don't have the answer. Life and death are truly mysteries. We don't like to live with mystery, we always want answers. But we must always conclude that God is in control—His way is not our way." Bishop Grutka would add during the eulogy, "Mr. Furman's words and deeds as a mortal, will ensure him a warm welcome at the gates of Paradise."

New Growth

In 1977, Bishop Grutka announced the formation of a new parish in Dyer. Situated in the north of the town, it would be carved out of the parish territories of Saint Joseph in Dyer and Saint Thomas More in Munster, which at the time was the largest parish in the diocese. Father Richard Ameling was given charge of organizing the community and building the church that would be named in honor of Saint Maria Goretti. A year later, Father John Savio was asked to form a new parish in the south of Porter County at Lake Eliza (as it was then called). The parish would serve the growing community on the Porter County side of the Lakes of the Four Seasons community. It would also care for new subdivisions being planned westward from Valparaiso. The parish, named for the latest canonized American citizen, Saint Elizabeth Ann Seton, met on Sundays for mass in the dance hall at Lake Eliza until they could build their church. It was dedicated in 1982 with a seating capacity of five-hundred. The growth of the area far exceeded expectations, and Bishop Grutka was heard to remark at a meeting of the Priests' Senate, "Where did all these people come from; it was too small on the day it was dedicated." Also in 1978, Father Timothy Benante was asked to direct a new spiritual center in the diocese that could be used for retreats, days of recollection, or spiritual direction. It was to be located at the former Brothers' Residence on the campus of Bishop Noll Institute and named the Seimetz Center after Father Frank Seimetz, a former principal of the school who died in 1965.

Groundbreaking at Saint Maria Goretti

Surgery

In 1976, Bishop Grutka was hospitalized at Saint Mary's Mercy in Gary where he was diagnosed with an ulcer. Two years later, at the age of sixty-nine, and for the first time in his life, he would undergo surgery at the Mayo Clinic. The surgeons there removed a tumor from his colon. This took place in June, 1978. He recuperated at Camp Lawrence for six weeks, staying at his cabin, while the Albertine Sisters, staying at the Sisters' Cabin on the hill, took care of his meals and general housekeeping. The camp proved to be the perfect place for his recuperation. As he had no car, he couldn't go anywhere, and the camp chaplain served as watchdog to keep visitors at bay. The absolute necessities of chancery work would be brought to him by the chancellor as needed. The rest proved to work well, and he was still able to preside at the ordination in July.

Permanent Diaconate Program

As the Second Vatican Council restored the diaconate to its full status of ministry in the Church, the diocese would come to accept permanent deacons as a blessing to the community.

The first permanent deacon was John Beda. As yet, there was no program of formation in the diocese. And so, at the age of sixty-two, he entered to study for ordination at Saints Cyril and Methodius Seminary, Orchard Lake, Michigan for a period of three years. Bishop Grutka ordained him on 9 May 1971 at Assumption Church in East Chicago, and he was assigned to work at Saint James the Less, assisting the pastor and community in works of charity and the Word. He died on Christmas day, 1972, at sixty-six years of age. Deacon Walter Stone studied for the Archdiocese of Chicago but later moved to Knox. His transfer being approved by Bishop Grutka, he ordained him at Saint Thomas Aquinas on 8 December 1972. He served at Saint Thomas until he was appointed to assist the pastor of Saints Peter and Paul on 30 October 1977 where he ministered until his untimely death in 1978 at the age of forty-nine.

It was at this time that Bishop Grutka announced the establishment of a diocesan program for the education and training of permanent deacons. Father William Martin was appointed the first director. The faculty would comprise the priests who taught in the Institute of Religion. Camp Lawrence was chosen as the first venue for the project. For a period of three years, candidates would spend weekends of formation at the camp taking classes in theology and scripture. Later, these weekend sessions would move to the Seimetz Center, which suited the program more appropriately. The program grew to three classes of candidates. In all, forty-two men from this program were ordained by Bishop Grutka between 1981 and 1984. The first class of permanent deacons was ordained on Sunday, 22 February 1981 at the Cathedral. Aside from being the memorable event it was, it was also the first time in anyone's memory that the bishop broke with his usual solemnity during the liturgy. During the ordination rite, after the homily, there would normally follow the commitment to celibacy before the examination of the candidates. Of course as these were not to be transitional deacons, candidates for the priesthood, the commitment would be omitted. Whether it was the bishop or the master of ceremonies who was distracted, the bishop launched right into it: "By your own free choice you seek to enter the order of deacons. You shall exercise this ministry in the celibate state. . ." and then he paused, realizing what he had just said, and then broke into a smile and said, "Oh, we can't be doing this."

The deacons, of these first three classes, were assigned to work in their home parishes for the most part, sometimes moving to other parishes because of work commitments. After the third class was ordained in 1984, the program was suspended with the advent of Bishop Gaughan.

Jubilees

The diocese celebrated the tenth and twentieth anniversaries of the diocese at the cathedral. These events while public in nature were more the marking of the bishop's episcopate. Many speculated at the twentieth, that the reason for the celebration was that the bishop would probably not be with us for the jubilee. But this was not the case. The silver jubilee of the diocese was celebrated on a grand scale. As the cathedral would not be large enough for the celebration, the new Genesis Convention Center in Gary was secured for the purpose. Busloads of the faithful from around the diocese arrived on Sunday, 21 February for the celebration of the Eucharist, concelebrated by the bishop, the priests of the diocese and twenty-two bishops from around the country. Among the honored guests, was John Cardinal Carberry, retired Archbishop of St. Louis. Archbishop Edward O'Meara of Indianapolis preached the homily, as his predecessor had done twenty-five years before. In his remarks at the end of mass, Bishop Grutka spoke of his immense debt of gratitude that could never be repaid except through prayer. He reminded the congregation that "more things are done by prayer than we can possibly imagine." At the end of mass as the recession made its way down the center aisle, it turned up a side aisle, passing the bleachers where the priests were seated. As the Bishop passed, the group of priests broke into spontaneous applause which surprised some, but was certainly seen as a fitting tribute. The next day another celebration took place at the cathedral with a dinner following for the clergy and the bishops invited guests.

December of 1983 marked another jubilee of a personal nature; the bishop's golden anniversary of his ordination to the priesthood. The celebration took place at Bishop Noll Institute. A concelebrated mass by the bishop, the priests of the diocese, and guest bishops was celebrated in the field house with a reception afterwards. The bishop remarked on his gratitude to God for the gift of fifty years in the priesthood and of his remarkable good fortune to pastor this diocese for twenty-six of those years.

Silver Jubilee Celebration at the New Genesis Center

Albertine Home established

In September, 1974, Bishop Grutka welcomed to the diocese four sisters of the Albertine Order from Krakow, Poland. Their arrival began the bishop's plan to establish a retirement home for the priests of the diocese. The sisters spent their first summer at Camp Lawrence. There, with the help of volunteers, they began to learn English. In the fall the bishop assigned them to different convents so that they could immerse themselves in the language and familiarize themselves with American customs and way of life. Until such time as a site would be chosen for the retirement home they took up residence at the convent of Saint Joseph parish in Hammond. It was here that they began their work; their first resident was Monsignor Schmid whom they cared for until his death in 1991.

The choice of the site of the home was proving to be a problem. While some of the priests suggested Camp Lawrence, Bishop Grutka felt the retirees should not be isolated. He wanted to build in an urban area near hospitals and in an area that would be convenient for travel. His choice was on the campus of Bishop Noll Institute. By appropriating the

Albertine Home

convent, work got underway in 1983 with the addition of a three storey wing connected perpendicular to the original structure. This addition was comprised of eighteen two room suites. Dining and other facilities, including the chapel would be housed in the convent section of the building. Bishop Grutka dedicated the building on 22 July 1984. While there have always been retired priests in residence at the Home, they have never filled the residential wing. Soon after its opening, relatives of priests or former diocesan employees were given the opportunity to retire to the Albertine Home.

Retirement

The beginning of 1984 brought with it great expectations for the future. Bishop Grutka, who reached his seventy-fifth birthday in November, 1983 submitted his letter of retirement to the Holy See as required. The next step would be the acceptance of that letter and the naming of a successor. Speculation was widespread; would it be someone from the diocese? Names of some of the priests were bandied about, some with hopefulness, others, with trepidation. But the prevailing attitude was that it would be a complete stranger. Bishop Grutka stayed away from these conversations. He spent his time in the normal daily occupation of his office, now on the third floor of the cathedral grade school, except now it was time to start organizing his personal files for packing and removal in order to prepare for his successor.

In one of his last acts as bishop, he named fourteen priests to honorary prelacies (monsignori), which he had not done since the close of the Vatican Council, and elevated two to a higher rank. This was seen as an act of gratitude to those who labored closely with him these many years in the work of the diocese; priests who not only worked in his curia, the chancery and tribunal, but also those who helped develop the programs and parishes that would foster the growth both spiritual and physical of the diocese. The date of the mass for their "installation" was announced for 19 July at Saint John the Baptist in Whiting. Ten days earlier, on 9 July, the Vatican would accept the bishop's resignation. With grateful thanks for his years of service he was given the title Bishop Emeritus of Gary, and asked to function as the Apostolic Administrator until such time as his successor was installed. An era of twenty-seven years was completed; now the wait truly began.

At his chancery desk

The Poor Handmaids of Jesus Christ
(The Ancilla Domini Sisters)

Founded in Germany in 1851 by Blessed Catherine Kasper; their first foundation in the United States was in 1868. Total number of professed Sisters in the United States is 149.

Their ministry is in the field of academic education on all levels, healthcare, parish ministries, retreat ministries, childcare institutions and retirement homes.

Their labor in the vineyard:

Saint Mary	East Chicago	1913-1994
Saint Mark	Gary	1931-1986
Saint Ann	Gary	1945-1987
Our Lady of Perpetual Help	Hammond	1943-1992
Saint Catherine of Siena	Hammond	1957-to the present
Catholic Central High School	Hammond	1921-1933
Saint Catherine Hospital	East Chicago	1928-to the present
Saint Mary Mercy Hospital	Gary	1913-1994
Saint Mary Mercy Hospital	Hobart	1973-2001
Holy Family Hospital	LaPorte	1900-1966
Bethany Retreat House	East Chicago	1992-to the present
Sojourner Truth House	Gary	1995-to the present

The School Sisters of Notre Dame

Founded in Germany in 1833 by Blessed Theresa of Jesus (Caroline Gerhardinger); their first foundation in the United States was in1847. Total number of professed Sisters in the United States is 2209.

Their ministry is in the field of academic education on all levels, Directors of Religious Education, Pastoral Associates, ministry to women, the poor, sick, and elderly.

Their labor in the vineyard:

Saint Patrick	Chesterton	1894-1973
Holy Angels	Gary	1909-1979
Saint Luke	Gary	1917-1970
Saints Peter & Paul	Merrillville	1905-to the present
Saint Stanislaus	Michigan City	1898-1986
Saint Mary, I. C.	Michigan City	1897-1934
Saint Mary High School	Michigan City	1897-1934

The Sisters of Providence of Saint-Mary-of-the-Woods

Founded in France in 1806 by Saint Theodora Guerin; their first foundation in the United States was in 1840. Total number of professed Sisters in the United States is 473.

Their ministry is in the field of academic education on all levels, Diocesan Offices, Parish and Pastoral Ministry, Health Care and Retirement Homes.

THEIR LABOR IN THE VINEYARD:

Saint Mary	East Chicago	1901-1913
All Saints	Hammond	1897-1972
Saint Joseph	Hammond	1886-1972
Saint John the Baptist	Whiting	1900-1987
Sacred Heart	Whiting	1895-1987
Saint Edward	Lowell	1915-1994
Marquette High School	Michigan City	1975-1980
Diocesan Marriage	Tribunal	1989-to the present

The Sisters of Saints Cyril and Methodius

Founded in the United States in 1909. Total number of professed Sisters is 122.

Their ministry is in the field of Academic Education, Parish ministry and Religious Education, Retreat and Spiritual Direction, Hospital chaplaincy, Homes for the aged, and prison ministry.

THEIR LABOR IN THE VINEYARD:

Holy Trinity	Gary	1911-1995
Immaculate Conception	Whiting	1926-1985
Andrean High School	Merrillville	1959-to the present

Carmelites

The Sisters of Saint Francis of Perpetual Adoration

Founded in Germany in 1863 by Mother Maria Theresia Bonzel; their first foundation in the United States was in 1875. Total number of professed Sisters in the United States is 208.

Their ministry is in the field of academic education on all levels, Health Care in Hospitals, Ecclesial Ministry at parish and diocesan levels.

THEIR LABOR IN THE VINEYARD:

Saint Bridget	Hobart	1927-1941
Saint Mary	Griffith	1928-to the present
Saint Casimir	Hammond	1901-1985
Our Lady of Grace	Highland	1954-1999
Saint Joseph	LaPorte	1896-to the present
Saint Edward	Lowell	1915-1971
Saints Cyril & Methodius	North Judson	1911-1970
Saint John Evangelist	St. John	1907-1901
Saint Francis Xavier	Lake Station	1965-1973
Saint Margaret Hospital	Hammond	1898-to the present
Saint Anthony Hospital	Michigan City	1903-to the present
St. Margaret Mercy Hospital	Dyer	1992-to the present
Saint Anthony Hospital	Crown Point	1999-to the present

The Sisters of Saint Joseph, Third Order of Saint Francis

Founded in the United States in 1901 by Mother Felicia and Mother Clara. Total number of professed Sisters is 374.

Their ministry is in the field of academic education on all levels, Pastoral Ministry, Health Care Services and Continuing care retirement community.

THEIR LABOR IN THE VINEYARD:

Saint Stanislaus	East Chicago	1923-to the present
Our Lady of Guadalupe	East Chicago	1930-1964
Holy Family	Gary	1926-1978
Saint John Bosco	Hammond	1952-to the present
Saint Bridget	Hobart	1996-2005

Class of St. Joseph's School, Laporte, in 1896

Our Lady of Victory Missionary Sisters

Founded in the Fort Wayne diocese in 1922 by Father John Sigstein. Total number of professed Sisters is 149.

Their ministry is in the field of catechetics.

THEIR LABOR IN THE VINEYARD:

Queen of Heaven Mission Center	East Chicago	1930s-1960s
Our Lady of Fatima Convent	Gary	1930s-1960s
All Saints	San Pierre	1925-1940s

Franciscan Sisters of the Sacred Heart

Founded in Germany in 1866 by Sister Coletta Himmelsbach; their first foundation in the United States was in1876 in Avilla, Diocese of Fort Wayne. Total number of professed sisters is 114.

Their ministry is in the field of academic education, Pastoral Ministry, Health Care Services and Social Work.

THEIR LABOR IN THE VINEYARD:

Saint Michael	Schererville	1900-to the present
Saint Joseph	Dyer	1901-1988

Missionaries of Charity

Founded in India in 1950 by Blessed Teresa of Calcutta. Total number of professed sisters is 4500.

Their ministry is in the field of Soup Kitchens, Emergency Shelters, Homes for unwed mothers, Homes for AIDS patients, Hospital and shut-in ministry, After-school and Summer Camp programs for children.

THEIR LABOR IN THE VINEYARD:

Saint Mark Convent	Gary	1999-to the present

Carmelite Home for Boys

Carmelite Home for Girls

Carmelite Sisters of the Divine Heart of Jesus

Founded in Germany in 1891 by Mother Maria Teresa Tauscher; first convent in the United States in 1912. Total number of professed Sisters in the United States is 70.

Their ministry is in the field of Homes for Children, Homes for the Aged, Day Nurseries, and mission work.

THEIR LABOR IN THE VINEYARD:

St. Joseph Home	East Chicago	1913-to the present
St. Joseph Home of the Divine Child	Hammond	1915-to the present

Congregation of the Sisters of Saint Agnes

Founded in the United States in 1858 by Mother Agnes Hazotte. Total number of professed Sisters is 319.

Their ministry is in the field of academic and religious education, hospitals, homes for the aged, parish ministry, social services, healthcare.

THEIR LABOR IN THE VINEYARD:

Saint Mary	Crown Point	1868-1995
Sojourner Truth House	Gary	1997-to the present

Congregation of the Sisters of Holy Cross

Founded in France in 1841 by Basil Anthony Moreau; first convent in the United States in 1843. Total number of professed Sisters is 506.

Their ministry is in the field of academic education on all levels, Adult Education Centers, Social Service Centers, Human Rights Centers, Hospitals and other Health ministries

THEIR LABOR IN THE VINEYARD:

St. John the Evangelist	St. John	1846-1907
Saint Patrick	East Chicago	1923-1974
Queen of All Saints	Michigan City	1952-2006
Notre Dame	Michigan City	1955-1981
St. Mary, I. C.	Michigan City	1886-1897 & 1934-1985
Saint Mary of the Lake	Gary	1949-1977
Saint Peter	LaPorte	1923-1972
Saint Paul	Valparaiso	1867-1987
Bishop Noll Institute	Hammond	1933-1987
St. Stanislaus	Michigan City	1891-1897
St. Ambrose Academy	Michigan City	1869-1886
St. Mary High School (Marquette)	Michigan City	1886-1897 &1934-1996
Angela House	Michigan City	1994-to the present
Our Lady of Holy Cross	San Pierre	1993-to the present

Franciscan Sisters of Chicago
(Franciscan Sisters of Blessed Kunegunda)

Founded in Chicago in 1894 by Mother Mary Theresa. Total number of professed Sisters is 71.

Their ministry is in the field of academic and religious education.

THEIR LABOR IN THE VINEYARD:

Saint John Cantius	East Chicago	1905-1979
Saint Adalbert	Whiting	1905-1913
Saint Joseph	East Chicago	1918-1968
Blessed Sacrament	Gary	1965-1986
Sacred Heart	Gary	1914-1968
Saint Hedwig	Gary	1917-1977
Saint Mary	Hammond	1912-1970
Sacred Heart	LaPorte	1916-1970
Assumption	New Chicago	1918-1969
Saint Anthony Home	Crown Point	1939-to the present
Saint Anthony Hospital	Crown Point	1974-1999

Congregation of the Sisters of the Third Order of Saint Francis, Servants of the Poor. *(The Albertine Sisters)*

Founded in Poland in 1891 by Saint Albert Chmielowski. First convent in the United States in 1974 in the Diocese of Gary.

Their ministry is in the field of health care.

THEIR LABOR IN THE VINEYARD:

The Albertine Home	Hammond	1984-to the present

Mantellate Sisters Servants of Mary of Blue Island

Founded in Italy in 1861 by Filomena Rossi and Giovanna Ferrari; first convent in the United States in 1916. Total number of professed Sisters in the United States is 13.

Their ministry is in the field of academic and religious education.

THEIR LABOR IN THE VINEYARD:

Saint Bridget	Hobart	1942-1992

Adorers of the Blood of Christ

Founded in Italy in 1834 by Saint Maria De Mattias; first convent in the United States in 1870. Total number of professed Sisters in the United States is 380.

Academic education on all levels, special and religious education, pastoral care, nursing homes, diocesan offices, homes for the aged.

THEIR LABOR IN THE VINEYARD:

Most Precious Blood	Wanatah	1888-1904
Holy Trinity (Croatian parish)	East Chicago	1917-1992
Immaculate Conception	East Chicago	1933-1977

Felician Sisters

(Sisters of Saint Felix of Cantalice, Third Order of Saint Francis)

Founded in Poland in 1855 by Blessed Mary Angela Truszkowska; first convent in the United States in 1874. Total number of professed Sisters is 1049.

Their ministry is in the field of academic education on all levels, Catechetical Centers and Religious Education programs, Health Care, Retreat Centers.

THEIR LABOR IN THE VINEYARD:

Saint Mary	Otis	1914-1965
Nativity of Our Savior	Portage	1965-1971

Daughters of Divine Charity

Founded in Austria in 1868 by Mother Franziska Lechner; first convent in the United States in 1913. Total number of professed Sisters is 81.

Their ministry is in the field of academic education, home for parish ministry, homes for the aged.

THEIR LABOR IN THE VINEYARD:

Saint Emeric	Gary	1922-1962
Holy Trinity (Hungarian parish)	East Chicago	1922-1956

Homework

In Class

Sisters of the Holy Family of Nazareth

Founded in Poland in 1875 by Blessed Mary of Jesus the Good Shepherd (Frances Siedliska); first convent in the United States in 1885. Total number of professed Sisters is 434.

Their ministry is in the field of academic education, hospitals and health care.

THEIR LABOR IN THE VINEYARD:

Saint Adalbert	Whiting	1913-1977

Company of Mary

Founded in France in 1607 by St. Jeanne de Lestonnac; first convent in the United States in 1926. Total number of professed Sisters is 46.

Their ministry is in the field of academic education, Religious Instruction Centers, Retreat Centers, Health ministries.

THEIR LABOR IN THE VINEYARD:

Little Company of Mary Health Facility	San Pierre	1941-1993

Sisters of the Blessed Sacrament for Indians and Colored People

Founded in the United States in 1891 by Saint Katherine Drexel. Total number of professed Sisters is 194.

Their ministry is in the field of academic education on all levels, catechetical schools, Adult Education and Social Service.

THEIR LABOR IN THE VINEYARD:

Saint Monica	Gary	1945-1985

Sisters of Saint Casimir

Founded in the United States by Mother Maria Kaupas in 1907. Total number of professed Sisters is 131.

Their ministry is in the field of academic education, foreign missions, hospitals, pastoral ministry.

THEIR LABOR IN THE VINEYARD:

Saint Francis	East Chicago	1927-1973
Saint Casimir	Gary	1928-1968

Sisters of Saint Benedict of Pontifical Jurisdiction
(Peoria, IL)

Erected by decree of the Holy See on 25 February 1922, with twenty monasteries in the United States and two in Mexico. Total number of professed Sisters is 904.

Their ministry is in the field of academic education, parish ministry, retreats and spiritual direction.

THEIR LABOR IN THE VINEYARD:

Saint Thomas More	Munster	1949-to the present
Saint James the Less CCD	Highland	1976-1979

Sisters of Mercy of the Union

Catherine McAuley founded the Sisters of Mercy in Dublin, Ireland, in 1831. In 1843 the Sisters established their first foundation in the United States at Pittsburgh. In 1929 several of the independent congregations amalgamated to form the Sisters of Mercy of the Union. In 1991 the members of the nine provinces of the Union and of sixteen other Mercy congregations founded the Sisters of Mercy of the Americas. Total number of professed Sisters is 4888.

Their ministry is in the field of academic education, parish ministry, healthcare.

THEIR LABOR IN THE VINEYARD:

Saint Ann Home	Hammond	1940s-1966
Mt. Mercy Sanatorium	Dyer	1940s-1992

Dominican Sisters, Saint Mary of the Springs

There are twenty-three Congregations of the Dominican Sisters of the Third Order of Saint Dominic in the United States. The Congregation of Saint Mary of the Springs is based in Columbus Ohio.

Their ministry is in the field of academic education at all levels, hospitals, care of the elderly, parish ministry, campus ministry, and social work.

THEIR LABOR IN THE VINEYARD:

Saint Mary Mercy Hospital	Gary	1989-1991
Saint Mary Medical Center	Hobart	1991-to the present

Dominican Sisters

THEIR LABOR IN THE VINEYARD:

Saint Thomas Aquinas	Knox	1955-1962

Sisters of Saint Francis of Christ the King

THEIR LABOR IN THE VINEYARD:

Saint Joseph the Worker	Gary	1921-1990

Dominican Sisters

Of Springfield Kentucky

THEIR LABOR IN THE VINEYARD:

Saint Mark	Gary	1927-1931

Sisters of Saint Anne

Founded in India by Bishop Louis Charbonneau in 1956. Total number of professed Sisters in the United States is 8.

Their ministry is in the field of health care and religious education.

THEIR LABOR IN THE VINEYARD:

Holy Angels Cathedral	Gary	1992-to the present
St. Margaret Mercy Hospital	Hammond	1992-to the present
St. Catherine Hospital	East Chicago	1992-to the present

Saint Francis Xavier Church, Lake Station

Norbert Felix Gaughan, D. D., Ph. D.

Born:	30 May 1921 Pittsburgh, Pennsylvania
Ordained a Priest:	St. Vincent Archabbey, Latrobe, Pennsylvania 4 November 1945
Consecrated a Bishop:	Blessed Sacrament Cathedral, Greensburg, Pennsylvania 26 June 1975 Consecrator: Bishop William G. Connare Co-Consecrators: Bishop Cyril Vogel, Bishop John McDowell
Motto:	*Grant a heart that listens*
Auxiliary Bishop of Greensburg PA	2 April 1975 – 24 July 1984
Second Bishop of Gary:	2 October 1984 – 1 June 1996
Died:	1 October 1999 Crown Point, Indiana
Buried:	9 October 1999, St Emma Monastery, Greensburg, Pennsylvania

CHAPTER 4

A New Administration

+Norbert Felix Gaughan, D.D., Ph.D. 1921 – 1999
Hospes Infelix

Mr. Edward Joyce taught at Bishop Noll Institute for thirty-four years and was something of an icon among both students and faculty. He would often preside in the Faculty dining room during the lunch period telling stories about former students or some of the priests who were part of the faculty. Toward the end of Bishop Grutka's episcopacy, talk among the teachers would often consider who his successor might be. Some of the faculty presumed he would be a priest from the diocese, as Bishop Grutka had been. Others, knowing that this was not the norm, could not imagine who he would be, but hoped for someone who would support Catholic education.

Mr. Joyce who came from Uniontown, Pennsylvania, would often remark about the young priest who attended his dying brother. How considerate he was, and what a reputation he had for preaching! Often, people attending mass at the parish in Uniontown would be standing outside the church during mass, because the building was full when Father Gaughan was the celebrant. "We were told that he became a bishop; wouldn't it be something to get someone like him?" Mr. Joyce would say.

Early in the morning, on 24 July 1984, Mr. Joyce received a telephone call from one of the priests on the faculty, "We don't know how you did it, but your horse came in. We just got word that Bishop Gaughan has been named the new Bishop of Gary."

Norbert Felix Gaughan never wanted anyone to know his middle name. Throughout his episcopacy, he used the middle initial only, and when people would ask what it stood for, he would either change the subject or give some flippant remark. Perhaps he saw the irony and did not want to share it. *Felix* is the Latin word for happy and it seemed that for much of his time in Gary, he was not very happy at all.

Born in Pittsburgh, Pennsylvania, on 30 May 1921, he was educated in the Catholic school system, entered Saint Vincent Seminary administered by the Benedictine Abbey at Latrobe and was ordained for the Diocese of Pittsburgh on 4 November 1946. He was assigned as an assistant pastor in Uniontown and later found himself a priest of the Diocese of Greensburg when that diocese was carved from Pittsburgh in 1951. In 1955 he was appointed to the Chancery and became Chancellor in 1960. During this time he earned a doctorate in Philosophy from the University of Pittsburgh. The office of Vicar General of the diocese was added to his responsibilities ten years later, and in 1975, he was consecrated the titular bishop of Taraqua to serve as an auxiliary to the bishop in Greensburg. Whether or not he had thoughts of one day succeeding as bishop of Greensburg, can only be imagined, but would certainly not be unthinkable. If he was disappointed when named to the see of Gary he did not say, but as he spent his years here, there was always a question among some people as to why he would accept an appointment he did not want. Something of his philosophy was uncovered during an interview with a priest who was in the process of being transferred. He told the priest, "as of July first, you are appointed pastor of

Saint **** Parish." The priest later related: "I thought about what he said for a second or two and then said to him 'I accept.' The bishop looked at me and said, 'I'm not asking you, I'm telling you you're going.'" To another priest, in discussion about a transfer, he related the attitude that when a priest is ordained he gives up his free will. Certainly all God's children work throughout their lives learning to surrender themselves to the will of God; still, God himself would not want us to compromise our consciences by giving up his gift of free will. Yet, the bishop indicated that this was so; perhaps telling us more about his own attitude as to why he came to Gary.

When he was appointed to the see of Gary in 1984, he had worked in Greensburg's chancery for just less than thirty years. He was a consummate bureaucrat; task oriented who got things done and expected no less from those around him. If he needed information, he picked up the telephone and called for it. When he got what he wanted, he hung up the phone. No thank you, no goodbye, so preoccupied was he in the task at hand. He seemed to enjoy and cultivate a contentious personality. If he didn't like something, or heard of a situation that irked him, you got a telephone call and heard about it. It was not unusual to see him wagging a finger at a deacon during a Confirmation mass if he felt the deacon had overstepped his bounds liturgically. The clergy, used to Bishop Grutka's style, were bowled over. Yet, there were some who gave back to him as good as they got from him. And he enjoyed it. It seemed he was just waiting for someone to stand up to him; and when you did, he was on your side.

When he became a bishop in 1975, the original motto on his coat of arms was: *Quis tibi penset amor*, which he translated as "What love can balance Thine?" With his coming to Gary, he decided to change the motto to: "Grant a heart that listens" hearkening to the prayer of Solomon that he may be granted understanding as he begins his reign. This was a sincere effort on his part. He actually enjoyed the company of priests and wanted them to be healthy in their work. He began an annual picnic for priests which he hosted at his home in Valparaiso. At parish gatherings such as Confirmations, he would prefer that only priests be invited to the dinner.

Yet he was that unhappy stranger. He chose to live away from Gary preferring the countryside west of Valparaiso. He built the new chancery, the Pastoral Center, in Merrillville because he wanted people to be able to come to the offices (particularly the Tribunal) without fear. A harpoon decorated his office wall; priests were never sure what this meant. Was he reminding himself of his situation or using it in contemplating yours? The cathedral was for the most part ignored. In its renovation in 1973 the cathedra was removed. This seemed to irritate him when he arrived to prepare for his installation. A suitable chair was borrowed for the occasion, but after that time he only used the cathedral when he had to, typically for the Mass of Chrism on Holy Thursday. Other celebrations would be held elsewhere. Ordinations would be celebrated either in an ordinand's home parish or one of ample size in different areas of the diocese for the faithful to attend.

He worked hard and enjoyed his hobbies, particularly photography. But these would not allay the stress of his situation. A diabetic, he suffered a minor stroke in 1989. While not leaving him seriously debilitated, it seemed to toughen his desire to remain independent. He often drove himself to various functions in the diocese and would invariably be late because he would lose his way. Trying to reason with him (as with any stroke victim) at times like these would only make matters worse. He was not careful with his diet which only exacerbated his situation. So it was no surprise to many when he suffered a more serious stroke in February 1992. He was hospitalized for ten weeks of rehabilitation.

He died on 1 October 1999 at Saint Anthony Home in Crown Point; fifteen years to the day he took possession of the diocese. His funeral took place at the cathedral he rarely used in the city he never lived in, in the diocese he did not want. He chose not to be entombed in the cathedral as his predecessor, but to be buried in the cemetery of Saint Emma Convent, the Benedictine Monastery in Greensburg where he had served as chaplain for so many happy years.

Preparations

Those who had the opportunity to attend the meeting at the chancery on 10 August in preparation for the installation of the new bishop knew immediately things would be very different. While Bishop Grutka often preferred to take time to mull over situations, Bishop Gaughan was decisive. There would be two liturgies to prepare. On 1 October, at Evening Prayer in the cathedral, he would take formal possession of the diocese. The next day, the feast of the Holy Angels he would celebrate his installation at 3:00 o'clock in the afternoon in the presence of Archbishop Pio Laghi, the Apostolic Delegate to the United States. After the evening liturgy, a dinner for clergy and guests would be provided at the Radisson Hotel in Merrillville; a reception in the school gymnasium would take place after the installation mass. He was very particular about the liturgies, especially the music. He didn't like long musical settings of hymns and preferred that they not take too much time. He wanted the booklets to not only be useful to the worshippers but also visually appealing. He had suggestions for the layout as well as the artwork for each booklet.

October 1984

In the estimation of the committee he should not be, nor would he be disappointed. Those days of October dawned bright and clear, and everything was in readiness. Evening Prayer was to be celebrated at 6:00 o'clock in the evening.

October 1984

Busloads of clergy and guests arrived from Greensburg to attend the festivities and wish both the bishop and faithful of the diocese well.

Those involved in the liturgy arrived at the cathedral rectory to vest while both Bishops Grutka and Gaughan disappeared upstairs to sign some documents. As it was getting late, one of the masters of ceremonies was sent to fetch the bishops. Not wishing to disturb them, but not having any choice, he approached the doorway. Both men had their backs to the door and did not see his approach. The emcee was about to address Bishop Grutka (as the Apostolic Administrator) whom he felt was still the authority. Instead, as he rapped on the doorpost, he just said, "Excuse me, Bishop." Both men turned toward him, but it was Bishop Gaughan who responded not happy at the disturbance: "Yes?" "It's getting late Bishop, we need to begin." He was told they would be there presently and the emcee would later report that he walked away ambivalent; relieved yet a bit taken aback at the experience.

A month later, in what would become a tradition, the clergy were called together to celebrate mass for the deceased priests of the diocese. This first observance took place at the Salvatorian Shrine in Merrillville with luncheon and a meeting afterward. This first clergy conference with the new bishop was an opportunity for the priests to get to know him. He would be "a heart that listens" according to his motto. Some of the topics broached would be the support of priests, as well as communication with the chancery.

Information from the chancery came in the form of letters that would be received, it seemed, on a daily basis. It was eventually determined that all chancery offices would send out any information weekly in one mailing; also, the Bishop would inaugurate the monthly newsletter, Libenter, where a pastor would find any new diocesan policies clearly written down. Every priest received one copy; pastors received two, so that one could be filed in the parish archives. One of the finest and most pastoral decisions made for the good of the faithful was in the area of the Marriage Tribunal. Since the Vatican Council and the revision of the Code of Canon Law that would not be promulgated until 1985, the process for annulments was "streamlined" yet there were many who found themselves bogged down in what seemed to be hopeless situations and pastors who were not trained in the details of marriage law could not help their situation. Sometimes, people found that a pastor would tell them that what would turn out to be a simple case was impossible, while others would hear that their case would be relatively simple, and then they would find themselves languishing. Bishop Gaughan firmly stated that parish priests would not be involved

Chrism Mass

in this process. They were to give no advice whatsoever, but direct any interested individuals to contact the Marriage Tribunal directly where they would get the adequate information they needed.

As a corollary to this, the bishop wanted people to be able to conduct their business at a chancery that was easily accessible to all; and the third floor of the cathedral school was not that place in his estimation. Ideas were bandied about for a new site. Suggestions were made to move the chancery to Valparaiso, the geographical center of the diocese. Some thought office space should be rented from someplace like the Gary National Bank, others thought a new building was in order, while still others thought that the diocese had plenty of empty schools and convents that could be remodeled appropriately. A decision was made, and ground was broken for a new facility that would be known as the Pastoral Center at Ninety-Third Avenue and Broadway, at the southern edge of Merrillville and the northern limit of Crown Point, on former farmland donated to the Church by the Wirtz family of Crown Point. The new building would house the chancery offices on the south of the building and the tribunal on the north. There would also be space for the Superintendent of Schools and for the Office of Worship. True to his nature, the bishop planned the undertaking meticulously, even down to the type of artwork on the office walls.

The Northwest Indiana Catholic

Bishop Gaughan had a national reputation as a syndicated columnist. Many of his essays were collected and published in book form, most notably *Shepherd's Pie*. He had a love for words and for writing and was chairman of the U. S. Bishops' Communication Committee. As bishop of a diocese he had the opportunity to fulfill the dream of establishing a newspaper of his own creation. That newspaper would be the *Northwest Indiana Catholic*. This was difficult for some people to accept. Many families could say they had subscribed to *Our Sunday Visitor* since its founding by Bishop Noll. And indeed it was our diocesan newspaper even in the new diocese when the national edition would be enfolded by our local news. While the local news would not be ignored, the new paper seemed to be more interested in the national scene.

This publication has proved itself on a national basis being the recipient of many awards, and people have grown to accept it as our diocesan paper; yet, you will still hear some of the old-timers refer to it as "the Sunday Visitor."

The Catholic Services Appeal

Every parish contributes to the support of the diocese by paying a tax which allows the bishop to promote the ministries within the diocese, operate his chancery and contribute to the needs of the universal church. In the diocese of Gary this tax is known as *The Quota* and is determined by a percentage of parish income. Early in Bishop Gaughan's administration, especially with the consolidation of chancery offices and the establishment of new programs, he felt that the quota was only about half of what was needed to keep the diocese functioning. His solution was not unorthodox. He would hold an annual fund appeal as many dioceses throughout the country were already doing. In Gary, it would be called the Catholic Services Appeal. Each pastor was given an additional quota and was expected to fulfill it. They were to contact each parishioner personally (either themselves or with the help of a committee) to secure a pledge that could be paid in six months. Of course all parishes were expected to participate and those falling short of their CSA quota would be billed by the chancery and the money taken from parish savings. The first year of the appeal was in 1987 and was extremely successful. Many today insist that they had misunderstood the bishop's

At work with flood victims in Highland

intentions. They say they believed that the diocese was in some sort of financial trouble and that this appeal was to bail them out. This of course was not the case, for it was the Bishop's intention to make this an annual appeal as many bishops had already done throughout the country. Despite the occasional grumbling by some, the appeal has been successful since its inception and has raised millions of dollars to benefit programs and ministries within the diocese and has allowed the bishop to fulfill our diocesan responsibilities in the support of the Church's world-wide mission.

The Heartland Center

In 1987, Bishop Gaughan invited the Jesuit Fathers of the Chicago Province to the diocese to develop a joint venture which would become known as The Heartland Center. Its mission is to "serve the people of Northwest Indiana through research on social issues, educational programs, leadership training, and community coalition building." This is accomplished through cooperation with the parishes of the diocese as the center works closely with Peace and Social Justice Commissions offering guidance and leadership training. Their research work has provided the diocese with necessary information on regional issues that enable the Church to work toward positive and just social policies. There work also liaises with the Indiana Catholic Conference; this enables parishes to be informed on pending legislation in Indianapolis that would affect the lives of Catholics in Northwest Indiana.

The Jesuit Fathers established their home, the Roque Gonzalez Residence, in the Indiana Harbor section of East Chicago and from there have provided needed assistance to local parishes.

Collaboration

While deaneries had always been in place, with the local dean established as the bishop's authority for that particular area, deanery meetings were rather rare during Bishop

Heartland Center and Habitat for Humanity project

Ordination of Peter Muha

Grutka's administration. He would often hold clergy conferences, usually at the cathedral, scheduled for late in the afternoon so that everyone, including priests teaching in the high schools, would attend. There he would conduct his business, and everyone would be informed of problems or solutions to problems at the same time. Under Bishop Gaughan, the monthly clergy conferences disappeared. Deans would convoke meetings of the clergy within the deanery, but they tended to be sporadic, and only when the need arose. In 1988, the topic of pastoral term limits was brought to the attention of the clergy. Would pastors be willing to accept assignments with a six year term and the possibility of renewing it one time for a total of twelve years in any one assignment? The matter was discussed at deanery meetings and many felt that such a program could not be fairly executed. What about special circumstances, especially in the area of ethnic parishes? Would those pastors be exempt, and if they were, would that be fair to the others? The bishop accepted the deliberation of the deaneries and did not press the issue. The idea of collaboration would always continue to operate during Bishop Gaughan's administration but would hit a roadblock later in the year.

In the fall of 1988, the diocese held the first Presbyteral Convocation. It was seen, as reported by the steering committee, as an opportunity "to create a climate of trust so that priests can talk to one another and be listened to by all members of the presbyterate –including the bishop as a member—and can experience the bonds of support and the beginnings of reconciliation, if that is needed. It is an opportunity to name the personal issues, the personal pain, that historically or presently weigh heavily in the lives of priests." Although he was not opposed to the idea it took Bishop Gaughan awhile to agree to the convocation. And so, all priests were expected to be in attendance for the three day conference at the Holiday Inn in LaPorte. Things went well until one session when an older priest took the bishop to task in regard to the bishop's courtesy when using the telephone. There was some misunderstanding, and the bishop was insulted. The convocation limped along to its conclusion, and the bishop determined never to convene another. And indeed, there would not be another until 1994 after the arrival of Bishop Melczek.

First attack

Bishop Gaughan suffered a "slight" stroke in April 1989. In the May issue of Libenter he reported: "I had a slight stroke which was probably brought on by a combination of factors: diabetes, an illness that runs in my family and for which I am taking medication, and low blood pressure, which may have been caused by a complication of medications. Both of the doctors who attended me suggested that what happened was caused primarily by genetic factors. Neither said anything about overwork, but one did suggest I might limit the amount of hours I work each day... . Even so, I am plagued with worries about some of the things that must be accomplished." A year later, in a letter of May 1990 to the clergy regarding Catholic Charities he wrote: "Last year at this time, I was recuperating from a slight stroke I had suffered in April 1989. Today, thanks to your prayers and those of your parishioners, my recovery continues and I am able to perform my duties. I am doing these carefully, with a view to not allowing anything to happen again." Some might not have agreed with this statement. He continued to work in his office and fulfill the engagements on his calendar. When he tired, he would sometimes get confused with directions and often be late for celebrations in parishes because he would insist on driving himself and then lose his way. He wanted his priests to be healthy, providing medical check ups for them, and surely he wanted to be healthy too, but "plagued with worries" would prove to be too much for his system.

We Can Change the Future

In 1987, a consulting firm was engaged to take a census and survey of all the Catholics in the diocese. Their report to the bishop would result in the program *We Can Change the Future* which would develop a five year plan of pastoral initiatives establishing pastoral councils and move toward renewal among the faithful. Sister Rosemary Hickman, O.P. was engaged in July of 1989 to work toward the development of such a plan. The proposed plan, 1990 – 1995 was presented in April, 1990 with the following goals:

Worship

1. The Diocese of Gary will provide personal and communal opportunities for spiritual growth.

2. The Diocese of Gary will encourage each parish to strive for on-going conversion of its members through a communal emphasis of liturgical life.

Parish life

1. The Diocese of Gary will see evangelization as a primary function of each parish in an on-going personal and communal conversion, calling the inactive, alienated, and the unchurched to membership in the Body of Christ.

2. Parishes of the Diocese of Gary will provide opportunities for "full, conscious, active participation" by all members in building the community life of the parish.

3. Parishes of the Diocese of Gary will model and employ the principles of collaboration and communication through joint ventures in ministry.

4. *The Northwest Indiana Catholic* will tell the story of Catholicism in northwest Indiana, as well as of the broader issues in the universal church.

Priestly Life & Ministry

1. The Diocese of Gary will establish and implement policies and practices required to improve priestly life and morale.

2. The Diocese of Gary will develop and define vehicles to improve communications among and between the bishop and priests.

3. The Diocese of Gary will initiate an aggressive campaign to promote shared responsibility for the mission of the church.

Social Concerns

1. The clergy and laity of the Diocese of Gary will actively participate in social justice and works of charity as a way of life.

2. The director of the office of peace and justice will collaborate with organizations administering social justice programs and works of charity to effect structural change within society.

3. The director of the office of peace and justice will design & implement a plan of social justice for the diocese.

Education

1. The Diocese of Gary will strengthen its commitment to religious education for Catholic school youth and for Catholic youth attending other schools.
2. The Diocese of Gary will improve, strengthen, and broaden its commitment to catholic schools in general.
3. The Diocese of Gary will provide opportunities for continuing education for adults for faith development and preparation for ministry.

Stewardship

1. The Diocese of Gary will provide an ongoing stewardship program for developing needed resources within the diocese.
2. To provide improved administration within the diocese (the objective of this last goal was the establishment of parish pastoral councils within all parishes).

The plan was approved and parishes were directed to begin the necessary work on their areas. While one cynic was heard to remark "Stalin had three five year plans" it is unfair to say the program failed. Indeed the most successful result of the plan besides pastoral councils was the establishment of the Lay Ecclesial Ministry Formation Program. One can't say the plan was sidetracked, but in the next year and a half, there would be major distractions.

Distractions

The government had been investigating gambling in general and bingo in particular at the end of 1989. The McBride Union Hall in Gary had been holding a weekly bingo that drew a large crowd and the union donated some of their profits to local parishes. Questions of accurate record keeping came up and there was talk of money laundering. A grand jury was convened to look into the matter. One of those called to testify was the diocesan chancellor whose parish was a recipient of some of these funds. As his lawyer would later state, "Monsignor had made some mistakes, but did not possess criminal intent."

The pastor was charged with lying to a grand jury, was tried in late 1990 and convicted in February of 1991. In a statement to the press, Bishop Gaughan stated:

"While the court has deemed this matter closed, there is another process that must begin and which I am already initiating: the healing of wounds that may have been caused as a result of Monsignor's alleged behavior and which have occurred as a result of the grand jury indictment and this trial. . . I am proud of the manner in the Diocese of Gary and its personnel, particularly the priests who were called to testify, conducted themselves in the investigation and on the witness stand. It must be noted that upon advice of our legal counsel, the Diocese of Gary cooperated *fully* with the federal government in its investigation. When they asked questions, we answered them. When they sought documents, we provided them. This past Wednesday afternoon, as the government concluded its case, an assistant U. S. attorney Bernard Smith stated emphatically to the jury: 'The Roman Catholic Church is not on trial.'... I pray that we can take the government at its word, and that in no way will this case become a precedent upon which constitutional separation between church and state would ever – for any reason – be violated in the country."

Parishes were directed to make sure that any games of chance operated by the parish would be kept strictly within the laws of the state, with accurate records kept for inspection, and that all applicable taxes be paid in conjunction with these enterprises.

The Pastoral Center Annex

The new Pastoral Center found itself too small for the expanding ministry offices necessary to serve the diocese. To remedy the situation, Bishop Gaughan directed an annex to be built that would contain four new offices, another conference room, and a storeroom. The addition was completed in time for its dedication on 6 September 1991 in the presence of the Apostolic Pro-Nuncio Agostino Cacciavillan.

Religious Education

In the early 1990s, Sister Jeanne McGue, SSND the Diocesan Director of Religious Education developed a new plan that would allow catechists accredited through the Institute of Religion an opportunity for enrichment courses. This program was called the Clock Hours program in which a catechist took a three hour course in various subjects of scripture, liturgy, theology, or history. It was seen as an opportunity to brush up on specific areas of catechesis and was wildly popular. Unfortunately it began to supplant the Institute of Religion. Since the courses were completed in an evening instead of a semester, it became popular with those working toward certification, who would forgo a thirteen week course in place of an evening's work. But this was just a prelude to what was to come. Both programs would soon be replaced by something more challenging and open to all interested parties in participating in the ministry of the Church.

Rite of Acceptance

At work

Second Stroke

Bishop Gaughan suffered a more serious and debilitating stroke that left him paralyzed on his left side in February of 1992. In the spring issue of the Libenter he wrote, "It is well known by now that I spent two and a half months in St. Anthony Hospital, the result of a stroke that was not brought on by overwork, believe me, but as the result of diabetes. . . I was not aware of its intensity and the need to take care of it. I was on a pill, but that did not seem to stop the damage. My sugar was high and that brought on the stroke. . . . I am grateful for your welcome back and your willingness to put up with a handicapped bishop. I am available for appointments." From now on, the bishop would not be able to live on his own. He would have a succession of caregivers who would see to his needs. He still dutifully attended to his work in the chancery, but the situation was getting more difficult. By the summer, something would have to be done.

Cardinal's Visitation

Saint Mary Church, Michigan City

Dale Joseph Melczek, D. D.

Born:	9 November 1938 Detroit, Michigan
Ordained a Priest:	6 June 1964
Consecrated a Bishop:	Consecrator: Edmund Cardinal Szoka Co-Consecrators: Bishop Arthur Krawczak, Bishop Harold Perry, SVD
Motto:	*To Know Christ*
Auxiliary Bishop of Detroit, MI	27 January 1983
Apostolic Administrator of Gary	19 August 1992
Coadjutor Bishop of Gary	28 October 1995
Third Bishop of Gary	1 June 1996

CHAPTER 5

Toward a Future Full of Hope

+Dale Joseph Melczek, D.D.
1992 – 1996 Apostolic Administrator
1996 Bishop of Gary

Bernardin Cardinal Gantin, Prefect of the Congregation for Bishops was aware of Bishop Gaughan's situation. Upon the bishop's release from the hospital in May, he asked the archbishop of Chicago, Cardinal Bernardin, metropolitan of the neighboring province to please visit his neighbor and give a report assessing his capability to administer the diocese. In the normal course of events our own metropolitan, the archbishop of Indianapolis would have been requested to accomplish this mission; but Archbishop O'Meara had died in January and the see of Indianapolis was still vacant. As such, it fell to Cardinal Bernardin who visited twice; in May and in June. Whether or not the visits went well, the archbishop's assessment was that Bishop Gaughan would not be able to continue his administration. The work would only exacerbate his physical condition making matters worse. By August a decision was made and he would have to be informed.

Meanwhile two-hundred twenty-five miles away, in Detroit an unsuspecting auxiliary bishop received a telephone call from the Pro-Nuncio in Washington. The Holy Father was asking if Bishop Melczek be willing to go to Gary and formally administer the diocese. When would the appointment take effect was one of the bishop's questions. The reply came in words to the effect "as soon as Bishop Gaughan is notified, which in fact was yesterday." Following the evangelical dictum to the apostles on the urgency of preaching the gospel "not to carry a traveling bag" Bishop Melczek came immediately, if still not a little shocked, to complete his new mission. He arrived in Gary on 19 August 1992. In meeting the press, it was revealed to the members of the diocese that he was Dale Joseph Melczek, born in Detroit on 9 November 1938 and ordained for the archdiocese on 6 June 1964. He served at Saint Sylvester Parish in Warren, Michigan for seven and one-half years after his ordination, received a Master of Arts degree in education, and was made pastor of Saint Catherine Parish in Detroit in 1972. He would become the Vicar for the west Detroit vicariate in 1973 and be made an archdiocesan consultor the next year. Cardinal Dearden would appoint him his secretary and Vicar General in 1977. When Cardinal Szoka succeeded as archbishop, he retained Bishop Melczek in his positions. He was appointed an auxiliary bishop of Detroit on 3 December 1982 and ordained bishop the following month on 27 January 1983. Capable in administration, he organized for the archdiocese the visit of Pope John Paul II in 1987.

At the press conference that introduced him to the diocese he remarked, "It's important for me to be with the people and not to remain behind a desk. I welcome the chance to meet with priests, deacons, religious and lay people to collaborate in building up the Church of Gary."

The clergy would later meet him at Saint Elizabeth Seton parish. There on Wednesday, 2 September, the priests celebrated a "Rite of

Welcoming for an Apostolic Administrator." During this ritual, the Diocesan Consultors attested to his authority in the diocese by signing a document accrediting his appointment to administer the diocese. In his talk, he desired to meet with the clergy in small groups in order to listen to their hopes and aspirations for the diocese. It would take time to get to know him, but the clergy would discover a great energy. He was delighted to be with us, and the priests would find a person with a highly competitive spirit who was willing to listen and collaborate with the presbyterate during what would be a difficult time for Bishop Gaughan.

In February of the next year he would write to the clergy: "I have said before, but I wish to reiterate, that it is a joy for me to be with you, the Presbyterate of Gary. Your deep faith, loyalty to the Church, and zeal for the Gospel is most edifying." And certainly the feeling was mutual. He lost no time in assessing the needs of the diocese, reviewing the five year plan that had been somewhat sidetracked, accomplishing the daily demands of the chancery, visiting all the parishes, and all the while remaining sensitive to Bishop Gaughan and respectful toward Bishop Grutka making sure he called upon both men on a weekly basis.

An Historic Funeral

Sixty years of faithful service to the Gospel came to a peaceful end on Thursday, 11 November 1993, when Andrew Gregory Grutka, first Bishop of Gary, entered into eternal life. He had succumbed, at his home at Camp Lawrence, to the cancer that had plagued him in his later years. Early in 1992, while attending the wake of a priest's mother, he apologized that he would be unable to attend the funeral as he would be at the Mayo Clinic that day. And then, characteristically, as an aside, "It doesn't look good." And indeed, it wasn't. For the next year and a half he would struggle until the end came that November morning one week short of his eighty-fifth birthday. Preparations had already been made for his funeral. As the diocese had never experienced an event such as this, it would be an historic occasion.

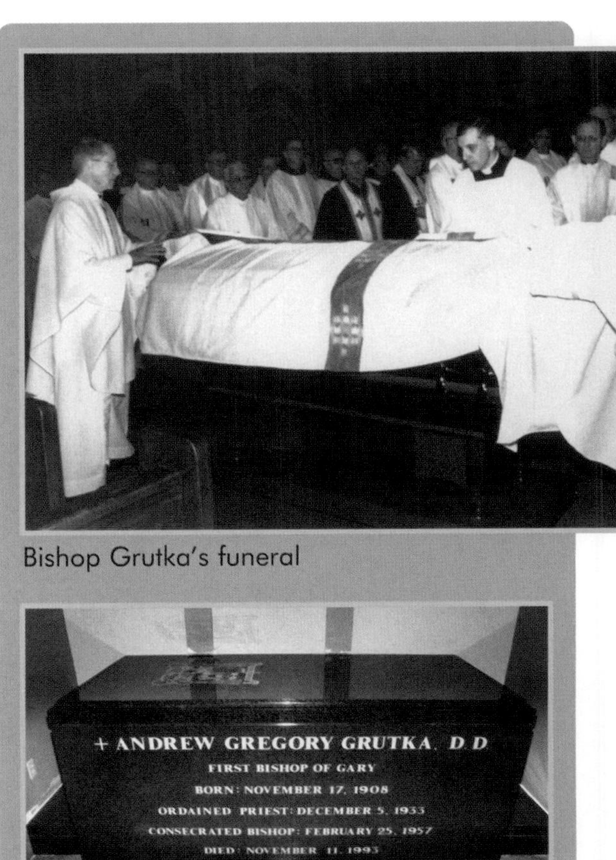

Bishop Grutka's funeral

Bishop Grutka's tomb

On Saturday, Bishop Gaughan presided over the reception of the body at Holy Trinity Parish, Bishop Grutka's former parish, with the wake continuing through evening prayer, which was celebrated by the pastor, Father Michael Yadron. On Sunday, the casket containing the bishop's remains was carried in procession to the cathedral, where Bishop Melczek presided over the reception of the body at noon with vigil prayer. The procession into the cathedral was met by an honor guard from both the Knights of Columbus and the Knights of Saint Peter Claver. Throughout the day mourners filed past the casket, stopping in prayer and paying their respects. The church was closed in the evening and reopened at 9:30 on Monday morning as mourners continued to arrive. Morning Prayer was celebrated at 10:00 o'clock with the Funeral Mass at 11:00 o'clock. The principal celebrant and homilist of the mass was Bishop Joseph Brunini, the retired bishop of Jackson, Mississippi, and one of Bishop Grutka's classmates from Rome. Concelebrants included the clergy of the diocese and visiting bishops and archbishops numbering over one hundred sixty participants. Bishop Brunini spoke of Bishop Grutka's love that drove him to do God's will, and that now "he is very much alive... he now enjoys the glory of God, what divine happiness." Following the final commendation, there was but a brief procession to an alcove next to the apse of the east transept where his remains would be entombed in a granite sarcophagus.

A Future Secured in Two Dioceses

Bishop Melczek continued in his responsibilities as Apostolic Administrator of the diocese throughout the next two years fulfilling his obligations to the people in diocesan liturgies, parish visitations at confirmation time, and in the ordinary duties of the chancery. In the fall of 1995, the announcement came that indeed his work would not be overlooked. The Holy See announced on 28 October, that Bishop Melczek would become the coadjutor Bishop of Gary with the right of succession, meaning that Bishop Gaughan's retirement would become effective on his seventy-fifth birthday, and that Bishop Melczek would succeed him as the third Bishop of Gary automatically.

Ten days later, on the seventh of November, came another announcement that would delight many in the diocese. Monsignor Carl F. Mengeling, pastor of Saint Thomas More parish in Munster, was nominated to become the fourth bishop of the diocese of Lansing, Michigan. Monsignor Mengeling, who had just celebrated his sixty-fifth birthday, was as surprised as anyone. "The Lord has drastically changed my plans. With total trust in the Lord, I humbly accepted, knowing that my frailties will be superseded by the Lord's sufficient grace." A member of the first ordination class in the diocese, he served at Saint Mark in Gary, received his doctorate in Sacred Theology in Rome then returned to teach at Bishop Noll Institute. He became pastor at All Saints in Hammond while at Noll, and later would be the pastor at Holy Name in Cedar Lake for a brief time before becoming the pastor at Nativity of Our Savior in Portage. During his fourteen year stay at Portage, the parish would witness the opening of the parish school as well as the building and dedication of their new church. He became the second pastor at Saint Thomas More in 1985. In the months following his nomination, there would be farewell celebrations in his honor hosted by his parishioners as well as by the priests.

Just as busloads of Pennsylvanians arrived in Gary in 1984 to celebrate with the faithful of the diocese Bishop Gaughan's installation, so did busloads of Hoosiers make their way to Michigan in January 1996 to celebrate with the people of Lansing the ordination and installation of their new bishop, which took place on 25 January. The new bishop was ordained by Adam Cardinal Maida, archbishop of Detroit, with Bishop Melczek and Bishop Povish, the retiring bishop, as co-consecrators. Since that time Bishop Mengeling has dedicated himself to the people of his new diocese, yet has found time to return to visit his family and at times to participate in our diocesan celebrations.

Golden Jubilee

With speculation as to the future of the diocese no longer in question as it had been in 1983 at the time of Bishop Grutka's golden jubilee, the faithful turned toward Bishop Gaughan's golden jubilee celebration with gusto. The date was set for 3 November 1995 at the Salvatorian Fathers' Shrine in Merrillville. A special ramp was constructed to allow the bishop to celebrate

Bishop Gaughan's Golden Jubilee

mass at the altar from his wheelchair. The church was filled with the faithful from the diocese as well as the bishop's family, invited guests, and bishops from surrounding dioceses. The bishop was in good spirits and fine form that day. Dinner was served in the social hall afterward with toasts and later, after dinner comments made by the guest dignitaries. In six months the bishop would be seventy-five years old and the celebration was a fitting "thank you" to one who had given his all to the people of the diocese.

Third Bishop of Gary

In a sense, June first dawned rather uneventfully. Yet for the diocese, the day would be historic; Bishop Gaughan's retirement had become effective and Bishop Melczek was now the Third Bishop of Gary in name and in fact. Because the succession was automatic, there would be no formal installation. Still, some type of public celebration was in order and this would result in what would be entitled a Mass of Pastoral Commitment. This became an opportunity for the diocese to celebrate the formal beginning of a new episcopate while giving Bishop Melczek the opportunity to publicly dedicate himself to the faithful of the diocese. Fifty-six archbishops and bishops which included the Apostolic Pro-Nuncio, Archbishop Agostino Cacciavillan, the Metropolitan of the Province, and three cardinals were on hand to congratulate the bishop and celebrate with the diocese. During the mass, Bishop Melczek hearkened to the preparation for the new millennium and called upon the faithful of the diocese to look upon the event as "a new springtime for this diocese and for each one of us who is a member of the body of Christ here in Northwest Indiana. This time of grace calls us to make a more deliberate genuine effort to reach out with loving concern to those who do not know Christ and who have no church affiliation." Also, for the first time since 1973, a new cathedra was installed and Bishop Melczek used it for the first time at the mass. The cathedra is fashioned from black walnut with an arched back reminiscent of the cathedral windows. The back is "woven" to represent the diverse cultures of the people of the diocese. A companion piece to the cathedra is a carved angel, reminding us of our diocesan patrons and, quoting Father Martin Dobrzynski, director of the Office of Worship, "the angel is also a symbol of the inspiration of

Congratulations to Bishop Melczek, third Bishop of Gary

the Holy Spirit for the Bishop of the Diocese as well as a sign of guidance in his decisions. The angel is offset by the colorful coat of arms on the left side of the cathedra."

Formation in Ministry: Lay Ecclesial Ministry Program

As a natural progression from diocesan programs that preceded it, the Lay Ecclesial Ministry Program was developed beginning in 1993 at the request of Bishop Melczek for the education and training of not just catechists, but of all wishing to serve the community of the diocese in some ministerial capacity. His commitment to such a program is reflected in the document *Workers in the Vineyard of the Lord* which was published during his tenure as Chairman for the Committee on the Laity of the United States Bishops' Conference. In the fall of 1994, Sister Helen Hayes, O.P., Bishop Gaughan's former Chancellor, became the first director of the Diocesan Lay Ecclesial Ministry Program. The program collaborated with both Calumet College of St. Joseph and Catholic Theological Union at Chicago, with the latter providing the instructors. The first class was graduated in the spring of 1997 and since that time one hundred twenty lay men and women have completed the program. In 1995, the Diocese of Gary collaborated with the Dioceses of Lafayette, Indianapolis, and Evansville in defining the scope of a Lay Ecclesial Ministry program that would guide the four dioceses in forming the laity for church leadership.

Under the guidance of a twelve member Board composed of priests and lay members, along with the program coordinator, Anne Verbeke, the Lay Ecclesial Ministry program has become a four year program which includes twenty-four hours of graduate level theology, monthly spiritual formation sessions, a pastoral development component and a ministry practicum. Every two years a new class begins; there are currently sixty-five lay men and women enrolled in the program. The Lay Ecclesial Ministry Program is a pre-requisite for the three year Diocesan Diaconate Program.

Invaluable Contributions

Throughout the history of the diocese, the community has been blessed through the talents and work of so many faithful members of lay organizations.

Knights of Columbus

Knights of Saint Peter Claver

Ladies of Saint Peter Claver

The Diocesan Council of Catholic Women, affiliated with the National Council, has striven to unite parish societies of women throughout the diocese in areas of education, devotion, and social ministry. Unsung, for the most part, members of the DCCW have become invaluable to the Office of Worship as they have assisted in the distribution of the Holy Oils after the Mass of Chrism at the Cathedral.

Devoted to praying for vocations, the Serra Club of the diocese, united with Serra International, has worked, often behind the scenes, in promoting vocations to the priesthood and religious life.

Councils of the Knights of Columbus in the area predate the diocese by almost fifty years. The oldest, St. Thomas Council, was chartered in Gary in 1908 with many councils being formed throughout the four counties of the diocese. Their works of charity and service to the diocese give a fine example to the community at large.

Many parishes have conferences of the Society of Saint Vincent DePaul.

These dedicated members seek to emulate Saint Vincent's spirit of charity through their efforts to help those in need, assisting them with food, clothing, shelter, medicine, or whatever situation they may be able to manage.

Serra Club

Restored Diaconate Program

Bishop Melczek also reinstituted the Permanent Diaconate Program in 1997. Men who fulfill the requirements and are graduates of the Lay Ministry Formation Program continue their theological studies and spiritual formation, and

Deacon Ordination, 2000

then are admitted to Holy Orders. Since the program has begun under the direction of Father J. Patrick Gaza and Father Michael Yadron who succeeded him, Bishop Melczek has ordained two classes for service to the diocese. In all, twenty men have been ordained since June of 2000. The current director of formation is Deacon Mark Plaiss.

Convocations and Communication

With Bishop Melczek's interest in collaboration came the opportunity for more communication with the priests and people of the diocese. The opportunity for convocations again presented themselves, and so in October of 1994, September of 1996 and 1998, the priests of the diocese convened with the bishop at Mundelein for meetings on the following themes: *Renewing Priestly Identity* in 1994, *The Priest and the Emerging Church* in 1996 and *Spirituality of the Diocesan Priesthood* in 1998. In the fall of 2000 the fifth convocation (since 1988) took place in Bloomington, Indiana in which the priests focused on the theme of the *Sacraments as Moments of Conversion*. The sixth convocation met in October, 2001 at Donaldson to discuss the *Sin of Racism*. It was from this convocation that a three year major diocesan program to combat racism developed as well as the Bishop's Pastoral Letters. The seventh convocation met in October 2002 at Swan Lake Convention Center in Plymouth to deal with learning healthy lifestyles and work habits to increase effectiveness. The eighth convocation in October of 2004 also at Swan Lake met to discuss the barriers that inhibit communication and healthy ministerial relationships. The ninth convocation met in October of 2005 at Swan Lake to discuss improved collaboration with the bishop, so that both bishop and priests might more effectively listen to each other and accomplish the dictates of the gospel message.

In 1996 Bishop Melczek broached the subject of term limits as his predecessor had done in 1988. The subject was again discussed in deanery meetings and then brought to the Bishop and the Council of Priests where it was rejected. The Bishop, although disappointed, accepted the advice of the Council and dropped the issue. Six years later, at the suggestion of one of the Deans, the matter was again brought before the deaneries and the council. Again it was rejected, and the bishop again took their advice. However, some weeks later, he reversed his decision, as is his right, and put the decision into effect. Pastors accepting new assignments would do so for at least one six-year term with the opportunity to renew for not more than one more term. This time it was the priests who were disappointed, thus the need for the convocation of 2005.

One of the goals of the diocesan five-year plan was to establish on-going communication between the bishop and the priests by establishing deanery meetings on a regular basis. Bishop Melczek quickly accomplished this. He also restored the Diocesan Pastoral Council that had not been convoked since 1984 at the end of Bishop Grutka's episcopacy.

Following the norms of the Second Vatican Council and the Code of Canon Law, the Diocesan Pastoral Council is a consultative group that meets with the Bishop to prayerfully discern matters pertaining to the pastoral activity of the diocese and to make recommendations that pertain to these matters. The members of the council reflect the age, gender, culture and race of the entire diocese. Included with the laity, are two priests and one religious. Membership selection has come from the pastoral councils of each parish to the Dean who then forwards six nominations to the Bishop for final approval. When approved, a member serves for three years. The formation of the Pastoral Council has discovered committed laity, eager to serve the needs of the Church, collaborating with the Bishop who sets the agenda and presides.

He has also promoted parish pastoral councils using the model of parish commissions who fuel the work of the council. In 2004, for greater communications between parishes, he established pastoral councils on the deanery level, bringing representatives together from parishes within the deaneries to share ideas and resources and bring appropriate matters before the bishop and his council of priests through their dean.

Pastoral Letter on diversity

These convocations, and the communication with the laity have resulted in two pastoral letters, the first, *The Many Faces of Our Church: a Letter to our Catholic Faithful Regarding Cultural Diversity* in 2002 on the celebration of diversity in the diocese, and the second in 2003 *Created in God's Image: a Pastoral Letter on the Sin of Racism and a Call to Conversion.* Bishop Melczek has been highly involved in the civic community and continues to serve as the founding co-chairman of the Race Relations Council of Northwest Indiana.

January 1998: Cathedral Dedication

The installation of the new cathedra in 1996 was just the beginning of new life for the cathedral. Not only would Bishop Melczek reclaim the use of the cathedral for major diocesan events, he would oversee a complete renovation of the building following the norms of the Second Vatican Council and subsequent documents on the liturgy. Some of the ideas from Bishop Grutka's original plans were put into effect but far more boldly: the sanctuary was moved further into the chancel on octagonal steps forming an island, and a Blessed Sacrament Chapel was formed this time from the west sacristy, rather than the eastern one. A large baptismal font was constructed in the main aisle, while the original font became the base of a new ambry for the holy oils. The former sanctuary now became the presbytery, a seating area for the priests, which would free more seating for the faithful as they came to celebrate diocesan functions. Rounding out four corners of the altar's steps, the faces of four angels carved in bas-relief were imbedded in the floor. While they were artistically appealing, they became a hazard often to unsuspecting priests who would trip over them. These were later replaced by angels done in mosaic tile. The original angels were moved to the Blessed Sacrament Chapel to adorn the area around the tabernacle. A new color scheme was developed in the painting of the walls, improved lighting was

Cathedral dedication

installed as well as a new sound system, and the stained glass windows were refurbished. In a solemn liturgy celebrated on 26 January 1998 Bishop Melczek blessed the font and consecrated the altar, while the walls were anointed by priest sons of the parish (the most notable being Monsignor Ferdinand Melevage, the parish's first vocation to the priesthood ordained in 1942) and former pastors and associates. The bishop invited the faithful of the diocese to look upon this event as an opportunity for self-renewal: "As we dedicate this symbol of the people of God of our diocese, we will re-consecrate ourselves to the Lord and pray for the grace to be ever faithful to our baptismal commitment. I urge you during your parish weekend liturgies to renew your own commitment to grow in the love of the Lord Jesus and to follow Him who is the Way, the Truth, the Life and the Light." This celebration marked only the end of the first phase of renovation. In November 2001, the completion of the second phase was an addition to the building that connected the cathedral to the school building. A spacious hallway stretches the length of the cathedral, leading those who enter from the north parking lot to the front of the building where they enter through the main entrance to bless themselves as they pass the baptismal font. On the opposite side of the hall sacristies for both the parish and the bishop were constructed, also adding new restrooms and a storage area. The whole area has come to be known as the cloister since the large windows on the east of the hall look out onto the lawn that has been enclosed on the west side of the cathedral. The planning and execution of the renovations have inspired and edified the faithful that have come to worship there.

Cathedral dedication: anointing the altar

Bishop Gaughan's Funeral

Father Charles Niblick was privileged to share a close friendship with Bishop Gaughan. In the later years of the bishop's life, Father Niblick would be his companion when the bishop traveled; he would see to his needs and make sure he had his medication. In 1993, on a trip to Rome, they met with the Holy Father. Bishop Gaughan wished to emphasize to the pope that while he was most grateful to the Holy Father that he was given help and that Bishop Melczek was most talented, surely he must be needed elsewhere, as he, Bishop Gaughan was perfectly capable of administering his diocese. Father Niblick relates that the pope rose from his chair, came to the bishop and kissed him on the forehead and said "your ministry now is to carry the cross."

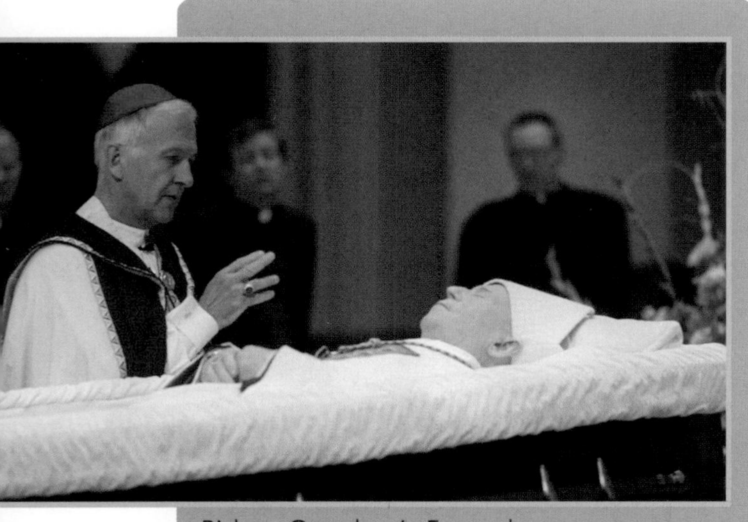

Bishop Gaughan's Funeral

On Friday, 1 October 1999, Bishop Gaughan was relieved of that cross. He peacefully entered eternal life at about noon, at Saint Anthony Home in Crown Point, where he had resided since his retirement. Typical of his nature, as one who did not desire fanfare, his funeral would be far simpler than his predecessor's. Visitation took place in the chapel of Saint Anthony Home the following Wednesday. His body was then taken to the cathedral for visitation beginning at ten o'clock

Bishop Gaughan's Funeral

the next morning, followed by the Mass of Christian Burial at noon. Bishop Melczek was the principal celebrant, assisted by the clergy of the diocese and twelve bishops from neighboring dioceses. Father Niblick preached the homily. Francis Cardinal George was in attendance and before the final commendation, spoke to the congregation which filled the cathedral.

On Saturday, 9 October, following a memorial mass celebrated at Blessed Sacrament Cathedral in Greensburg, his body was taken to the Benedictine Monastery of Saint Emma in Greensburg where he had resided during his years working in Greensburg's chancery, serving the sisters as their chaplain, and buried in the monastery cemetery.

While administering the diocese for only eight of his twelve year episcopate, he worked tirelessly to update diocesan policies and welcome the opportunity for new ministries that would be open to all interested in answering God's call to serve his family. The diocese he initially did not want became very important to him. Father Jon Plavcan, also a native of Pennsylvania and a student of Bishop Gaughan, relates the story of his coming to join the diocese as a seminarian, having been recruited by the bishop. He was assigned to live at Father Niblick's parish. One evening at dinner to which the bishop had been invited, the bishop told his fellow Pennsylvanian: "The beauty of the hills of Pennsylvania is not here but there is a different kind of beauty here. You will find it. Just look and you will see."

Viability committee

What is known in some circles as a "graying presbyterate" has forced the diocese to consider how parishioners will be cared for in the future. In 1999, the Priests' Council established a subcommittee to look into ways of accomplishing this. Bishop Melczek, having experienced the emotional distress of the faithful in Detroit when many parishes were closed, is determined to look for ways to keep viable parishes open. The viability committee has discussed different methods of grouping parishes in clusters under the administration of one pastor. Retired priests could help in the administration of the sacraments, wherever possible. Competent laity, graduates of the Ministry Formation program, would assist in the daily administration of communities. Since 1997 the pastors of Holy Angels, Saint Mark, Saints Monica and Luke, Holy Rosary, and Saint Mary of the Lake in Gary have formed the "Gary Cluster" and have worked in cooperation with each other, pooling talents and resources to keep communities active. This consortium of cooperation of the five pastors has proved itself constructive for these parish communities. When Holy Rosary lost its resident pastor, the community continued under the care of the priests who remained.

Homecoming Missions

In Whiting, four parishes, Saint Adalbert, Saints Peter and Paul, Immaculate Conception, and Sacred Heart pooled their resources under the direction of Father Stanley Dominik. With the aid of an assistant, the communities continued to function. In 2002, the people of Saints Peter and Paul recognized the need to close the parish and merge their talents with the other communities. Since Father Dominik's retirement, Saint John the Baptist has joined the cluster and has taken charge of the administration of the parishes. In the convocation of 2005, the viability committee's final plan which was discussed on the deanery levels by both clergy and laity was submitted for final discussion. The plan of clustering parishes was accepted by the bishop and will be put into effect as the need arises. Yet one important point remained. The diocese would continue in its program for the active promotion of vocations to the priesthood and do everything possible to assure the faithful of the diocese that their spiritual and sacramental needs would be met.

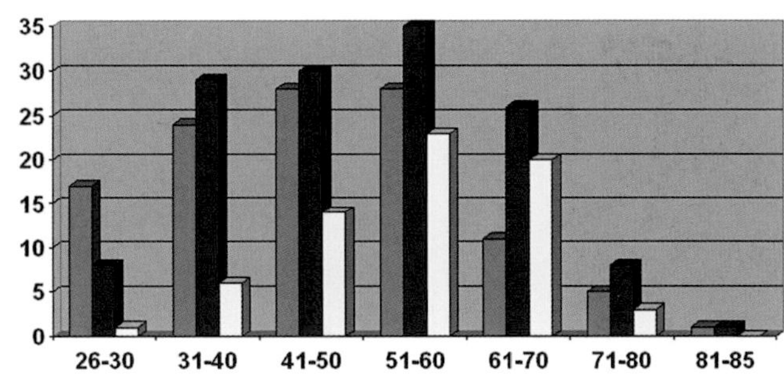

Millennium

As the Church approached the dawn of the third millennium, the diocese began a program of preparation for the event. A three year program of faith sharing was provided to all parishes in which groups would gather for discussion focusing on one person of the Holy Trinity in each year of the program. In promoting the program, Bishop Melczek stated, "The Diocesan Millennium program offers us an opportunity of rooting ourselves more deeply in the mystery of the Trinity. We and the people we serve are constantly seeking to identify that which gives meaning and purpose to our lives. The answers to our deepest yearnings are found in the person of Jesus Christ, the Son of God. Faith in Jesus Christ gives us the ability to see life anew and to keep the tasks of life in perspective."

As part of the celebration in 2000, clusters of parishes in each deanery hosted missions (seventeen in all) dedicated to the theme of "Homecoming." These three-day missions were designed not only to kindle a deeper faith in parishioners, but also to "welcome home" those who for whatever reason had wavered in their faith. Each three-day mission concluded with a liturgical penance service in which hundreds of people participated. The culmination of this successful program came on the feast of the Body and Blood of Christ, 25 June 2000. The faithful throughout the diocese gathered at Gary's Genesis Center for an afternoon celebration of reflection and Eucharistic worship, ending with a Corpus Christi procession, the edifying spectacle of nearly three thousand of the faithful marching in procession, singing hymns and praying while Bishop Melczek carried the Blessed Sacrament down Broadway to Seventh Avenue, from the Genesis Center to the Cathedral. Benediction was celebrated under a canopy in the south parking lot next to the church. Afterward, there was ethnic music, food, and fellowship for the rest of the day. Chartered buses, which brought the participants from their parishes to the Genesis Center, were on hand to meet the people at the Cathedral when it was time to return home.

Millennium Celebration

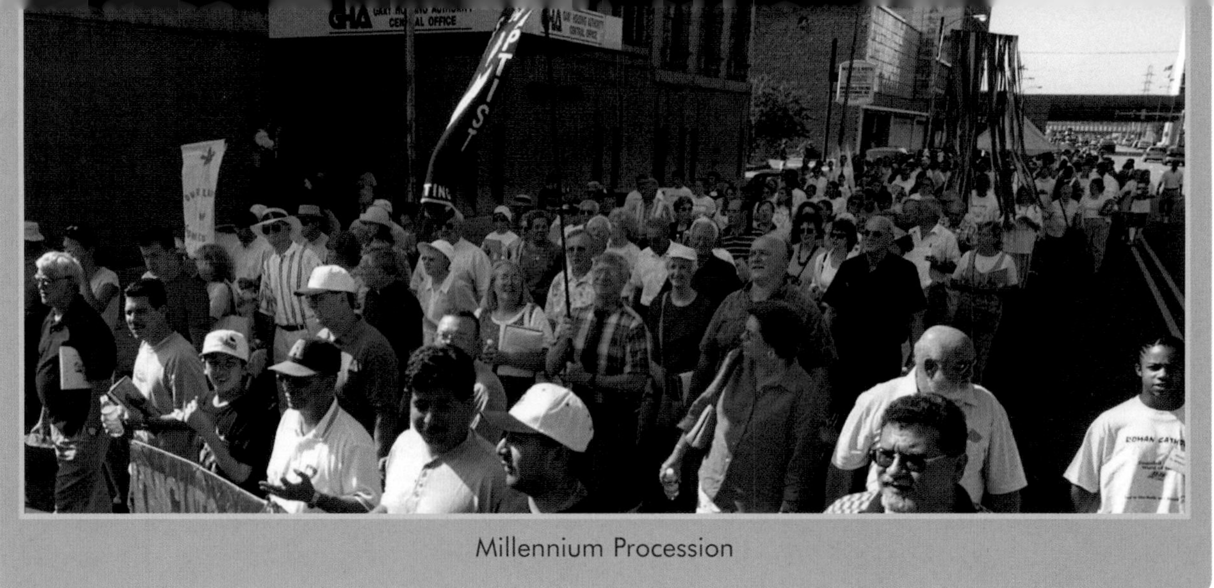

Millennium Procession

Protecting God's Children

When Bishop Melczek came to the diocese, he made sure there was a contingency plan in place to deal with the problem of the sexual abuse of minors, should the problem ever arise. Sexual Misconduct toward Minors & Others at Risk was published 10 July 1993. Talk of the scandal of child abuse by clerics had been whispered throughout the nineties. Such talk came to national attention in Boston, with similar scandals snowballing throughout the country. In 2003, The VIRTUS Program was begun to educate everyone in the diocese on how to keep children safe from this problem. Anyone working in a diocesan institution that had any contact with children was expected to be part of this program which would include not only ongoing education through use of the internet, but also criminal background checks.

The bishops of the country met in Dallas, Texas, for their June 2002 meeting to determine their protocol. The Charter, published by the United States Conference of Catholic Bishops, set about a comprehensive set of procedures in dealing with accused members of the clergy, the healing process, and a program for prevention. Bishop Melczek stated that the diocese would fully cooperate with the Bishops' plan. The results of independent audits beginning in 2004 have revealed 100% compliance within the diocese. Sadly, the diocese would not be spared the grief surrounding these scandals.

A Future Full of Hope – toward the jubilee and beyond.

In February 2006, Bishop Melczek invited all of the parishes to participate in a process titled "A Future Full of Hope: Looking Back and Moving Forward." In his letter of invitation he wrote, "Our communion with God and one another is nurtured and expressed in our parishes and institutions. It is there that we grow in holiness and are challenged to extend God's kingdom of truth, peace, justice and love into our families, neighborhoods, workplaces and the world. We as individuals and as a diocese are vibrant when parishes and institutions are vibrant."

The program is designed to help the faithful, especially those involved in leadership positions on Parish Pastoral Councils and Commissions, to reflect upon the various aspects of the mission of the parish and then assess current strengths and weaknesses with a view to developing a concrete plan of action, which will lead to a more vibrant parish over the coming years. The process focuses on five areas of the parish: parish life, stewardship, peace and social justice, education and formation, and spirituality and worship. As parishes are not isolated from one another, the goals and recommendations of each parish will be shared with other parishes in the clusters, the clergy, and deanery pastoral councils. Realizing that the area of the Lord's vineyard known as the Diocese of Gary, cultivated by clergy and laity for fifty years, will have positive impact on succeeding generations working toward the diocesan centenary, 2057.

Catholic Charities

The origins of the Office of Catholic Charities in the diocese dates back to its foundation in the Fort Wayne diocese in 1936. The Reverend W. Edward Sweigart organized the ministry that would include offices in Gary and Hammond. In 1949 an additional office was established in East Chicago. At the time the agency was primarily oriented toward child welfare, dealing with adoptions and the placement of children in foster homes and institutions.

Monsignor Sweigart, who was administering Saint Mary parish in East Chicago at the end of 1956, would continue the work of Catholic Charities as its Director in the new diocese in 1957. Looking toward the future, Bishop Grutka directed Father Joseph Semancik to obtain a Master's Degree in Social Work from the University of Chicago while assisting Monsignor Sweigart. He would later earn a Doctorate in Social Work (in 1977) and was appointed to succeed Monsignor Sweigart in 1962.

The work expanded beyond child welfare to include work with parish conferences of the Saint Vincent DePaul Society. An early success was the establishment of the DePaul Salvage Bureau which processed clothing and furniture for sale or donation to the needy.

Under Monsignor Semancik's direction, the work of Catholic Charities continued to expand with the creation of four divisions: **Catholic Family Service,** which deals with social work including individual and family counseling; the **Senior Volunteer Program,** which includes opportunities for retirees to volunteer in a variety of ministries as well as the Senior Companion Program; **Family Life Ministry** included the program for Marriage Preparation, and hosts the annual Wedding Anniversary Mass at the cathedral; and **Parish and Community Services** which worked to develop parish and community organizations and created the Pastor's Emergency Fund.

The Office of Catholic Charities has also been responsible for refugee resettlement on behalf on the United States Catholic Conference.

The laity of the diocese have always been actively involved in guiding the work of Catholic Charities through Lay Boards of Directors for all the divisions and major programs of the office. Monsginor Semancik was succeeded by Doctor Kenneth Flanagan in December of 2000 and continues to oversee the work begun in this area over seventy years ago.

THE PARISHES OF THE GARY-HOBART DEANERY

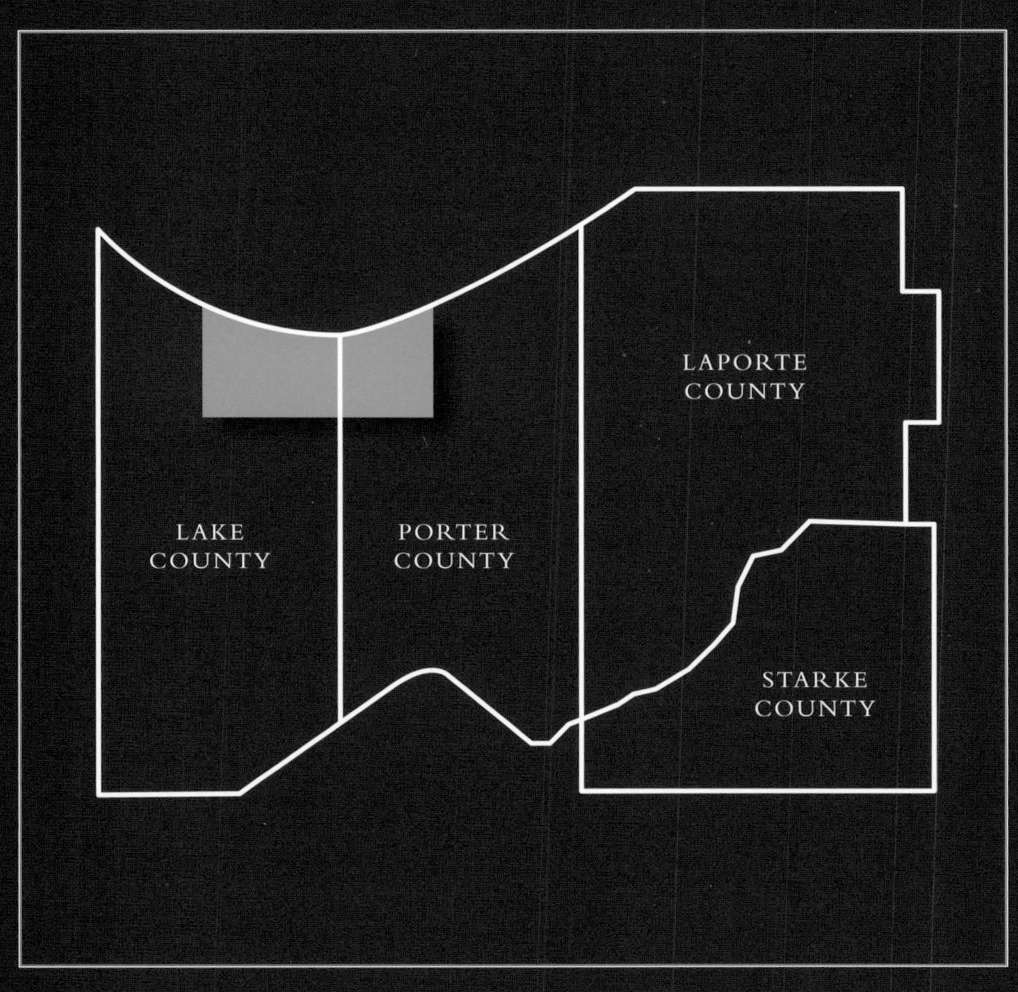

Holy Angels Cathedral

The history of Holy Angels Parish parallels the history of the city of Gary. In 1906, with the planning and building of the city by the United States Steel Corporation, the Church would be visible and active from the first appearance of its new citizens.

Father Francis Thomas Jansen, who used his middle name so as not to be confused with Father Francis J. Jansen, had been pastor at Saint Bridget in Hobart since 1903. Young and vigorous, he accepted Bishop Alerding's request to organize a parish for the new city, just seven miles distant from Hobart. The first mass was celebrated at Binzenhoff hall, a tavern located at Fourth Avenue and Broadway. Father Jansen would continue to care for the fledgling community from his parish at Hobart until he took up residence in the city in 1908. By this time land was secured from the Gary Land Company at Seventh Avenue and Polk Street. The story is told that when Bishop Alerding visited the site, he was disappointed because it seemed that the parish was at the edge of the city in what was still undeveloped wilderness. He was assured that it would not be wilderness for long. On Thanksgiving Day, 1908 the cornerstone was laid for a two storey building that would accommodate a school on the first floor, with the church on the second. The school was ready for occupancy with the beginning of the 1909 school year staffed by the School Sisters of Notre Dame.

The tremendous growth of the city found Father Jansen sending out assistant pastors to found other parishes in the city, while Holy Angels continued to grow. In 1934 Father Jansen was made a domestic prelate and dean of the new Gary deanery, celebrating also the twenty-fifth anniversary of the completion of the church/school building. In 1942 after a fruitful ministry of thirty-six years serving the people of Holy Angels, Monsignor Jansen died suddenly at the age of sixty-nine. His successor would be Father John Anthony Sullivan who would continue to the foster and harness the energy of the community. After World War II, he supervised the construction of the present church, a

magnificent structure in the gothic style which was dedicated on 29 January 1950 by Bishop Noll. It is said that on the day of the dedication the parish was debt free.

In 1957, Monsignor Sullivan was informed that his parish, the Mother Church of Gary would become the Cathedral of the new diocese headed by Bishop Grutka. Monsignor Sullivan retired in 1963 and was succeeded by Monsignor John Witte who built the new parish school in 1965. After Monsignor Witte's transfer in 1968, the parish would have the following rectors (later called pastors):

- Monsignor Casimir Senderak, 1968-1971;
- Father Don C. Grass, 1971-1983;
- Father Richard A. Emerson, 1983;
- Father Joseph J. Viater, 1983-1985;
- Father William E. Vogt, 1985-1986;
- Father Andrew Daniels, OFM Cap., 1986-1992;
- Father Matthew Iwuji 1992-1997; and
- Father Robert Gehring since 1997.

The parish would witness the consecration of its first bishop in 1957, the installation of its second bishop in 1984, and the pastoral commitment of its third bishop in 1996.

In 1994, the parish consolidated with other parishes in the formation of the Sister Thea Bowman School located at Holy Angels. The diocese ceased operation of the school in 2002, and then the Drexel Foundation would operate it as a Charter School.

Holy Rosary

As the city of Gary grew, the west side of Holy Angels would be divided in 1931 to form Holy Rosary Parish. Father Arnold Wibbert, coming from Mercy Hospital, would organize the community and use a rented storefront to celebrate mass for forty-seven families. Father Louis Ratajczak would become the first resident pastor in 1933 and build the church, which was dedicated by Bishop Noll in 1934. Father Joseph Smith (1944-1966) would succeed him. He would remodel the church and build the parish school which opened in 1956 under the direction of the Sisters of Saint Joseph, Third Order of Saint Francis. By 1961, because of overcrowding, the parish would celebrate mass simultaneously in the church and the church hall. As the membership decreased, this would be discontinued by 1968. Father Smith would be succeeded by Father John Daniels (1966-1967), Father William Peil (1967-71). Fathers Carl Mengeling, John Hogan, and John Siekierski would administer the parish until Father David Gosnell was appointed in 1973. The growing Hispanic population would see the addition of devotions such as the Our Lady of Guadalupe novena. The school closed in 1975 because of declining enrollment. Father Fernando DeCristobal would replace Father Gosnell in 1973 and would care for the community until he was transferred in 1997. Father Frank Torres would administer the parish until his transfer in 2003. The parish has been a member of the Gary Cluster and is currently under the administration of Father Robert Gehring.

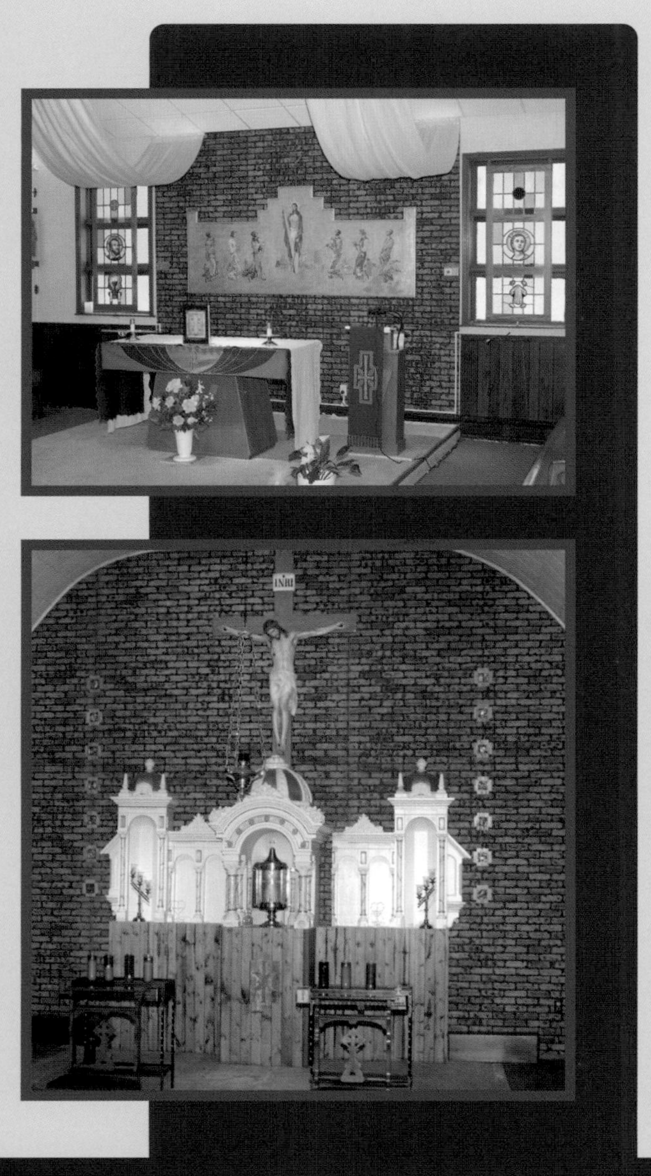

Saint Ann

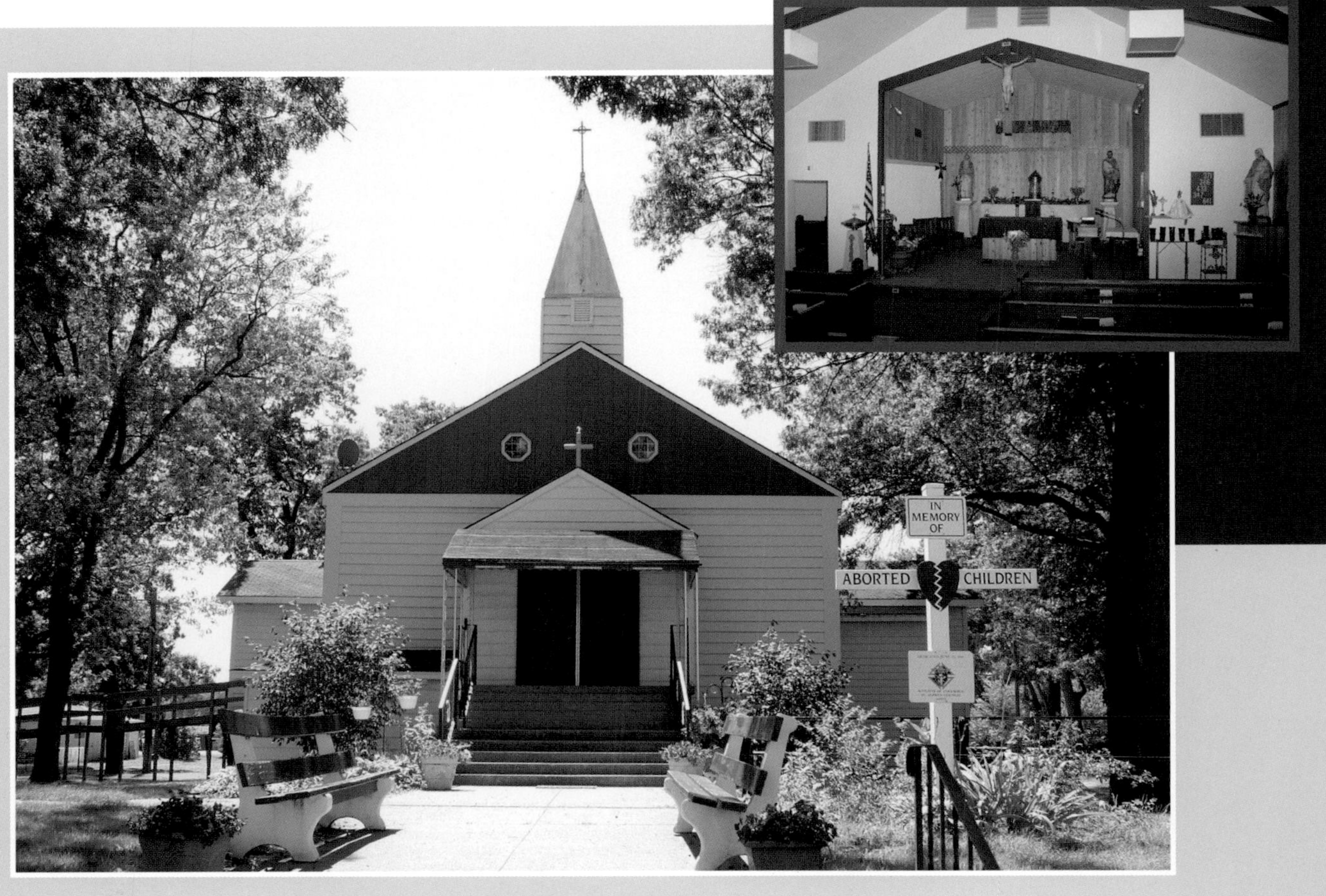

Father John Beckmann, the founding pastor of Saint Ann Parish, recounts that during his time as an assistant at Saint Mary in East Chicago, he would, on his days off, often take drives in the country with Father Emmons.

One such occasion found them passing through Black Oak while driving back home. They were both struck by the growth of the area and thought it important to discuss the matter with Bishop Noll, who allowed the area to be canvassed to determine the number of Catholics. The community began to gather in a rented hall on Colfax Street for Sunday mass. The jubilation of the first mass for the community (7 December 1941) turned to sadness as the group emerged from the hall after mass and heard the news that Pearl Harbor had been attacked. Although many thought that the ensuing war would delay the founding of the parish, others were just as eager to do whatever they could to get the parish established.

Father Beckmann was appointed pastor in June, 1942. Land was donated on Twenty-Seventh Avenue, a block east of Burr Street. Bishop Noll granted permission to build a church and added $1,000.00 to the building fund. Permission was obtained from the War Production Board that a church could be built provided it cost no more than five thousand dollars; so the congregation banded together to accomplish the task themselves. Bishop Noll dedicated the church in honor of Saint Ann that year. The building of Interstate 80-94 would force the community to move the church to the present site where a new rectory would be built in 1947.

The school was built in 1945 and staffed by the Poor Handmaids of Jesus Christ until it closed in 1987. Father Beckmann was transferred to Saints Peter and Paul in 1955 and was succeeded by Father Andrew Mattieu (1955-1956), Father John Frawley (1956-1958), Father James Stapleton (1958), Father Walter Mastey (1958-1963), Father Philip Fusco (1963-1965), Father John Minnich (1967-1996) and Father Stephen Kosinski (1996-2003). With Father Kosinski's transfer, the parish is without a resident pastor and has been placed under the care of the pastor of Saint Mary, Griffith. The parish community, fearing the church would close, has worked diligently to maintain a vibrant community spirit and continues to thrive.

Saint Hedwig

Spring of 1908 was the target date for the completion of the second parish church in Gary: Saint Hedwig built for the Polish community who had come to work in the new steel mills.

Early on the parish was organized by Father Anthony Stachowiak from Indiana Harbor. A small frame structure was completed by parishioners donating the time and talent, which Bishop Alerding dedicated on 4 July 1908.

Father Peter Kahellek was the first resident pastor arriving in March of 1909 and built a rectory in 1910. A two storey brick school was built in 1917 and staffed by the Franciscan Sisters of Blessed Kunegunda.

Father Michael Swiatkowski was the second resident pastor arriving in August 1929 and with the community endured some troubled times during the great depression.

The new and present church was started in 1940, but took two years to complete because of the war and shortage of materials; shortly after the dedication Father Swiatkowski died and was succeeded by Monsignor Louis Michalski who made many improvements to the Church property.

Father Casimir Senderak became pastor in 1965 and was succeeded by Father John Murzyn. Father Hilary Halter, OFM became pastor in 1976, and was succeeded by Father Henry Lazarek in 1983 until 1987. In May of 1978 the Parish School was closed.

The parish has become a small but fervent community who are currently under the care of the Salvatorian Fathers.

Saint Joseph the Worker

Croatian immigrants coming to Gary at the beginning of the twentieth century settled in a neighborhood of their own west of Broadway in the vicinity of Twenty-First Avenue. Their parish was one of the five national parishes that received a grant from the U. S. Steel Corporation to build their church which would be located at Twenty-Third and Adams. This occurred in 1912 and the parish was dedicated to the Holy Trinity, and would be the second parish of that name in Gary as the Slovaks organized their parish the year before. The first pastor was Father Luke Terzic who came from Croatia. Consequently, all of the ten pastors, both diocesan priests and Conventual Franciscans, were sent to Gary either from Croatia or Slovenia.

Rev. Charles Jesih started the parochial school in the church hall. In 1919 the school had 200 students. In 1921 Sisters of the Third Order of St. Francis of Lemont, IL, took over the teaching duties of the school and continued their work in the school for a long time. A Society dedicated to the Sacred Heart of Jesus, a nucleus of Croatian Catholic Union with the Home Office in Gary, was founded in this parish in 1921.

Father Vjenceslav Ardas, well known as Croatian "Moses of Gary," secured property in the Glen Park area. When the community moved to Glen Park, the property would become Saint Monica parish.

Father Ardas built the new church between 44th and 45th Avenues and built the new parochial school and sisters' convent. The church was renamed to honor Saint Joseph the Worker in 1944. Father Ardas came back to take over the Parish from the ailing pastor Father Victor Rogulj in 1954. He built a much larger and impressive church in a Romanesque style which was dedicated in 1956, the year of the Golden Jubilee of the city of Gary. The church has a seating capacity of 780. The sanctuary has some sculptures made by famous Croatian sculptor, Ivan Mestrovic, who taught art at Notre Dame. Shortly after the untimely death of Father Ardas in 1959, Father Mirko Godina was named pastor. He led the parish to celebrate its golden jubilee. He also had the stained glass windows installed, would

build the new Convent for the Sisters in 1967, and remodel the school in 1970, which was closed in 1987.

Father Benedict J. Benakovic was the pastor of the Parish from 1972 to 2000. He has seen the parish in its peak as well as through its decline in numbers in those twenty-eight years. Father Benedict was the voice of reason and calm during these times of crisis.

There is a long tradition of an annual "Parish Day" in July when all celebrate with lamb, sarma, sausages, tamburitza music and dance. Twice a year Holy Rosary Sodality cooks a delicious Sarma Dinner. Several times a year ladies from the Altar Society make the best apple and cheese strudels in Indiana. The Cookie Sale for Christmas draws the customers with a sweet aroma of kolacici and povitica baked by many parishioners.

Father Stephen Loncar, who became pastor in 2000, leads the parish into the new Millennium with a youthful enthusiasm. He is trying to reconcile past and present, nationalities and races, distances and differences, hoping to increase its dwindling membership. He wants to keep Roman Catholic tradition, devotions and religious education in the parish, but also strives to uplift it with diverse cultural events and with openness to new possibilities.

SAINT MARK

With the foundation of the catechetical centers and the Gary-Alerding Settlement House, the spiritual and social needs of new immigrants to the city were attended to as they assimilated into society. Father John DeVille, who directed the Settlement House, would go on to organize a fledgling community in 1921 that would become Saint Mark Parish.

With the draining of the swampland around the Little Calumet River, and the landscaping of a three hundred acre park, the city began to develop southward, and found the area that would be called Glen Park, an appealing place to live. The distance to the local parishes, (Holy Angels and Saint Luke) while not considered difficult today, found Catholics with limited transportation options at a loss.

A committee of concerned Catholics knew of an abandoned German Evangelical church building on Twentieth Avenue and Grant Street. They purchased it from the Missouri Synod and moved it to the location at Thirty-Ninth and Broadway in 1921. In meeting with Bishop Alerding they were told that no priest was available for a new parish. However, if Father DeVille at the Settlement House would be willing to care for them until a resident pastor could be appointed that would be fine. Father cared for the community until the appointment of Father Joseph Ryder as the first resident pastor in 1923.

A rectory was built for him on Broadway next to the church building. It was the community's hope however, that these would be temporary since property was purchased on Ridge Road for a permanent church and school.

This project was completed in 1927, and Bishop Noll would dedicate the church and school on 31 July.

Monsignor Ryder would lead the community until his death in 1947; he would be succeeded by Father Francis X. Guerre (1947-1956) who would build a new rectory in 1949 and an additional school building that was ready for the 1951 school year. Father Frederick Westendorf would be the third pastor from 1956 until his sudden death in 1963. He would be succeeded by Monsignor Alvin Jasinski (1963-1969), Father Richard Zollinger (1969-1972), Father John Morales (1972-1985), Father James McGrogan (1985-1986), Father Roy Beeching (1986-1993), Father Robert Gehring (1993-1997) and the current pastor, Father John Ambre, since 1997.

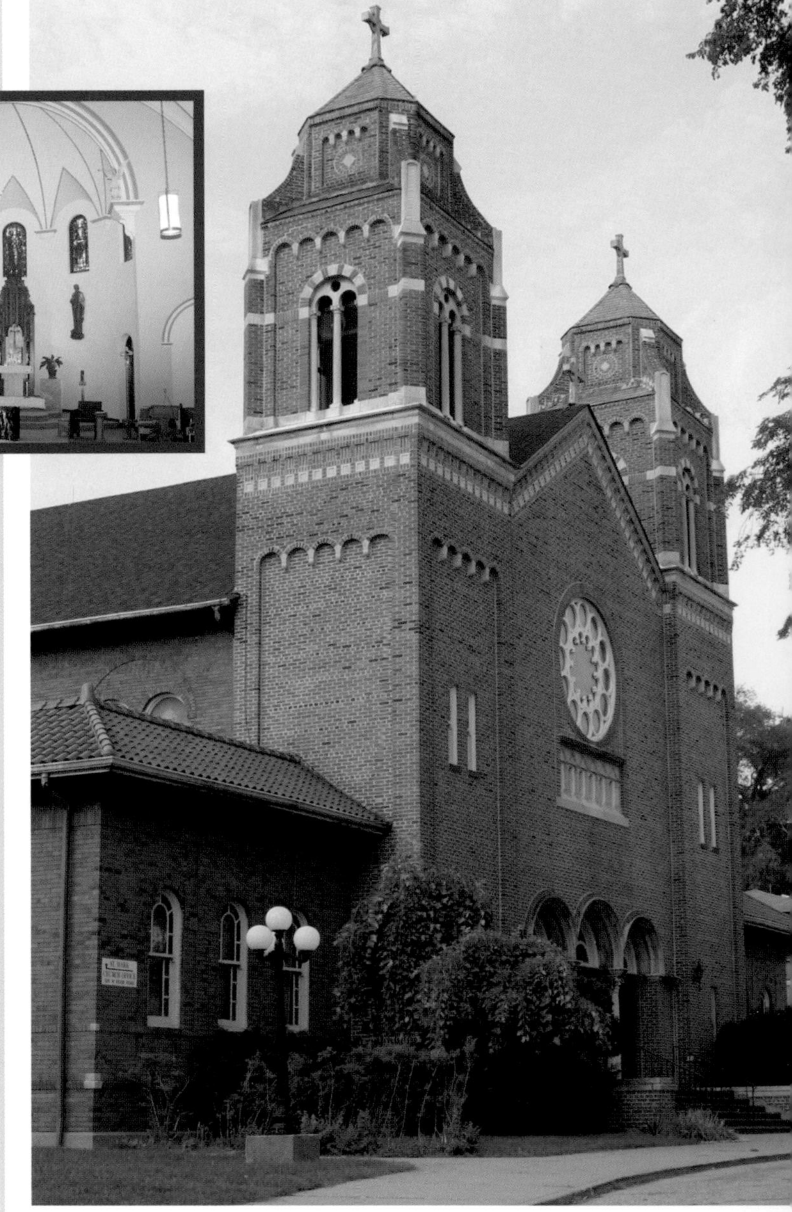

The parish suffered much because of the racial unrest beginning in the 1960s.

Glen Park, considered a fashionable area in the 1940s and 1950s, would be a victim of white flight. Beginning around 1973, the parish, once with a membership of two thousand families would fall to less than five hundred.

The parish would be forced to close the school in 1999. Now, a much smaller congregation than before, it is a mixture of White, African-American, and Hispanic families, working and worshipping together.

Saint Mary of the Lake

The Town of Miller, which predated the foundation of Gary, would be annexed by the city. So too, as the population grew, the Church in Gary would take responsibility for the development of a new parish in the area. Father Francis Guerre, an assistant at Holy Angels, would organize a parish and build a church on land provided by the James Ansbro family in 1929. He would remain at the parish until 1942 when the death of Monsignor Jansen would cause him to move to Valparaiso, as Father Sullivan would be going to Holy Angels. The next resident pastor would be Father H. James Conway who would build the school and ask the Sisters of Holy Cross to take charge of it beginning in September of 1949. Six years later, through the work of parishioners Adrian and Edmund Lessard, a gymnasium was erected that would also serve as a parish hall. This building was providential as the church was lost to fire on 15 November 1956.

Father Ferdinand Melevage became the third pastor in 1959 and set about the task of replacing the church. The building program was begun in May of 1961.

Through the dedication of the community, Father Melevage built an imposing modern edifice that conformed to the liturgical directives of the time. The church was dedicated on 16 September 1962, just one month before the beginning of the Second Vatican Council. There is no doubt that had he and the community known what was coming, the new church would have been a model for post-conciliar parishes. Father Ralph Hoffman became pastor in 1966 and would serve the community for twenty years until his retirement in 1986. During these years the parish would sustain the loss of many families moving to the south or east of the county. The Holy Cross Sisters would withdraw from the school in 1977; the school would be closed in 1977. Father Joseph Pawlowski became the parish's fifth pastor in 1986 and he would be succeeded by the present pastor, Father Thomas Mischler, in 1998. The parish currently belongs to the Gary Cluster of parishes which support each other through the sharing of resources.

Saints Monica and Luke

The Saint Monica Story

Late in 1927, African Americans living in Gary petitioned the bishop for a parish of their own. Father H. James Conway, chaplain at Saint Mary Mercy Hospital, volunteered and began ministering to the fledgling congregation celebrating mass in a building located at Twenty-Fifth Avenue at Jackson Street. Father Conway became the first pastor in June 1928 and was followed by Father Thomas Daley in 1934 who served the community until 1939, when Bishop Noll invited the Oblates of Mary Immaculate to work in the diocese. The Congregation was noted for missionary work among Catholics of African American descent. They established their headquarters at 3620 Jefferson Street and Father Daniel Finnegan, OMI was appointed pastor. In April of 1944, he was succeeded by Father Joseph Barry, OMI. It was at this time that the Croatian parish of Holy Trinity bought property in Glen Park, and Bishop Noll would give the vacated property at the corner of Twenty-Third and Adams to Saint Monica Parish. In the meantime, Father Barry made great efforts to open up

a school, but was unable to obtain sisters. Through the cooperation of Bishop Noll, the Sisters of the Blessed Sacrament agreed to staff the school which would open on 14 September 1945. The newly acquired church building was redecorated and officially dedicated of 21 May 1947.

In January 1953, the Saint Monica Federal Credit Union was established. During this time, the Legion of Mary, Holy Name Society, the Sodality, Boy Scouts, Altar Guild, and the CYO were organized. In 1963, the Oblate Fathers left the diocese and Bishop Grutka appointed Father Patrick Meehan pastor who served the community until 1968 when he was succeeded by Father William Martin who immediately initiated a massive improvement program of the entire parish plant. It was during this time that the parish school received a First Class Accreditation by the State of Indiana. It also became one of the first schools in the area to use a closed circuit TV system as an instructional aid.

With all these successes, a crossroad occurred for the church in the early 1980s . It was at this time that Saint Monica merged with Saint Luke parish and became known as Saints Monica and Luke. The merger was a trying time for parishioners, especially in the consolidation of the parish school with the cathedral.

Father William Martin (1979-1985) became pastor of the merged parishes followed by Father Sammie Maletta, Administrator in 1985, Father Joseph Viater (1986-1994), and currently Father J. Patrick Gaza (1994 to present).

The Saint Luke Story

In 1917, Bishop Alerding divided Holy Angels parish, directing Father Jansen's assistant, Father Frank Gnibba to form a new community on the east side of Broadway. This parish would be known as Saint Luke, following the plan to name the daughter parishes of Holy Angels after the evangelists. Father Gnibba built a combination church and school building on the corner of Seventh Avenue at Rhode Island Street. The church was in the basement, with the school on the first floor. After his untimely death, he was succeeded by Father Raphael Donnelly, (1925-1942) who added a second floor to the school. Succeeding pastors were Father Carl Schnitz (1942-1950), Wilfred Mannion (1951-1959) who built the present church in 1954, Father H. James Conway (1959-1968), and Father Henry Ameling (1968-1970). Saint Luke School which had been directed by the School Sisters of Notre Dame since 1917, officially closed on 12 June 1969, and was demolished in October 1972. Father John Morales (1970-1972), and Father Seraph Menello (1972-1979) were the following pastors before the merging of the parishes.

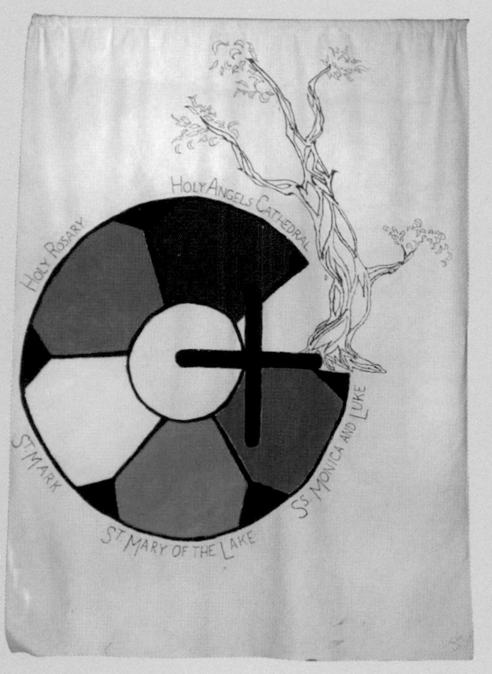

SAINT BRIDGET OF KILDARE

The city of Hobart was founded in 1847 on the eastern edge of Lake County. Hobart was one of a handful of settlements that developed around the area's rich farmland. Many of those who settled here were German farmers.

The city grew slowly until 1858 when the Pittsburgh and Fort Wayne Railroad was constructed through Hobart mainly by Irish immigrants, making Hobart a major shipping point for the county. As the community developed with mainly German and Irish immigrants, the number of Catholics also grew until 1873, when Father Michael O'Reilly, the pastor of Saint Paul in Valparaiso decided the time was right to establish a parish in the city. Before this time, priests would come from Valparaiso to celebrate mass in private homes. Father O'Reilly bought three lots on Main Street from George Earle the founder of Hobart. On one lot was a building used as an art gallery that proved perfect for the parish's first church. He placed the fledgling Catholic community at Hobart under the patronage of Saint Bridget of Kildare, a sixth century disciple of Saint Patrick and the first abbess of Kildare. At first the pastors of Saint Paul cared for the parish; later it would fall to the pastors of Saints Peter and Paul in Turkey Creek sometimes referred to as Lottaville, which was only six miles away to the southwest and closer than Saint Paul. The first resident pastor came in 1903 in the person of Father Francis Thomas Jansen, who used his middle name so as not to confuse others with Father Francis J. Jansen who was about the same age. He was ordained three years previously, and full of energy. But he would not remain very long, for in

1906 he founded the parish of Holy Angels in the new city of Gary. He would be succeeded by Father William Hoff in 1908 who would build the combination church and school building in 1911. He would remain at the parish until 1922. Father Joseph Lynn succeeded him but would care for the parish for only two years. His successor, Father John Steger, was pastor from January to September 1925. Father Paul J. Roederer would become the fifth pastor and stay at Hobart for twenty-one years. He opened the school in 1927 and invited the Franciscan Sisters of Perpetual Adoration from Lafayette to staff

the school. In 1941, because of some disagreement, he asked the Mantellate Servites, an Italian order whose Motherhouse is in Blue Island, Illinois to care for the school. He energized the parish and saw to it that the parish organizations functioned as they should. He was considered well organized but a tough personality. In 1946, he was transferred to Saint John a smaller parish at the time, because of his health. He was succeeded in 1946 by Father John Schaeffer who would remain for twenty-two years and change the face of the parish. In 1954, the present church was dedicated. In 1953, at the cornerstone laying ceremony, he invited the young pastor from Holy Trinity in Gary, Father Andrew Grutka to preach the sermon. In newspaper articles reporting on the ceremony, Father Grutka was quoted as saying that Saint Bridget parish was the mother of all the churches in the city of Gary, since Holy Angels was founded from the Hobart parish. In 1966 a new parish school would be built. Because of poor health, Father Schaeffer retired in 1968 at the age of sixty-eight. His successor was Father William Vogt, a popular individual who brought the parish through the revisions of the Second Vatican Council. He remained as pastor until 1983. From 1983 to 1985 Father William Peil would be pastor. This would be the second Father Peil to serve the parish as his brother Father Daniel Peil had been Father Roederer's assistant in the forties. Father John Strebig came back to Hobart in 1985 to serve the community as its pastor until 1990. He had been an assistant to Father Schaeffer and was very popular. In 1987 he built the Parish Center/ Gymnasium and remodeled the convent as a rectory and parish office building. His successor is the current pastor, Father Dominic Bertino. During his tenure the Servite Sisters ended their relationship with the school because of limited vocations. The parish paid the debt to the diocese for the parish center and has been able to keep the school producing students of academically high caliber. Since 2000, he also serves as the Dean of the Gary-Hobart Deanery.

SAINT FRANCIS XAVIER

Many people remember this community as East Gary, Indiana, but Lake Station was the original name of the settlement. There was a chapel here from about 1882 and eventually pastors from Hobart were charged with its care and the cemetery there. The building was destroyed by fire in 1917. And no activity would occur until 1930, when Father Francis X. Guerre, the founding pastor of Saint Mary of the Lake the year before, would build a church in honor of his patron. The parish continued in the care of the Miller parish until 1941 when Father Francis Quinn became the first resident pastor. He remained for two years and was succeeded by Father John Schaeffer in 1943 who invited the Missionary Sisters of Our Lady of Victory to work as catechists. Father Schaeffer left for Saint Bridget in 1946 and was succeeded by Father Clemens Koors who served the parish until his retirement in 1973. During this time he was instrumental in organizing the expansion of the parish. He purchased a home for the catechists, built the rectory in 1946 and installed a new pipe organ in 1948.

With the growth of the parish, assistants were assigned to the pastor, the first being Father Dominic Pallone who came in 1953. The Franciscan Sisters of Perpetual Adoration who by this time had moved their Motherhouse from Lafayette to Mishawaka were engaged to staff a new school for the parish. Ground was broken in the summer of 1955 and the new building was ready for the school year beginning in September of 1956. The school was formally dedicated by Bishop Pursley, the Apostolic Administrator of the diocese.

In 1963, an Italian priest, Father Seraph Meneghello, invited by Bishop Grutka to work in the diocese, was assigned to the parish to aid the influx of Spanish-speaking families joining the parish.

Father Koors retired in 1973 and was succeeded by retired Air Force Colonel, Monsignor Paul Haney. The sisters left the school in 1973 but were replaced by a lay faculty. Monsignor Haney retired in 1984. Father Richard Orlinski was appointed to administer the parish until the appointment of Father Robert Barry Evers in 1984, whose proficiency in Spanish encouraged the Hispanic members of the parish to greater participation. Father Evers retired in June, 2004 after twenty years of serving the parish. He was succeeded by Father J. Anthony Valtierra the present pastor. He had the unhappy responsibility of closing the school in June of 2005. In August of that year he fell ill. Father Jon Plavcan administered the parish from March to June 2006. On 8 July 2006, Father Eduardo Malagon was appointed by Bishop Melczek as coadjutor pastor to care for the community.

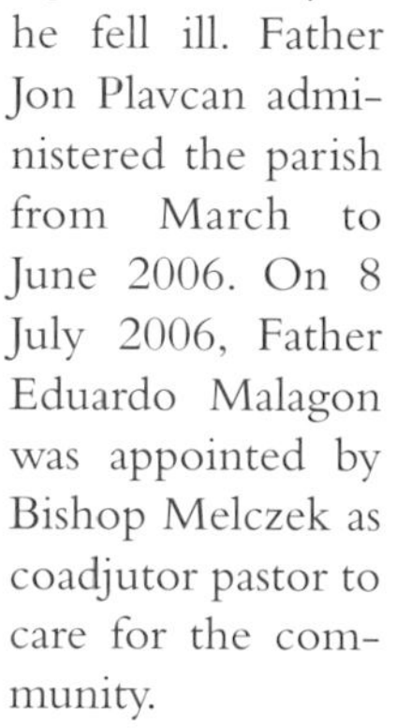

ASSUMPTION OF THE BLESSED VIRGIN MARY

In a small area tucked between Gary to the west and Lake Station to the east on the northern border of Hobart, lies the community known as New Chicago which formed in the early part of the twentieth century. Many of the settlers there were of Polish origin and they petitioned Bishop Alerding for the opportunity to have their own parish. In 1917, thirty-three families formed the Assumption of the Blessed Virgin Mary parish with Father Peter Kahellek of Saint Hedwig parish in Gary celebrating the first mass. He cared for the parish for a year until Father Ignatius Gapczynski from Sacred Heart in Tolleston on the southwest side of Gary was given the responsibility. In December 1918 Father Anthony Gorek was appointed the first resident pastor. During his pastorate land was acquired for the building of the church. In the fall of 1918 the Franciscan Sisters of Blessed Kunegunda (of Chicago) arrived to begin teaching in the parish school. By 1945, because of the community's growth, the convent was built along with additional classrooms. The growth of the community also necessitated the need for a new church. Permission was granted by Bishop Noll in 1939. Later that year, Father Valerian Karcz would be appointed pastor and given the responsibility for the building project. The new (and present church) which also included a classroom behind the sanctuary, was dedicated on 6 August 1940. Father Karcz would remain the pastor for thirty-six years, caring for the needs of the community but also saddened to see the departure of the sisters and closing of the school in 1967 because of a declining enrollment. With Father Karcz's retirement in 1975, Father John Murzyn was appointed the next pastor. He oversaw the project of using the school as a Pre-School and early learning center for three and four year old children. In 1978 plans were made for a parish hall which was erected and formally opened with a parish New Year's Eve party on 31 December 1979. The parish hall has become a popular place for wedding receptions not only because of its facilities but also because of the talent of the parishioners who cater the banquets. Parish activities, fish fries, and festivals put the building to good use.

In September of 1990, approval was given to renovate the Church. The sanctuary was enlarged, a new vestibule was added, and new lighting and windows installed. Bishop Gaughan blessed the completed project and dedicated the altar on 3 November 1991. The parish would welcome him a year later as he celebrated with them their seventy-fifth anniversary.

Poor health forced Father Murzyn to retire in 1994. He was succeeded by Father Martin Dobrzynski, the Director of Liturgy for the diocese. With his expertise for the liturgy, he infused a new fervor in the parish community.

In 2001, the parish completely renovated the parish hall, making it more appealing for its use by the community.

Father Dobrzynski was transferred to Saint Michael in Schererville in December of 2002. His successor is Father Jon Plavcan who also functions as the bishop's Administrative Assistant and Moderator of the Curia.

Nativity of Our Savior

The city of Portage was incorporated in 1964. Before this time, the settlements in northern Porter County attended either Saint Patrick in Chesterton, Saint Bridget in Hobart, or Saint Francis Xavier in East Gary. Father Clemens Koors secured the present site of the parish by buying a twenty-two acre site that was originally a pig farm.

As the city began to grow because to the growth of steel mills and the Port of Indiana at Burns Harbor, the community was certainly large enough for the establishment of a parish. As the first parish established by Bishop Grutka in the diocese of Gary, it received the title Nativity of Our Savior in commemoration of the Bishop's nomination as bishop of Gary on Christmas Eve, 1956. The first mass was celebrated on 3 May 1964 by the Diocesan Chancellor, Monsignor John Charlebois at the "Chapel on the Mall" a ten foot by fifty foot trailer placed at the north end of Portage's shopping mall. The first parishioners attended mass from their cars parked in the parking lot.

Father Joseph Till became the first resident pastor on 1 July 1964. He secured the Felician Sisters of Livonia, Michigan to organize a program of Religious instruction for the children of the parish. Ground was broken for a multi-purpose building on 31 October 1965 and dedicated by Bishop Grutka on 12 March 1966. Father Till was succeeded in 1969 by Father William Spranger who stayed for two years. On 30 July 1971 Father Carl Mengeling would become pastor. During his tenure, he would oversee the foundation of the Catechetic and Activities Center which would become with an addition, the parish school in 1975. An addition to the school was completed in 1977.

In 1979, a committee was formed to develop a plan for a permanent church. Bishop Grutka was invited to celebrate Midnight Mass on Christmas in 1981 and ground was broken before the celebration of that mass. The church was completed and dedicated on 18 September 1983 by Bishop Grutka.

Monsignor Mengeling would be succeeded by Monsignor John Morales. With the departure of Monsignor Morales, Father Joseph Gazarkiewicz would administer the parish until Father John Scott was appointed in 1991. He would remain pastor until he was succeeded by his associate, Father Patrick Kalich, in 1999. The present pastor, Father Walter Rakoczy arrived in 2000. Since then, with his various associate pastors and permanent deacons who assist him, he has worked to strengthen the community liturgically, through prayer, and the administration of both the parish school and religious education program.

The parish festival, which occurs each July, is one of the largest in the state of Indiana, and certainly one of the most popular in the diocese.

THE PARISHES OF THE NORTHLAKE COUNTY DEANERY

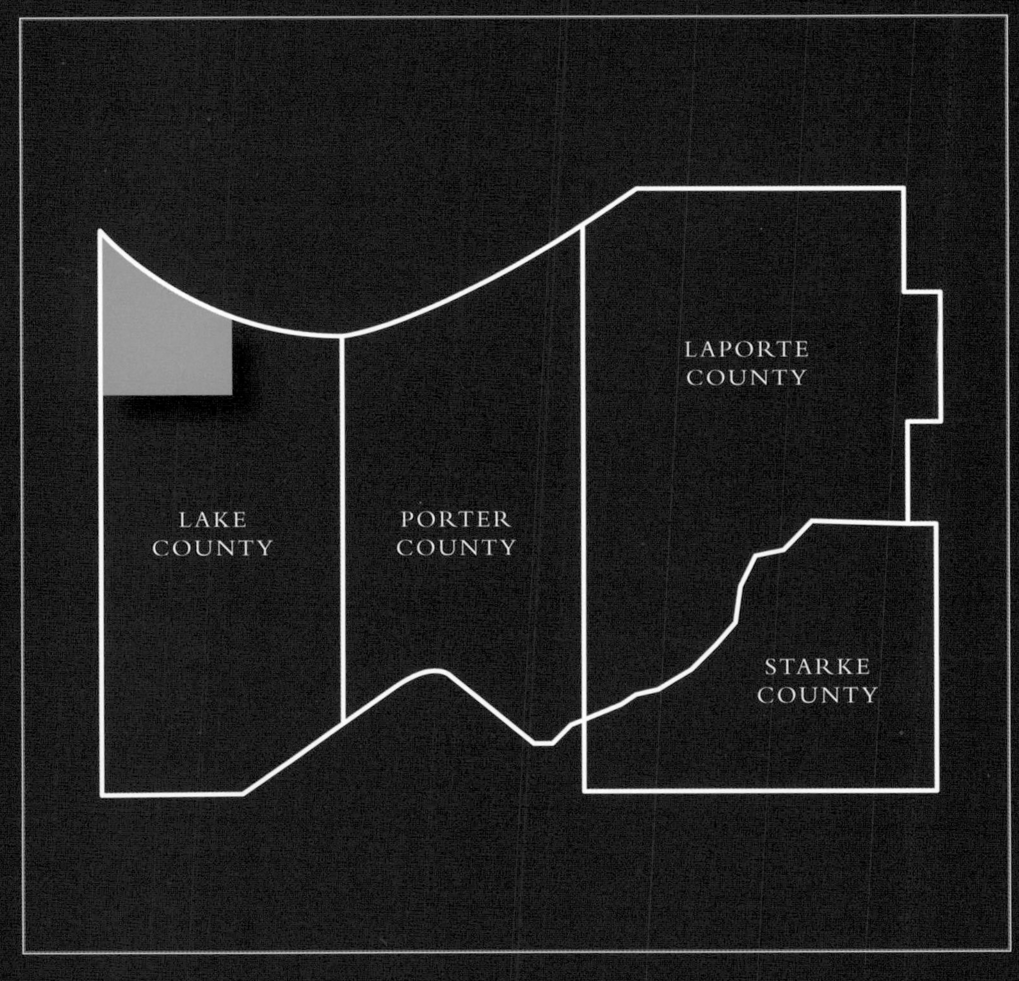

Holy Trinity (Croatian)

Although plans were considered for a parish in East Chicago for Catholics of Croatian descent, they did not come to fruition until 12 November 1916 with the celebration of the community's first mass. This took place at Holy Trinity Church, the parish founded for Hungarian speaking immigrants. Subsequently the community would travel to Saint Mary as well as Saint Stanislaus in East Chicago for their needs. At Christmas time 1917, the present combination church-school complex was completed under the direction of the first Pastor, Father Joseph Judnic and dedicated by Bishop Alerding on Trinity Sunday, 26 May 1918. Father Judnic would also build a convent for the Sisters Adorers of the Precious Blood, and oversee the opening of the school. He would remain pastor until 1922 when he was succeeded by Father Francis Bahoric until 1924. Father Francis Podgorsek would serve the parish from 1924 until his death in 1946. In 1941, as his health began to fail, the pastor was sent a newly ordained assistant in the person of Father Paul. He was a student at the Josephinum Seminary in Ohio, when Father Paul Schmid, a priest of the diocese on loan to the seminary as a spiritual director, recruited the young man for Fort Wayne, as there was a need for Croatian speaking priests. He came to East Chicago and remained at Holy Trinity for the rest of his life. From 1941, the year of his ordination, until Father Podgorsek's death in 1946, he was the associate pastor. In 1946, he became the pastor and served the community until his death in 2002. In 1957, he became the first *officialis* or presiding judge of the new diocese's Tribunal. In 1963, he was given the rank of Papal Chamberlain. For sixty-one years Monsignor Bogovich saw to the spiritual needs of the community and guided it through its difficulties through the loss of the Sisters and the closing of the school in 1992 and its transformation from a purely ethnic parish to one that served the entire neighborhood.

After his death a resident pastor would not be assigned to the parish. The community would come under the care of the Vicar General, Father Stanley Dominik, pastor of Sacred Heart in Whiting. Upon his retirement the administration of the parish would be the responsibility of the new Vicar General, Monsignor John Siekierski, pastor of Saint Stanislaus.

Today the parish counts about one-hundred fifty families in its membership who have been most devoted to the physical care of the property and the familiar atmosphere of the community as they gather on Sunday.

Holy Trinity (Hungarian)

The Hungarian priest, Father Benedict Rajcany, who was pastor of Saint John the Baptist Church in Whiting saw to the needs of the Hungarian immigrants who came to settle and work in East Chicago.

Between 1904 and 1910 a group of Hungarians formed a committee to canvass and solicit pledges for the building of a Hungarian parish. In 1905 six lots were purchased at Alexander Avenue and 148th Street. The cornerstone for the building was laid on 11 November 1906 and the completed building was dedicated on the feast of the Holy Trinity in 1907. Father Oscar Szilagyi, a Benedictine monk, arrived as the first resident pastor on 24 December 1907. In 1909 he was succeeded by Father Paul Bognar. In December 1911 the church was destroyed by fire.

A new building replaced it in 1912 and Father Francis Fekete became pastor that same year. A year later, Father Stephen Varga would become the pastor until 1916. He was replaced in 1917 by Father Alexander Schaffer. During his tenure, more property was secured and the third and present church was built and dedicated on 22 May 1921. The parish school was opened in 1922 and staffed by the Daughters of Divine Charity.

Father Schaffer remained until 1927 when illness forced him to resign the parish. He was succeeded by Father Joseph Toth. It has been said that during his tenure as pastor the parish, although not able to advance materially because of the depression, grew stronger spiritually. He died as a result of a fatal heart attack while preparing to hear confessions on 15 December 1934. Six weeks later, his successor would be a former assistant of his, Father Joseph Sipos.

The parish celebrated its golden jubilee on 11 November 1956 with Father Sipos celebrating a solemn high mass in the presence of a full church. The school would close two years later with the

departure of the sisters, but, as a result of a fire at Saint Stanislaus School, the building would be used for their students until 1960.

Father Sipos was transferred to Our Lady of Perepetual Help in 1962, and was succeeded by Father Stephen Vrabely who had the responsibility of executing the new liturgical directives of the Second Vatican Council. Also during his pastorate, the Missionary Sisters of Our Lady of Victory arrived to establish catechetical programs for the children of the area. Besides catechetics, they organized a choir for the liturgy. In 1966, Father Vrabely was followed by Father Stephen Varga (no relation to the pastor in 1916). While pastor, he remodeled the church and rectory, but suffered with the parish the loss of the parish hall and school by fire. Father Joseph Vamos administered the parish for a short while until the arrival of the present Father Alphonse Skerl, who came to the parish on 1 February 1971.

One of the most memorable events in the life of the parish was the visit of Joseph Cardinal Mindszenty, who visited the parish on 22 June 1974 and blessed the church bells which had been recently repaired.

Undoubtedly, our most exhilarating and historic experience occurred on July 10, 2004, when His Eminence, Péter Cardinal Erdő, Primate of Hungary visited our parish. He was accompanied by Auxiliary Bishop László Rigó and Rev. László Süllei, Chancellor. They participated in the celebration of Holy Mass at 5pm, followed by a reception in our hall. Everyone was in awe of his presence and his out-going personality. He indeed did his homework, for he presented to Father Skerl a bottle of Hungarian wine and a book on Railroad Trains.

In October we were pleased with the arrival of Deacon Fransis Magung from the Society of Divine Word Missionaries. He came from Indonesia and had requested that after ordination he be assigned to perform his ministry in Hungary. In order to learn the Hungarian language and become familiar with Hungarian culture, he has been asked to minister to our Holy Trinity Hungarian Parish and St. Stephen King of Hungary Parish in Chicago until his ordination in June, 2005.

The 22nd October of 2006 the church has celebrated her 100 years anniversary and the Hungarian freedom fight of 1956.

Through the thirty years of Father Skerl's pastorate, the joys and sorrows of a parish community have been shared; jubilees and anniversaries, the arrival and departure of bishops, and the dawn of a new millennium of Christianity.

Our Lady of Guadalupe

One of the results of increased production in industry during and after World War I was the rise of the Mexican community in Indiana Harbor. Attending mass at the various ethnic parishes in the city did not give them comfort and they hoped to one day have a parish of their own.

This hope was realized in the person of Father Octavio Zavatta, C.PP.S. an Italian missionary of the Precious Blood who worked among the people and said mass for them originally in the basement of Saint Demetrius Church.

In a year, property was purchased at 3855 Pennsylvania Avenue in order to build a church which was completed and dedicated by Bishop Noll on 30 January 1927.

Father Apolinar Santa Cruz, a Mexican priest seeking asylum from the religious persecutions occurring in Mexico arrived in 1927 and succeeded Father Zavatta in August of that year. Father Jose Lara, also from Mexico replaced him in July of 1929.

The parish worked closely together, particularly during the depression and made sure that everyone was cared for and had the basic necessities for their families.

In April of 1937, with the departure of Father Lara, the administration of the parish was given to the Priests of the Sacred Heart, whose Motherhouse was in Hales Corners, Wisconsin. With their arrival, Father Patrick O'Neill, S.C.J. would become the new pastor. A fire caused damage to the church and the community desired to build a new church closer to their neighborhood. This was done on the Feast of Our Lady of Guadalupe, 12 December 1939, when the cornerstone was laid at the new site on One-Hundred Thirty-Fifth and Deodar Street. The former church became the parish of Saint Jude for African Americans. The new church would be completely remodeled in 1976.

The Sacred Heart Fathers would serve the parish until 1986 when the Precious Blood Fathers would take charge. Father Leo Huber, C.PP.S. arrived on 1 September 1986. His successor would be Father Juan Gonzalez, C.PP.S., who came to this country from Chile in 1990 and would become pastor in 1994 and serve the community to the present day. In 2004, the church was again remodeled and enlarged to accommodate more seating and add a new Blessed Sacrament Chapel.

Sacred Heart

At the beginning of the twentieth century, with the growth of heavy industry in Lake County, many eastern Europeans, including Slovaks would come to work and find a new life. Father Clement Mlnarovich started Assumption Parish in Indiana Harbor in 1915, building a school and a church. In 1926 he established "Assumption Mission" in East Chicago since the Slovak people living there often had to walk to the Harbor for mass. Masses were celebrated for them at the Byzantine parishes, first at Saint Basil and the then Saint Nicholas.

Father Andrew Sucek, a teacher at Catholic Central High School, cared for the community until 1929, when Father Alexius Machacek, a Benedictine monk came from Saint Procopius Abbey in Lisle, Illinois. He came each week for Mass, heard confessions and gave instructions to the children. He was a zealous priest, known also as a taskmaster. By the 1930s the people were anxious to have their own church and they petitioned Bishop Noll for permission to build a church. Eventually they received permission and built a church. The parish was placed under the protection of the Sacred Heart of Jesus and the first mass was celebrated on 8 December 1940 though the formal dedication did not occur until 10 May 1941.

Sacred Heart Church is a church of devotion and prayer; a small church on a quiet street, a beautiful church of charm and warmth, befitting the warmth of its Slovak heritage. It was built during the later years of the great depression, during difficult economic times. Much of the work of construction was done by the parishioners themselves.

The first resident pastor would come from Elkhart in the spring of 1942 in the person of Father Andrew Grutka. As there was yet no rectory, he would live in a rented apartment for the two years he served the fledgling community. To quote a parish history: "Father Grutka's years at Sacred Heart were the war years, and everything was limited and rationed. But there was no limit on prayer, no limit on dedication. Father Grutka spoke at the dedication of memorials to the boys in service. Almost twenty years after his departure, a parishioner who was a child at the time recalled of his sermons that he always said, 'As you pray, so shall you live.' " His successor would be Father Louis Duray who would care for the parish until 1957. During his tenure a rectory was purchased and the church was beautified.

In 1957, Father Duray's predecessor, as the new Bishop of Gary, would appoint him to Holy Trinity in Gary. Father Milan F. Bach who taught at Bishop Noll High School would care for the parish until he succeeded the late Father Lach in 1960 at Immaculate Conception in Whiting. Father Joseph Semancik would become the next pastor while working as the Director of Catholic Charities until his transfer to Holy Trinity in 1969.

For the next five years, the parish would be cared for by Fathers Anthony Ficko, John Siekierski, and Clare Hendricks. When Father Hendricks became a Navy Chaplain in 1974, Monsignor Semancik returned and remains the present pastor.

Saint John Cantius

The beginning of the twentieth century brought the development of heavy industry to the area that would be called Indiana Harbor. Because of this, an influx of people came to the area seeking work. The greatest percentage at that time was of Polish descent. The area was marked by modest wooden structures, erected on scattered knolls. Seeking religious consolation, the people of the area went to the other side of East Chicago to Saint Stanislaus Church or to Saint Adalbert Church in Whiting; to the Polish Churches that already had been established. Each Sunday these pilgrimages were made afoot and started to become tiresome.

A group of fourteen men, who were pioneer settlers, met to discuss and to select a site for the Church. It was these men who selected the location of 139th and Main Street, and this site is where the Church and parish building are still located. At its inception, the parish consisted of twenty-six families.

Five parcels of land were contracted and the Land Company donated two additional parcels. Finally in June of 1904, Father Kubacki of Saint Stanislaus in East Chicago brought the good news that the bishop had approved permission for the organization of Saint John Cantius parish. In the latter part of 1904, preparation for building the church came to fruition.

In the spring of 1905 construction of the Church and school were completed and the first Mass was celebrated in March of 1905 by Father Anthony Stachowiak, who was also the first pastor. The school building consisted of four rooms; two rooms housed school children and the other two rooms as the temporary rectory for the pastor. In 1907, a rectory was constructed. Over the years, the rectory was enlarged and became a convent for the Franciscan Sisters who taught at the parish school, and a new rectory was constructed.

In 1917, plans were launched for a new church. However, because of World War I a substructure was placed under roof, and remains so today.

Between the years of 1925-1928, Father Theofil Chemma, who served as pastor from 1925 to 1932, had extensive remodeling done to all the parish buildings. To help off-set the debt, the pastor asked the parishioners for help. Many organizations were established for the sole purpose of liquidating the indebtedness. Events were held that would appeal to both young and old as well as arouse the parishioner's charitable qualities. Father Michael Petzold, the third pastor, served the church from 1932 until his death in 1965. He is best remembered for his leadership and guidance of the spiritual needs of the parish.

Due to a decline in the enrollment in the Catholic schools in Indiana Harbor, Bishop Grutka decided that the consolidation of the catholic schools in the Harbor was necessary. In 1967, under the tenure of Father Anthony Balczun, the parish school was remodeled and renamed Indiana Harbor Catholic Elementary School. The Sisters teaching at the school were not only the Franciscans from Lemont, but now also included the Sacred Heart Sisters from Saint Patrick Parish. Father Balczun was the pastor from 1965 to 1967 with Father Stanley Dominik succeeding him for one year.

Father Michael Tomaszewski became pastor in 1968. During his time he made many improvements and repairs to the church. He was succeeded by Father Vladimir Janeczek who was pastor for fourteen years. 1978 brought the first elected parish council and the remodeling of the rectory. At the end of the 1978 – 1979 school year the Franciscan Sisters of Chicago, who served the parish school since it inception were called back to their community.

In July 1992, Father Robert Tokarz became the next pastor. He reached out to all the parishioners to get more involved in the various parish ministries. His success brought parishioners from all ages and walks of life joining different ministries. He was succeeded in 1996 by Father Joseph Niezgoda who has kept up with the Polish traditions of the Corpus Christi procession outdoors on the church grounds as well as the Eucharist Devotions in October. He has made much needed improvements to the rectory and a continuing project of improvements to the church. In 2003, failing health caused Father Niezgoda to give up the responsibilities of administration at which time Saint Stanislaus parish, as in the beginning, sees to the care of the community.

Saint Mary

As the new city of East Chicago developed, the Catholic citizens were hoping for a parish of their own. The first mass was celebrated at the Todd Opera House by Father Henry Plaster, the pastor of Saint Joseph in Hammond. He built the first church which was dedicated 26 October 1890. The parish continued as a mission of Saint Joseph for ten years until Father George Lauer became the first resident pastor. In 1901, he built the parish school which was staffed by the Sisters of Providence for a brief period, when the Poor Handmaids would take charge in 1913. In 1921, the parish school provided the new Catholic Central High School (the future Bishop Noll Institute) with classroom space until their building was completed. Father Lauer was succeeded by:

- Father E. Werling (1923-1927),
- Father Edward Vurpillat (1923-1935),
- Father Michael Shea (1935-1956),
- Father Carl Holsinger (1956-1965),
- Father John Charlebois (1966),
- Father Stephen Vrabely (1966-1969),
- Father Joseph Till (1969-1975),
- Father Robert Gehring (1976-1985),
- Father Theodore Mens (1985-1993),
- and the current pastor Father Stephen Gibson.

The second half of the last century saw a dramatic change in the cultural makeup of St. Mary Parish, with a large Hispanic immigration into the East Chicago area. This immigration came primarily from Puerto Rico and from Mexico, but other Hispanic cultures were also represented. Since St. Mary's parish from the beginning was a territorial parish, one could say that it was natural for St. Mary's to be the parish that became the home for most of the Hispanic immigrants on its side of East Chicago. In 1971, the Spanish language began to be incorporated into the liturgy, and many aspects of the Latin culture began to be incorporated into parish and school life.

The last ten years has seen a continued growth of the Hispanic population in East Chicago, and this continues to affect greatly the cultural makeup of Saint Mary Parish. New immigrants continue to come monthly from Mexico. Most are young single people and young families. A large number of people have also come from the largely Mexican neighborhoods of South Chicago. The direction the Church takes in its pastoral work in East Chicago in the near future will have to reflect this reality. Under the direction of Father Gibson, the parish built a new church in 2000 which needed to be considerably enlarged in 2006.

Saint Patrick

Saint Patrick Church was founded in 1902 in the year old settlement of Indiana Harbor. Eight families comprised the first congregation. The original frame church was built on the corner of 138th and Hemlock and was completed for the first mass which was celebrated on 25 January 1903. Father Thomas Mungovan organized the community and remained as pastor until 1911 when he was replaced by Father John Wakefer who remained until 1917. The new pastor, Father James Connelly, initiated a fund drive for a new church and school upon his arrival in 1917. The present church was completed in 1923 and was dedicated in April of that year by Bishop Noll. The school also opened in that year staffed by the Sisters of Holy Cross.

Father Fernando de Cristobal, the current pastor, working with the Parish Council, developed a mission statement in the year 2000. It states: "We, the baptized believers of St. Patrick Parish will: make the celebration of the Eucharistic liturgy and the Word the foundation of all parish activities; strive to be a welcoming community celebrating our cultural diversity; foster harmony and reconciliation among parishioners and the community; encourage the use of the gifts the Spirit has given to serve our parishioners' needs and the needs of the community at large."

Over the years, the Parish has made many renovations. Revenues for these repairs/renovations came from a number of activities. The annual Church festival was re-implemented. The revenue from these festivals has helped to finance many of the renovations. An annual Super Bowl party is sponsored by the Saint Pat Boosters. Not only do the Boosters raise money, but they also supply most of the manpower for the renovations. An annual Fruit Sale is another fundraiser that helps meet some of the parish financial needs.

Saint Stanislaus

Before the turn of the century, Lake County was becoming an industrial center. The East Chicago area in particular, was found to hold great possibilities. This marshy, swampy bog advertised as "the twentieth century wonder where rail and water meet" attracted industries to locate within its borders. Workers and residents came from the Pennsylvania textile mills and coal mining towns. Immigrants from the European Balkans, specifically Poland also came in notable numbers in 1886. In order to fulfill their religious obligations, these devout Poles came to worship at St. Casimir parish in North Hammond. They traveled by foot, horse and carriage to a place of welcome where Frs. Casimir Kobylinski and Peter Kahellek ministered to their spiritual needs. Their numbers grew. In 1896, Father Kobylinski gained permission to build a church in East Chicago; a wood-framed structure located at 150th and Baring Avenue which was dedicated to Saint Michael. Father John Kubacki, who arrived in 1900, was assigned to be the first resident pastor. As his growing congregation already needed more space for a rectory, convent and school, land was purchased on 150th and Magoun Avenues.

The Church structure was moved to its new site and its name changed to Saint Stanislaus of Krakow, Bishop and Martyr. Father Peter Budnik assumed the duties of pastor in 1908.

In 1922 construction began on the last and final phase: a new school equipped with a gymnasium that would double-up as a hall and community center with two bowling lanes, pool and billiards and a 300 seat auditorium.

While the construction was underway, Father Julian Skrypinski was appointed the fourth pastor in 1923. He saw the project to completion and to full payment. The community center became the social gathering place. The school became recognized as a nurturing ground for good, honest, qualified citizens, workers, and community leaders. Tragedy struck the parish in January 1958, when fire broke out and destroyed the Memorial Hall and School Building. In April 1961, a new structure arose from the ashes. Father Henry Krysinski and Father Joseph Niezgoda, a native son, the fifth and sixth pastors inherited a great stewardship responsibility in their caring of the buildings, particularly in paying for the new school, and the building of the people of God following the Second Vatican Council. The final payment for the new school was realized in 1985 as the parish celebrated its 85th Anniversary. The current pastor since 1996 is Monsignor John Siekierski, the Vicar General of the diocese and Dean of the Northlake Deanery since 2005.

The Centennial Celebration was held on Sunday, 22 October 2000. The theme chosen to mark that milestone was "Honoring Our Past-Believing in our Future."

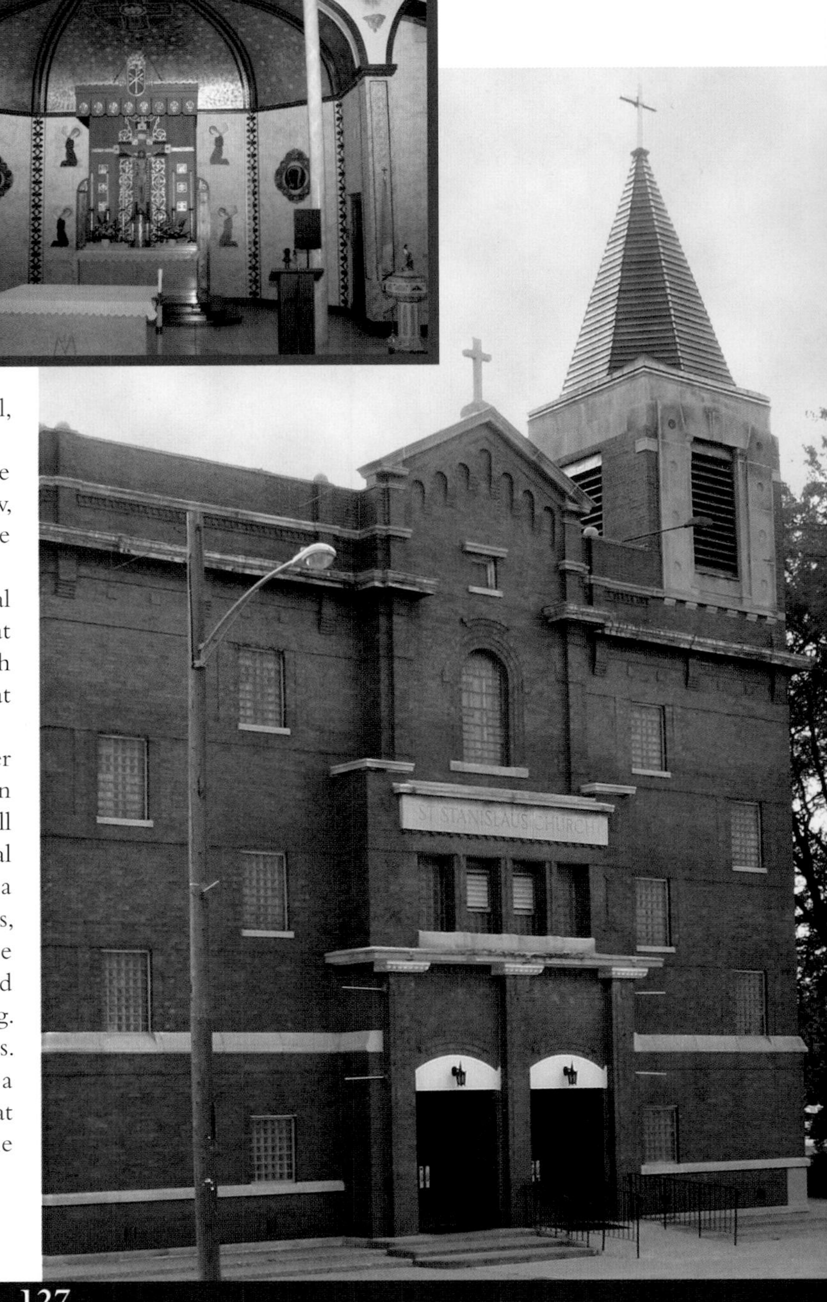

All Saints

As the priests at Saint Joseph preached in German, All Saints Parish was established in 1896, primarily for people moving into Hammond that could not speak German.

Father John Cook was asked to organize the community. He rented a home on Fayette Street and began to have a small church built. In 1897, he was replaced by Father Edward Barrett who established a school that year inviting the Sisters of Providence to staff it. By 1908 a larger combination church and school building was erected, as so many parishes at the time were doing.

In 1917 the parish would provide a new convent for the sisters. Father Barrett would remain pastor until his death in 1928 and would be succeeded by Monsignor Edward Mungovan, who in 1940 would be named Vicar General of the Fort Wayne diocese. Upon his arrival in Hammond he undertook a project to build a new church. In 1930 the parish built the present church, an imposing brick edifice. During his tenure the parish developed into a large and active community. Monsignor Mungovan would remain pastor until his death in 1954. Father Charles Seeberger would become the next pastor. In 1966, the parish school was consolidated with Saint Joseph School. Father Seeberger would care for the community until his death in 1969. Father Carl Mengeling succeeded as pastor while still continuing on the faculty of Bishop Noll Institute. While pastor, he would renovate the church according to the liturgical norms of the Vatican Council. Father Robert Barry Evers succeeded him in 1970, the year the parish school closed. He would be transferred to Saints Peter and Paul in 1980 when Father Edward Moszur would be named administrator and then pastor while remaining in the administration of Bishop Noll Institute. During his tenure he continued the practice started by Father Evers, of celebrating mass for the growing Hispanic population in the area. In 1991 he would be succeeded by Father J. Anthony Valtierra. He continued to spur the community into social as well as spiritual activities and was much beloved. In 2002, the administration of Saint Margaret Mary would be added to his responsibilities and he would reluctantly accept a new assignment in 2003 when he would be succeeded by the current pastor, Father Stephen Kosinski.

Our Lady of Perpetual Help

Hessville was a town settled by Joseph Hess around 1851, rural in area, it would eventually be annexed by the city of Hammond as it expanded and Hessville developed. By 1927 the growing number of Catholics clamored for a parish of their own. The first mass was said by a visiting priest in a building on Summer Street in 1933. In 1937, Bishop Noll appointed Father Alfred Reinig the community's first pastor and he would place the parish under the protection of Our Lady of Perpetual Help.

Property was purchased in the 7100 block of Arizona Avenue and the former Morton Middle School gymnasium was purchased and moved to the site for use as the first church, which Bishop Noll dedicated on 6 November 1938.

In 1943 the Poor Handmaids of Jesus Christ would be engaged to staff the parish school. The combination church and school building was completed in 1949. The school continued in operation until 1992.

Father Reinig would remain pastor until 1962 when he would be transferred to Saint Mary, the Immaculate Conception. His successors would be Father Joseph Sipos (1962-1968), Monsignor Timothy Doody (1968-1976), Father Stephen Vrabely (1976-1982), Father Joseph Murphy (1982-1996) who would build the present church in 1987, Father John Winterlin (1996) who was parish music director before entering the seminary in the early 1960s, and the current pastor Father Charles Mosley who succeeded Father Winterlin in 2005.

While the school is no longer open, the parish continues to operate an active Religious Education program that annually teaches over 200 students. Within the church a variety of ministries maintain a bustling parish life.

The parish's Saint Vincent DePaul Society operates an extensive food pantry and also supports Habitat for Humanity projects and other community drives for social and economic justice. Besides offering classrooms for religious education, the former school is home to social service agencies that support community life in Northwest Indiana.

SAINT CASIMIR

At the end of the nineteenth century, the nearest Polish Catholic parish was located in Otis, Indiana. This was Saint Mary, and the pastor of the time, Father Urban Raskiewicz, would travel to Hammond to care for the spiritual needs of the Polish community, many of whom had come to the area to work at the George Hammond Meat Packing Plant. The community centered around the north of the developing city and desired to form a parish of their own.

The parish was formed in 1890 under the patronage of Saint Michael the Archangel. Nowhere in the parish archives is there listed an official change to the parish title, but it is believed to have happened within the first year to honor the first resident pastor, Father Casimir Kobylinski who served the parish from 1890-1897. The community numbering about fifty families, obtained eight lots at Huehn and Cameron Streets in North Hammond and built a two-storey combination church and school with a residence for the pastor on the first floor.

Father Peter Kahellek then served from 1897 through 1909. Under his pastorship three nuns representing the Sisters of Saint Francis of Perpetual Adoration were invited to the parish to teach in 1901. The teaching order remained with the parish until 1986. The parish school continues to this day with the dedication of lay teachers. When Father Kahellek left in 1909 to help with the establishment of Saint Hedwig

Parish in Gary, he was succeeded by Father John Kasprzykowski who remained until 1911.

In 1911, Father Felix Seroczynski became pastor and embarked on a building campaign. In 1920, a new rectory was built and the old rectory was made into a convent. And most importantly, the foundation was laid for the present church in 1923.

The cornerstone for the present church was blessed by the first Polish bishop of the United States, Bishop Paul Rhode of Green Bay, Wisconsin on 15 August, 1924. Construction was completed in 1925. The interior of this church was completed in 1928 under the guidance of Father John Hosinski who came in 1927 as pastor. Much of the original furnishings, consisting of statues and accessories were added through the generosity of the parishioners.

In 1929, a new school building, complete with gym, was constructed. On August 15, 1932, Monsignor John Biernacki became pastor. He served as pastor from 1932 until his death in 1960.

In 1940, the parish celebrated its golden jubilee with a mass celebrated by Bishop Noll on 19 May. In 1951 Monsignor Biernacki continued the building program with the construction of a three story convent with ample quarters for the teaching Franciscan Sisters. The parish was youthful and thriving, averaging 12 baptisms every Sunday. In 1955, ground was broken for a new school addition which is in use today as the primary classroom sites. By 1960, the parish numbered well over 1,000 families.The next pastor was Monsignor Stanley Zjawinski. Under his direction major repairs were made to the exterior of the church and the interior was entirely redecorated. The present altar and sanctuary furnishings were imported from Europe over a year long program of installation. The new rectory was built in 1966.

Upon the death of Monsignor Zjawinski in 1968, Father Anthony Balczun became the pastor and continued to make parish improvements which included the installation of air conditioning within the church.

Monsignor Casimir Senderak came as pastor in March of 1977. He had previously served as an assistant from 1944 to 1960. Monsignor began an energetic improvement program with the installation of a new heating system for the school and church, new roofs, tuck pointing of buildings, the cleaning and repairing of the church windows, the replacement of the church pews and kneelers, and also the replacement of the church floor and the installation of carpeting throughout the church.

Upon the retirement of Monsignor Senderak in 1992, Father Vladimir Janeczek was pastor until his retirement in 2004. He was succeeded by the present pastor Father William O'Toole.

SAINT CATHERINE OF SIENA

Saint Catherine of Siena parish would have the distinction of receiving the first three pastors from three bishops. In May of 1956, Father Dominic Pallone, the assistant of Father Koors at Saint Francis Xavier, received his appointment to found a new parish on the eastside of Hessville. While doing so, he would reside with and assist the pastor of Our Lady of Perpetual Help. A site was chosen at 165th and Kentucky Avenue, and ground was broken in April of 1957 for a school and gymnasium which would serve as a temporary church, named Saint Catherine of Siena in memory of his mother Caterina Pallone. The church was dedicated by Bishop Grutka on 13 April 1958 and the parish school would open in September staffed by the Poor Handmaids of Jesus Christ. The rectory was completed in 1960. Father Pallone cared for the community as a father for twenty-seven years until his death in 1983.

His successor, appointed by Bishop Grutka, would be Father Timothy Benante, who would implement many of the reforms of the Second Vatican Council. He would remain until 1985, when Bishop Gaughan would appoint Father Patrick Connolly, the third pastor of the parish.

During his tenure, the decision was made to abandon plans for a separate church building and renovate the current structure as the permanent church. The plan would turn the axis of the church centering the sanctuary along the north wall in the middle of the nave. Seating would surround the new sanctuary on three sides, and the former sanctuary would become a chapel for the Blessed Sacrament. Stained glass windows would also be installed. Bishop Gaughan would rededicate the church in 1987. That same year, Father Richard Orlinski would become pastor and care for the community until 1998; Father Lawrence Kew, the present pastor would succeed him. During this time the school would close its junior high school department to the benefit of the Bishop Noll Institute program, but would bring it back in 2002.

SAINT JOHN BOSCO

Under the direction of Father Paul Schmid, the principal of Catholic Central High School, Missionary Catechists located in Indiana Harbor, would help catechize the children of this area using a rented basement apartment on Columbia Avenue. The first mass was offered in that place on 15 April 1934.

Two weeks earlier on Easter Sunday, 1 April 1934, Pope Pius XI canonized the Italian priest John Bosco and Father Schmid dedicated this parish on the very same day in honor of the newly canonized saint, thus becoming the first parish in the world named in honor of the saint. Father Schmid would be appointed Spiritual Director at the Josephinum Seminary in Worthington, Ohio, later that year and would be replaced by Father H. James Conway. He would care for the small community until 1936, when Father Richard Grunenberg would succeed him

In 1937, Bishop Noll gave permission to move a portable classroom building, purchased from the Hammond School Board, to property owned by the Church on 171st Street and Columbia Avenue. Additions and remodeling was accomplished in 1938 to transform the building into a church for the community. Bishop Noll administered the sacrament of Confirmation for the first time at the parish on 19 October 1939 to one hundred sixteen children and adults.

In 1940, Father John Bartkowski was named pastor of the fifty family community. Ten years later the community had grown to six hundred families and plans were made to build a new church and school. The project was completed in 1952. Also that year the parish received four Sisters of Saint Joseph, Third Order of Saint Francis to staff the school. In 1956 the rectory was enlarged, and a new convent was completed in 1964. This building currently houses the parish office, the school library, and the Saint Vincent de Paul Society food pantry.

Monsignor Everard Klein would care for the parish from 1966 to 1982 and steer the community through the reforms of the Second Vatican Council, remodeling the sanctuary for that purpose. Upon his retirement, Father Michael Heimer would care for the community for three years until 1985, when he was succeeded by Father Stanley Dominik (1985-1998). During his tenure the church would be completely renovated, moving the sanctuary among the people and installing a new baptismal font. Father Richard Orlinski was appointed pastor in 1998 and also given care for the parish of Saint Mary of Czestochowa on the east side of Hammond.

SAINT JOSEPH

In 1879, Father Francis X. Baumgartner, a young Swiss priest with boundless energy would organize Saint Joseph parish in the new city of Hammond. He was at the time the pastor of Saints Peter and Paul at Turkey Creek with responsibilities also at Saint Bridget in Hobart. Upon receiving land donated by Caroline Hohman, a member of the Episcopal Church, he and the young community built a small frame church. Father Baumgartner would be transferred to Kentland in 1880 and the fledgling community would be placed in the care of the priest at Saint Michael in Schererville. In 1883 Father Baumgartner would return as the first resident pastor and would remain so until his death at the age of thirty-four in 1885. Father Henry Plaster was appointed second pastor in the summer of 1885 and would serve the community for thirty-one years until his retirement in 1916. Soon after his arrival he would build a school which would open in the fall of 1885. The Sisters of Providence would not take charge until the next year. In 1893 a second frame church would be built, but the growing congregation would soon need a new church. Under the direction of their pastor a plan was developed in 1910 to build the third and present structure, a magnificent Romanesque style brick church that would seat one thousand people. The cornerstone was laid on 16 June 1912 and the completed building was dedicated by Bishop Alerding on 22 March 1914. Father Plaster was succeeded by Father John Berg (1916-1927) who struggled with illness and the business community who wanted the church moved from the main street because it was in the way of business. Father Berg died in 1927 and was succeeded by Father Francis Jansen who would care for the community for almost forty years. During his tenure he would enlarge the sanctuary and have the church frescoed, a new convent would also be built. He was succeeded in 1966 by Monsignor Vincent Lengerich who would be forced to close the parish school before his transfer to Crown Point in 1972. The parish was administered briefly by the Principal of Bishop Noll Institute, Father James McGrogan, until Father Matthew Kish would become the next pastor (1972-1973). He would be succeeded by Father Joseph Vamos (1973-1979) who would lead the community in celebrating the parish centenary in 1979. He would be followed by Father William Spranger (1979-1985), Father Stephen Vrabely (1985-1993), and the current pastor, Father Roy Beeching. In the fall of 1985, under Father Vrabely's direction, the parish began the Saint Joseph Soup Kitchen, an inter-parish and ecumenical venture that has become a popular and important apostolate in the life of the parish community.

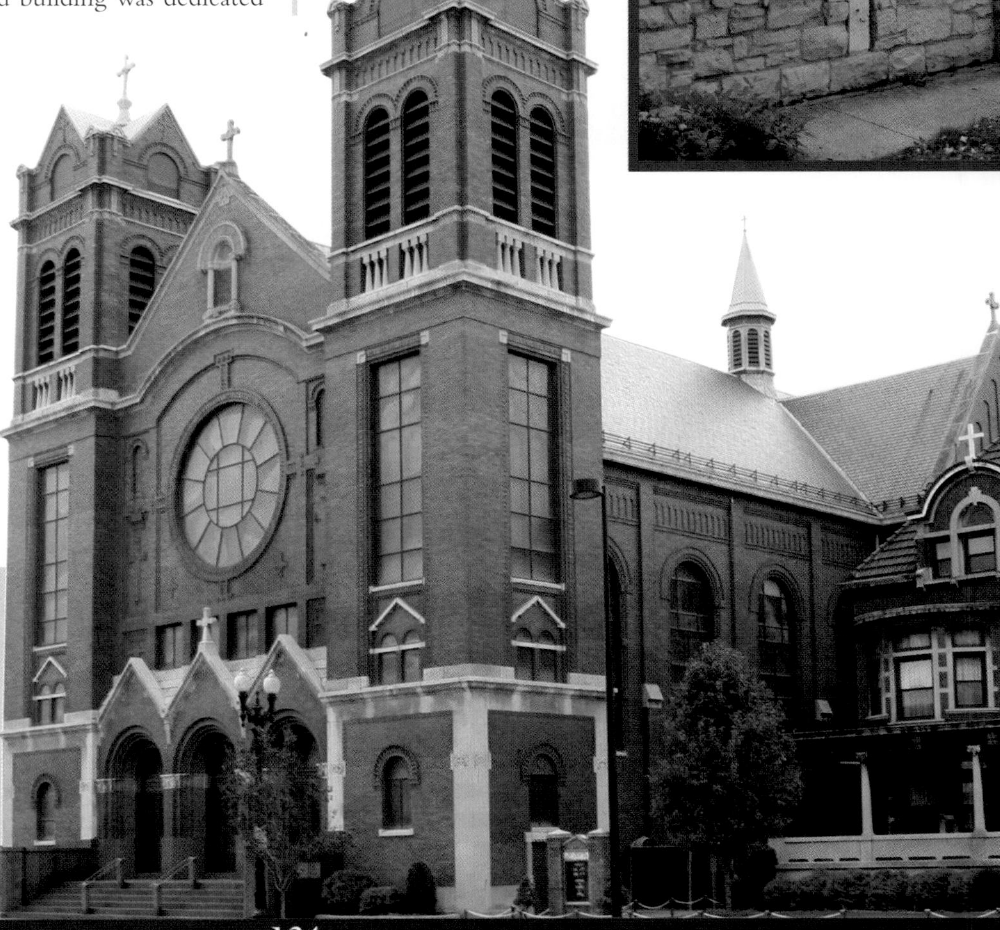

Saint Margaret Mary

Saint Margaret Mary parish, on the campus of Bishop Noll Institute, was dedicated by Bishop Noll on Sunday, 21 September 1952. It was organized by Father Everard Klein, who at the time was on the faculty of the school. The parish was seen as an opportunity for the families of the area who had their children at the high school to form a more tightly-knot community.

Speaking at the dedication, Father Klein talked of the future of the parish stating the desire that it will always remain a symbol of the deep faith of its parishioners; his prayer was that the church be an inspiration for all present and future parishioners.

Some one hundred families composed the initial parish with the count today of about 300 families. From the time of its founding, a number of pastors have served the community, supporting the sacramental life of the people: Monsignor Ferdinand Melevage (1966-1971), Father William Spranger (1971-1979), Father Joseph Murphy (1979-1982), Father Albert Zimmerman (1982-1984), Father Joseph Pawlowski (1984-1986), Father Joseph LaMere (1986-1991), Father Stephen Gibson (1991-1993), Monsignor Joseph Viater (1993-1997), Father Matthew Iwuji (1997-2002), Father Alfred Dettmer (2002-2003), and the current pastor, Father James W. Schulz, S.J.

Parish ministries have been fulfilling to its parishioners over the years. A strong religious program of faith for the children was supervised by Sister Francis de Sales, other sisters from Bishop Noll Institute, and many dedicated lay people.

Care for those in need has been the apostolate of an active Saint Vincent DePaul Society.

The parish continues to carry out the mission of personal and communal conversion, worship, stewardship and social justice, along with providing a place for religious functions for the students of Bishop Noll Institute.

Saint Mary of Czestochowa

Father Felix Seroczynski, pastor of Saint Casimir, organized the parish community for the Polish people who lived in the area of Hammond's eastside.

The original frame buildings were erected in 1913 during the pastorate of Father Anthony Gorek, the first resident pastor and would remain in use until the 1960s when Father Walter Mastey would convert the school gymnasium into a permanent church. The Franciscan Sisters of Blessed Kunegunda would serve the parish as teachers until the school was closed in 1970. Father Gorek would be succeeded in 1926 by Father John Chulewski until 1926 when Father Ignatius Gapczynski would arrive to care for the community. He would be replaced in 1931 by Father Ladislaus Szczukowksi (1931-1939) and Father Joseph Zobel (1939-1962). During Father Zobel's tenure the parish had much of its growth and development, when a new school and auditorium would be built. Father Casimir Senderak (1962-1963) would briefly replace the retiring Father Zobel. Father Walter Mastey (1963-1987) would then arrive to care for the community for twenty-four years. The old church was demolished during his tenure; a steeple would be added to the newly renovated gymnasium turned church to give the building a more recognizable identity as a place of worship. Father Louis Wozniak (1987-1995) became pastor when Father Mastey retired. When Father Wozniak retired, the community would be placed under the care of the pastor of Saint John Bosco parish.

THIS BUILDING ERECTED AND SUPPORTED
BY THE PARISHIONERS TO TRAIN THE MIND,
DEVELOP THE BODY AND CHARACTER
OF THE YOUTH UNDER THE PROTECTIVE MANTLE
OF OUR GREATEST MOTHER. A. D. 1950.
REV. JOSEPH ZOBEL

Immaculate Conception

A new parish for Slovak Catholics was organized in Whiting on 13 August 1922. They chose to attend the Croatian parish down the street with Father Francis Podgorsek ministering to their needs rather than Saint John the Baptist on the other side of town until their combination church and school building was completed in 1924 on property bought from the Schrage family. Father Michael Kosko was appointed the first resident pastor by Bishop Alerding.

He remained until 1926 when he was succeeded by Father John Lach who would guide the parish for thirty-four years until his death in 1960. During his energetic pastorate, parish societies would be active; athletic teams were organized for adults as well as a band that performed at the White House and also made a European tour in 1937.

Father Lach was succeeded by Father M(ilan) Fred Bach, a teacher a Bishop Noll High School. He guided the parish for twenty-three years from 1960 until his retirement in 1983. During his tenure he established the Center of Apostolic Prayer.

Father Anthony Ficko, although debilitated by illness, became pastor in 1983 and served the community until his death in 2000.

The school was opened under the direction of the Sisters of Saints Cyril and Methodius in 1926. The school functioned for fifty-nine years until its closing in 1985.

Currently the parish belongs to the Whiting cluster under the administration of Father John Kalicky C.PP.S.

A prominent feature of the parish is the Lourdes grotto, of which the community is very proud. It was dedicated in 1928 and depicts the apparition of Mary, the Immaculate Conception to Saint Bernadette Soubirous. This grotto is characteristic of the community's devotion to the Church through the intercession of the Blessed Virgin Mary.

Sacred Heart

The first community of Catholics was organized by the pastor of Chesterton, Father H. F. Kroll. He would celebrate mass in the homes of the faithful until property was purchased. The first resident pastor was Father Michael J. Byrne who built a frame church which was dedicated in 1891. The Sisters of Providence staffed the first school in 1895. There were 150 students. After a fire destroyed the school (1897), a two story brick building was built. Later a convent and rectory were built.

In 1898 Father Charles Thiele became the second pastor and as Whiting continued to expand, he purchased lots on LaPorte Avenue for a new parish church. Father John Berg, his successor, built a school building, convent and rectory. This was completed in 1910. The church was on the top floor of the school. A short time later the old Sacred Heart Church on Center Street was rededicated as Saints Peter and Paul Church.

Father William Miller succeeded as the fourth pastor in 1917. The present church, Romanesque in style, was built by his successor, Father Norbert Felden. It was dedicated by Bishop Noll on 9 October 1927. Beautiful stained glass windows from Munich, Germany were added and Father Joseph Lynn, a son of the parish, added a pipe organ. Father George Moorman, the seventh pastor, retired the parish debt, decorated the church, and a mural over the sanctuary arch was painted.

Monsignor F. Raymond Fowerbaugh served as an associate and pastor for almost thirty years. Extensive renovations of the parish complex were accomplished under his pastorate. New mosaics were installed in the church. The centennial of the parish was celebrated during his tenure. He retired in 1998 because of ill health.

Father Stanley Dominik was appointed as the tenth pastor. During his tenure, the community would undergo a renovation of the church. The original terrazzo floor was restored and the altar was extended into the body of the church according to liturgical norms. Due to declining enrolment, the school closed in 1999.

Currently the parish belongs to the Whiting cluster under the administration of Father John Kalicky C.PP.S.

SAINT ADALBERT

Around 1900, about thirty-five Polish families were settling in the growing community of Whiting, which incorporated in 1895. The growing industrial base and the incorporation of cities offered work and stability for the local residents, some of whom would soon be working together to start their own place of worship. These families had to travel by foot and by wagon to neighboring Hammond, East Chicago or South Chicago to attend Mass. Eventually, they decided it was time to have a church of their own. They petitioned the bishop who asked Father Peter Kahellek of Saint Casimir to organize the community and care for it as a mission from North Hammond.

A wooden structure, patterned after a church in Otis, Indiana, was built by the community and dedicated by Bishop Rademacher in 1902. Father Peter Budnik was assigned as the first pastor in April, 1902. He served until 1907. Not having a rectory of his own, he resided at St. John the Baptist rectory, where Father Benedict Rajcany was pastor. The parish founded their school which was staffed by Franciscan Sisters. In November of 1927, a youth group, the "Rose Buds," was introduced into the community. The young members were given an opportunity to learn Polish folk dancing and singing, to wear beautiful Polish costumes, and to attend youth conferences and conventions. Their annual project was the Mother's Day Program.

Father Felix Seroczynski served as the second pastor from1907 to 1911.

The new pastor also bought two plots of land and a new rectory was built.

The third pastor, Father Julian Skrzypinski, arrived here in September of 1911 and remained until February of 1922. Father Skrzypinski had a convent built for the new order of nuns, the Sisters of Nazareth, who arrived in 1913.

The school expansion entailed turning the original school building around, moving it back from the street, and adding a two-story building with four new classrooms at the front. During this time the rectory burned, and the present one was built.

The fourth pastor, Father Joseph Zielinski, arrived in 1922. He paid all the debts of the parish and even managed an excess in the treasury. Fr. Zielinski left the parish in 1926. The fifth pastor, Father John Chylewski served the parish from 1927 until 1950, when ill health forced him to retire. Father Walter Pawlicki became the sixth pastor and built the present church which was dedicated on 20 April 1952 by Bishop Pursley.

St. Adalbert Parish, at the time of its golden jubilee in 1953, consisted of 380 families. The enrollment in the grammar school, kindergarten through eighth grade, was around 260 students.

In February of 1955, Father Pawlicki was transferred, and on March 1, Father Stanley Zjawinski was assigned as the seventh pastor. During his tenure, stained glass windows and marble walls were added to the church. An ornate, stenciled wallpaper was put on the sanctuary walls and the beautiful altar was added.

The ninth pastor, Father Joseph Smith served the parish from 1966 until his retirement in 1979. During this time, Sisters of Nazareth were recalled by their superiors. Father Smith was succeeded by Father Michael Tomaszewski, who would close the school in the mid-eighties as enrollment dwindled.

In 1990, the Father Walter Rakoczy was assigned as pastor and had little choice than to undertake needed repairs to both church and rectory.

The lower hall was also renovated. The parish grade school, originally built in 1926, had been abandoned since the school's closing. In September of 1997 demolition was begun and the building, which had served the educational needs of the parish for sixty years, was razed shortly thereafter. While Father Rakoczy was on sabbatical, Father Andrew Corona was appointed acting pastor.

On 1 July 2000, the parish welcomed its twelfth pastor, Father John Zemelko. At the time of his transfer, the parish was placed under the jurisdiction of the Whiting Cluster which is currently administered by Father John Kalicky, C.PP.S.

SAINT JOHN THE BAPTIST

The parish of Saint John the Baptist, founded for Slovak immigrants who came to the area to work in the oil refineries, has its beginning in 1897 with the arrival of Father Benedict Racajny, who was sent to the area by Bishop Rademacher. The first congregation consisted of 50 parishioners and the original church was the social hall of the Slovak Catholic Union. A spire was later added to the building to create a religious atmosphere. It was dedicated on 4 July 1897 and named in honor of Saint John the Baptist.

A frame building was erected for a school by 1900, and the Sisters of Providence were invited to staff it. Enrollment grew rapidly and by 1909 the student body was nearly two-hundred eighty students.

As church membership continued to grow, Father Benedict sought the assistance of a priest from Saint Joseph College, Rensselaer, Indiana for weekend help with confessions and Masses. Father John Kostik, C.PP.S., Professor at the College made the weekly trip to Saint John's beginning in 1921. He would succeed Father Benedict as pastor from 1927 to 1945. From that time on the Precious Blood Fathers would be charged with caring for the parish.

It was early in Father Kostik's pastorate that the need for a new church building was apparent. Construction began in 1930, during the Great Depression. Hard-working parishioners made generous sacrifices to contribute to the fundraising efforts. Everyone contributed in some fashion and the current imposing Romanesque style structure was dedicated in 1931.

The current educational complex was begun by Reverend John Lefko, pastor from 1945 to 1953. Under his leadership and inspiration, construction began in 1950 and was completed by 1956.

Father Gabriel Brenkus served as pastor from 1953 to 1957; he was succeeded by Father Edward Homco who cared for the community from 1957 to 1990; Father Andrew O'Reilly in 1990, and the current pastor Father John Kalicky C.PP.S. who succeeded in 1991 and is currently in charge of the Whiting cluster of parishes.

THE PARISHES OF THE SOUTHLAKE COUNTY DEANERY

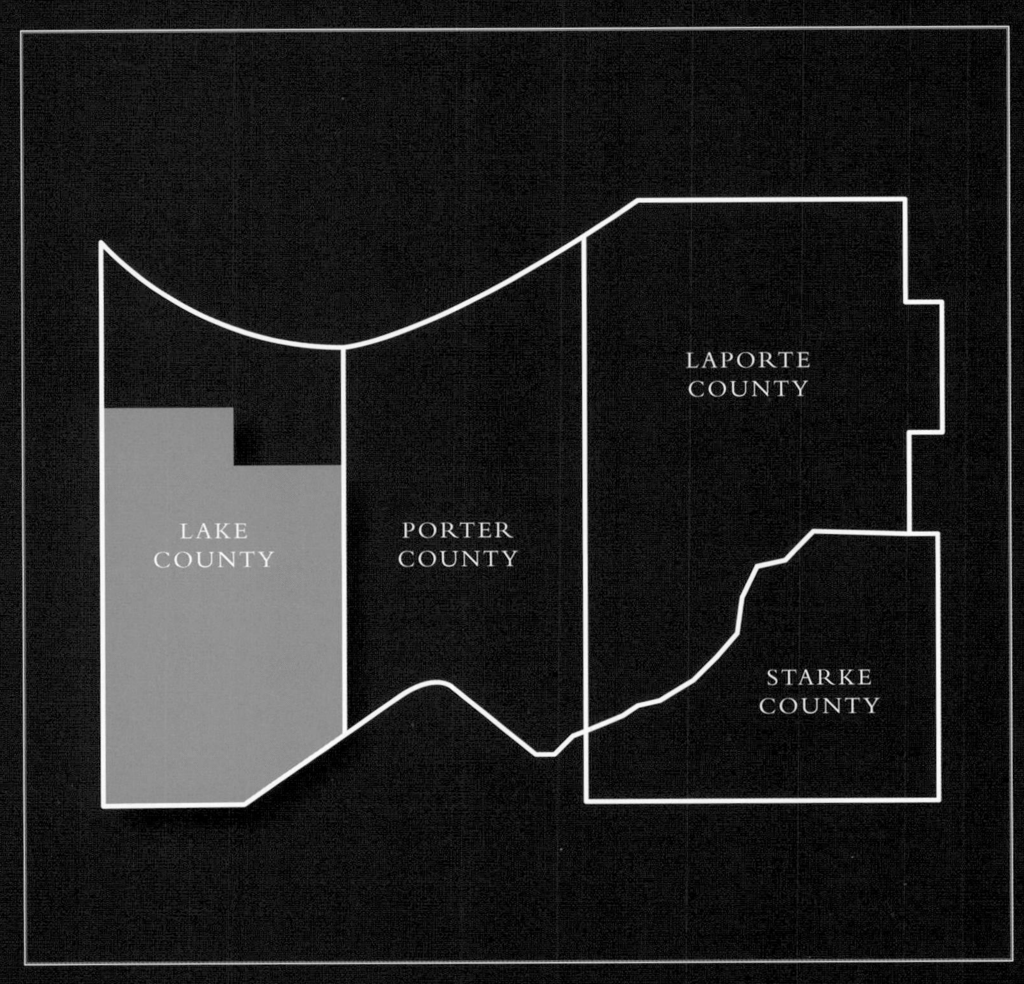

Holy Name

The beginnings of Holy Name Parish date back to the 1840s, when visiting priests would celebrate mass in the home of Matthias Geisen in Hanover Centre. In 1853 he donated five and a half acres of land to the diocese of Vincennes for use as a cemetery. And in 1859 a church would be built by Father Francis Xavier Nigh, and dedicated in honor of Saint Matthias. This church was destroyed by fire in 1866. The community moved the new building to the area that would be called Cook. There they would build a frame church and dedicate it to Saint Martin. This time Matthias Geisen would have three bells cast at Rappweiler, Germany where he was born, to be sent to the parish where they would ring out from this new church and subsequent foundations. A year later the parish would receive its first resident pastor, Father Francis Siegelack.

In 1881, the parish bought a school building and moved it to the parish grounds. The teachers were supplied from the parishioners for the purpose of teaching catechism and German. Later, another school building would be purchased for the use of the parish with the original one becoming the convent for the Franciscan Sisters of Perpetual Adoration from Lafayette. They would staff the school until 1932 when the School Sisters of Saint Francis (from Milwaukee) would take over. They would remain until recalled in 1980, being replaced by a staff of lay teachers. In 1986 because of decreasing enrollment the school was closed, and those few families who wished a parish education for their children would send them either to St. John or Crown Point.

Between 1911 and 1913, the parish built a church from brick as well as a two storey brick school. This church would be in use by the parish until it too was destroyed by fire in 1930. The community would then celebrate mass in the school hall until in 1932 the foundation of a new building would be used as a basement church. This building was completed in 1940 and dedicated to the Holy Name of Jesus on Thanksgiving Day by Bishop Noll.

Another modern school was built in 1952 as well as a convent in 1956.

The building now houses a day care center and preschool.

Cedar Lake itself has taken on something of a resort atmosphere and the parish finds itself in a developing bedroom community as new residents come not for agricultural work, but to reside here and work elsewhere.

The parish community is resilient and has weathered the ordinary difficulties of life: experiencing loss through two fires, the closing of the parish school and the experience of nine pastors in ten years.

Still, it has remained vibrant with new programs such as RENEW 2000 and Generations of Faith, social activities and parish picnics.

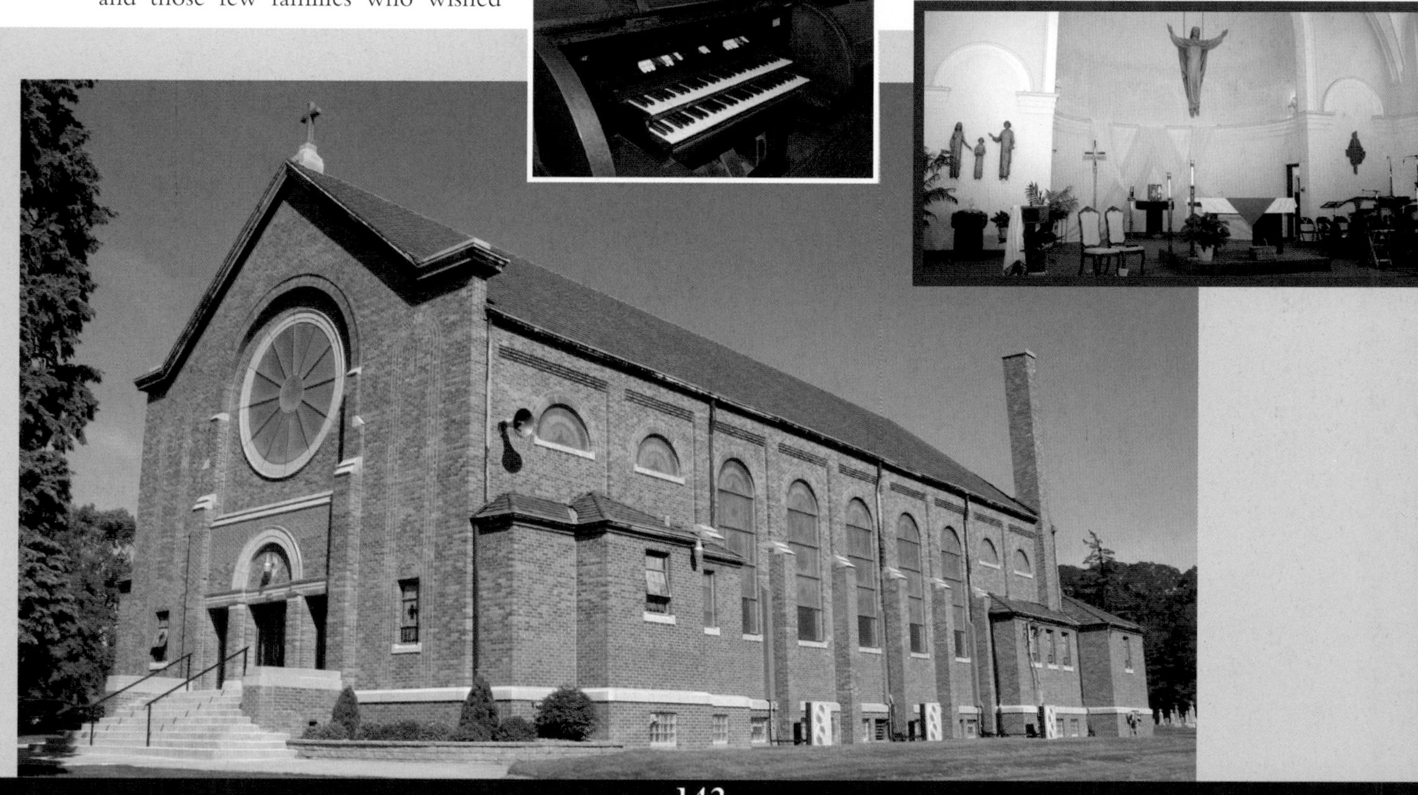

Saint Mary

In 1865, Bishop Luers directed Father H. Paul Werhle, the pastor at Turkey Creek to organize a parish in Crown Point, the county seat of Lake County. He would become the first resident pastor of the community. The church on South Main Street was dedicated to Saint Mary. He was succeeded by Father L. Weiser (1868-1871), and then Father Henry Meissner (1871-1875). From 1878 to 1889 the parish was given to the Benedictine Fathers in the hope that a seminary would be established in the city. The sacristy of the church doubled as the parish school until a proper building could be built. The Sisters of Saint Agnes staffed the school from its inception. Until the convent was completed they lived in a house on Walnut Street and they paid $6.00 a month rent. In its first twenty-four years the parish would see many priests, both diocesan and Benedictine, care for them until 1889, when Father Philip Guethoff would be appointed to care for the community. He would remain pastor for fifty-four years until his death in 1943, though the last four years would be the responsibility of his assistant since 1926, Father Joseph Hammes.

Father Guethoff realized the church, only thirty by sixty feet, was too small for the congregation. With a little opposition from some parishioners who were quite satisfied with what they had, he was able to convince the community to build the present church which was dedicated in 1890 on Joliet Street. A convent and the present rectory were built in 1911. The former church was then converted into the parish school. According to Father Guethoff, by 1916, it was in such a sorry state it would have been condemned if inspected by the authorities, so the Bishop reluctantly consented to the project even though no money had yet been raised.

In 1926 Father Joseph Hammes came as an assistant and stayed on to become the pastor in 1943. Under Father Hammes, the convent was remodeled and the new school building and gym were constructed in 1959. When Father Hammes retired in 1972, the parish purchased a home for him on South Court Street, and a grateful community hosted his golden jubilee in 1976. He was succeeded as pastor by Monsignor Vincent Lengerich who cared for the community until his transfer to Knox in 1984.

In 1984 Monsignor Don Grass became the pastor. He supervised the project the parish undertook for a complete restoration of the church. Due to the commitment of the parishioners, the community razed the old school building and enlarged the 1959 building in 1992. Monsignor Grass retired in 2003 and was succeeded by the current pastor, Father Patrick Kalich.

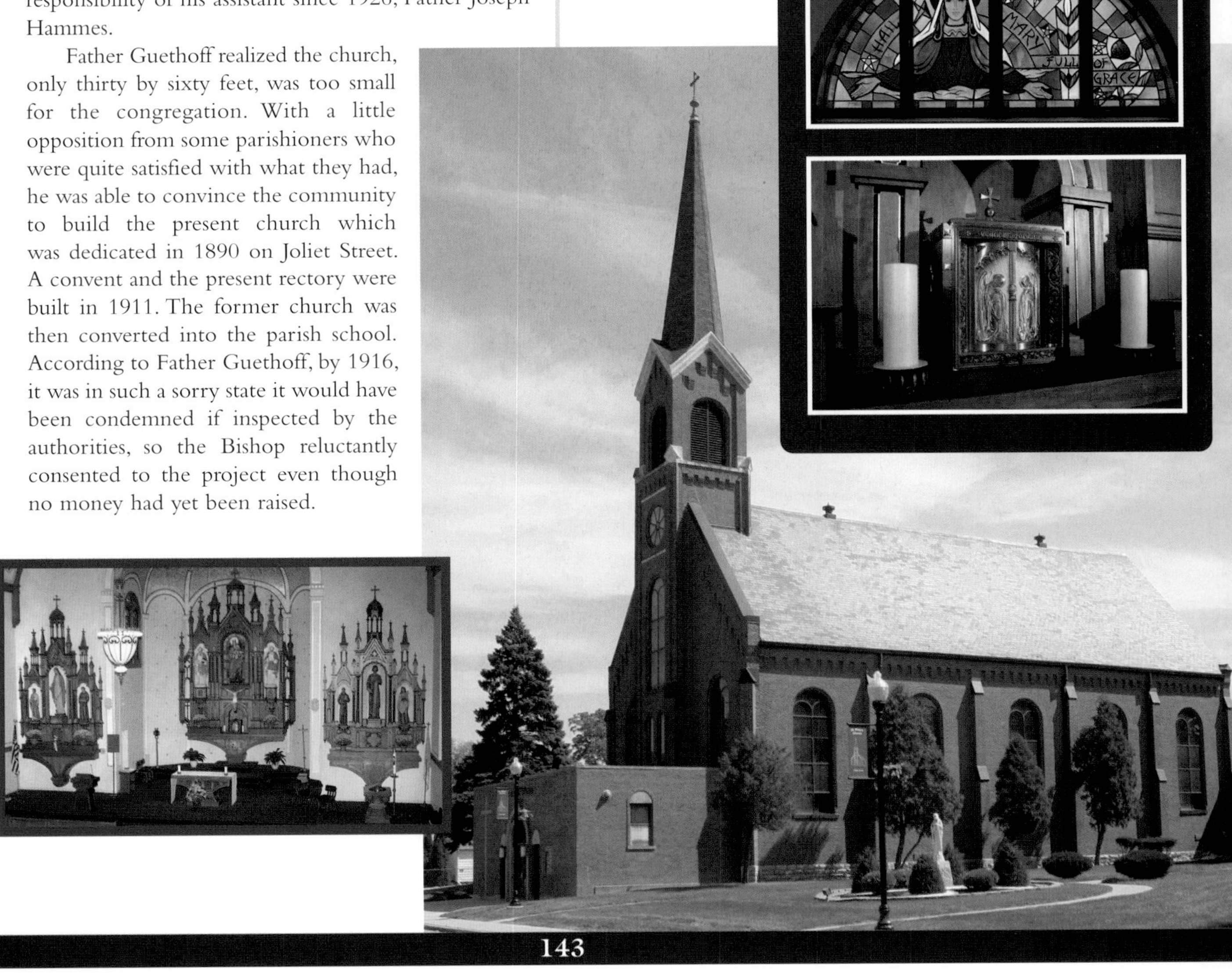

SAINT MATTHIAS

By the time Saint Mary parish celebrated their golden jubilee, it was evident the community was outgrowing the parish facilities. With the collaboration of Father Hammes, Bishop Grutka divided the parish in 1967 and assigned Father John Strebig, assistant at Saint Bridget in Hobart, to assist Father Hammes while organizing a new parish on the southern edge of the city. The parish would be named in honor of Saint Matthias, secondary patron of the diocese as it was on his feast day, 25 February (on the former liturgical calendar) that the diocese came into existence.

Until the first structure was built, the chapel of Saint Anthony Home was used for the new parish community, which met together for the first time on 8 January 1967. A social hall that would double as a temporary church would be completed in the fall of 1970. Parish offices would be housed at the rectory, down the road. Diligently the parish set about the task of a permanent church. Their hard work was realized with the dedication of the church by Bishop Grutka on 22 May 1983.

Father Strebig would return to Hobart in 1985 as pastor, and be succeeded by Father Timothy Benante until his untimely death in 1988.

The parish offices were moved from the rectory to the hall during his tenure. Father Gerald Schweitzer would arrive in September of 1988 and minister to the spiritual needs of the parish until he was succeeded in 1994 by Father Terrence Steffens who would care for the community until 2005. The current pastor, Father Mark Pavlina arrived in July of 2005.

The community has an active pastoral council and a variety of ministries. They also contribute in the support of the parish school located at Saint Mary's which has been named Saint Mary's Catholic Community School to reflect its inter-parochial use.

SAINT JOSEPH

Before a parish was established for the town of Dyer, residents would travel to either St. John or Turkey Creek for mass. This continued until 1867 when the community received Father Jacob Schmitz as their first pastor. On four acres of land he had the first frame church built.

There have been sixteen pastors who served the spiritual needs of the community since its founding. The successors of Father Schmitz were:

- Father Theodore Borg, 1870;
- Father H. Meissner, 1871;
- Father Bernard Wiedau, 1872;
- Father Anthony King, 1872-1874;
- Father F. J. Freund, 1874-1875;
- Father Charles Steurer, 1875-1878;
- Father Joseph Flach, 1878-1883;
- Father Charles Stetter, 1883-1888;
- Father Joseph Flach, 1888-1923;
- Father Georg Lauer, 1923-1932;
- Father Edmund Ley, 1932-1954;
- Father Ambrose Switzer,1954-1967;
- Monsignor Edward Litot, 1967-1983;
- Monsignor Ferdinand Melevage, 1983 to 1992;
- Father Mark Pavlina, 1992-2005;
- and the present pastor, Father Terrence Steffens since 2005.

By 1893 the original frame church needed repairs. The church was re-plastered, frescoed, and painted. Stained glass windows were installed and in 1899 a basement chapel, new altars, and an organ was installed. Three days after Christmas of 1902 a fire destroyed the original church.The present Gothic style church was dedicated 26 November 1903.

In 1878, Father Flach was transferred to the parish for his "first term" as pastor. He oversaw the opening of the school with the Sisters of the Sacred Heart staffing it. The first school building and convent were erected in 1901.The present brick building was started in 1939 and dedicated in April of 1940. It provided four classrooms. In 1956 a large basement and school room section extending south of the original building was added. Father Switzer then added a second floor of classrooms in 1963. Monsignor Melevage added a gymnasium in 1984. In 1991, Monsignor Melevage started the St. Joseph School Foundation. The Foundation was established to help with the financial obligations of the school. Money collected is invested and the profit goes toward the school budget. In 1992 Saint Joseph Parish celebrated its one-hundred twenty-fifth anniversary with a solemn mass celebrated by Bishop Gaughan. The celebration continued with a banquet following the mass. Since this time St. Joseph parish has made improvements to the church and school. The church received a new roof and the school received new windows, lights, ceilings and remodeled restrooms. The parish continues to look forward to building upon the foundations that have already been laid and serving the needs of the community.

SAINT MARIA GORETTI

In 1975, with the growth of south Lake County, the need was evident for another parish on the north end of Dyer that would also relieve Saint Thomas More parish, which had by this time become the largest in the diocese. Bishop Grutka had someone in mind at the time but did not act upon it until 1977 when he asked Father Richard Ameling to begin canvassing the Catholics in the Dyer-Schererville area. Until the parish received a proper name, it was referred to as the "North Dyer Parish."

As plans were being developed for a building, the early celebrations of the mass were in neighborhood public schools, which had a significant influence in the forming of the faith community that cannot be overestimated; everyone had a part in the liturgy.

The church, under the patronage of Saint Maria Goretti was dedicated by Bishop Grutka on 20 September 1981. Through the work of the children of the parish, a bell tower was erected in 1983. A Blessed Sacrament Chapel and administrative wing was added to the church in 1984. This sacred place, the church building, became a home for people not related by blood but by faith, who cooperated as a faith community to accomplish the work of the gospel. Religious Education, the RCIA and works of charity have been developed in the parish as well as the liturgical ministries necessary for the growth of the community. This has taken place under the direction of the founding pastor, Father Ameling, who was succeeded in 1994 by Father Michael Yadron, who was replaced by Father Alfred Dettmer in 1996, and the fourth and current pastor, Father Charles Niblick in 2002 who has dedicated the parish toward the works of social justice.

Blessed Sacrament

Although the pastors of Blessed Sacrament Parish have been of Polish extraction, the parish itself is a mixture of ethnic groups that comprised the city of Gary. In 1947, Father Louis Madejczyk, the assistant pastor at Saint Hedwig was appointed to form a new parish on the south end of Glen Park which was beginning to develop after the close of the world war. The new parish would be carved out of the parishes of Saint Mark and Saint Joseph the Worker in Glen Park and Saints Peter and Paul in Turkey Creek.

By August, 1947, a building was secured at Forty-Fifth Avenue and Cleveland Street (S. R. 55). The building had been used as a dance hall and café, and was originally built as a barn for school buses. Its open area made it ideal for the communities needs, and although rudimentary, the fifty-five families that made up the new community united to beautify their parish church that became their home for the first thirteen years of their existence.

A house was acquired at Forty-Fifth Avenue and McKinley Street for use as a rectory. A picnic grove also served for community functions, fund-raisers and even masses celebrated in the open air.

The children of the parish attended either Saint Hedwig school or the public schools in the area with the Sisters from Saint Hedwig teaching catechism on Saturday mornings.

As the congregation grew the necessity for property to accommodate the community was a prime objective. On 19 April 1959 ground was broken for a new church, school and social hall on newly acquired property at Forty-First Avenue and Garfield Street. The school was ready for occupancy with the beginning of the new school year, September 1960. The Franciscan Sisters of Blessed Kunegunda (of Chicago) staffed the school until 1987. From that time until the school was closed in 2003 two Sisters, Poor Handmaids of Jesus Christ and lay teachers dedicated themselves to the children of the parish.

The first mass in the new church was celebrated on Christmas Eve of 1960. One of the novelties of the new building was that the back wall of the sanctuary was retractable, opening to the social hall which could accommodate overflow crowds for mass (and allow them to celebrate mass facing the priest!). The parish plant was completed in 1972 with the building of a new rectory on the property.

Father Lou, as he came to be known with affection retired in 1983 having served the parish for thirty-six years. He was succeeded by Monsignor John Siekierski who cared for the parish until 1996. Father Robert Tokarz became the third pastor in 1996. The parish celebrated its golden jubilee in 1997 in the presence of its founder and former pastors. The fourth pastor, Father Krysztof Bugno, S.D.S. arrived in 2003 and cared for the community until recalled by his superiors. The administration of the parish was given at this time to the pastor of Saints Peter and Paul, Father Dennis Teles. And though for a brief time in 2005, when Father Lee Purcell became the fifth resident pastor of the community, Father Teles has continued to care for the parish.

Saint Mary

The town of Griffith was established in 1904 and was an interchange point for five railroads. Many families living in Griffith were employed by the railroads or worked for companies that used the railroad system. Other families settled in Griffith to work in industries located nearby.

The majority of the founding parish families were predominantly of German descent, with some Irish families among them. The effort to establish Saint Mary Parish began on 21 June 1921 when thirty-four women organized the "Catholic Ladies Social Club" and began an organized effort to form a Catholic church in Griffith.

In October of that year, joining with Catholic men, the group proceeded to form a corporation. Their purpose was to select a site for a Catholic church and end the travel to and from Saint Michael Church in Schererville for the sacraments and the education of their children. During the next several years, parishioners worked hard to raise funds to build a combination church and school.

The first Mass celebrated in Griffith took place in the Franklin School Gymnasium. On 21 December 1927 the Catholic families of Griffith chose the name Saint Mary for the parish.

Bishop Noll appointed Father Joseph Suelzer as the first pastor in June of 1928. He would begin to organize the community and supervise the building projects of a combination church and school building, rectory, and convent. The school was placed under the administration of the Franciscan Sisters of Perpetual Adoration. Father Suelzer was succeeded by Father Leo Hildebrandt who would remain as pastor until his retirement in 1972. Upon his retirement Monsignor Hildebrandt was succeeded by a former assistant, Monsignor Richard Zollinger (1972-1992). The present pastor is Father Theodore Mens.

In 1939, most of the school was destroyed by fire. The parish immediately began to rebuild and also made plans for the current church which was completed and dedicated by Bishop Grutka in 7 April 1958. The parish continued to beautify the church in the next number of years, renovating the sanctuary according to the norms of the Second Vatican Council, and installing new stained glass windows in 1981.

The community, which had the tradition of never locking the church building, would end that tradition in 1988 because of an arsonist who set fire to the church, seriously damaging the sanctuary. In 1989 the parish built a gymnasium and social hall and named it Saint Mary-Hildebrandt Hall honoring Our Lady and their pastor of forty years.

Our Lady of Grace

Bishop Noll had great confidence in the talents of Father Alvin Jasinski. In 1947, he asked the returning army chaplain to found the parish of the Immaculate Heart of Mary in Independence Hill (the current Our Lady of Consolation parish in Merrillville). Two years later, in 1949, Father Jasinski was asked to organize another community in the developing town of Highland. The parish was to be located at Highway and Fifth Streets, on land purchased by the diocese. The name of the parish was chosen, Our Lady of Grace, because of Father Alvin and the parishioners' devotion to Mary, the Blessed Mother of God. The parish had been taken from the northern section of Saint Mary Parish in Griffith, which is considered the mother parish of the area.

The community comprised of just over two hundred families gathered at the Towne Theater for their first mass on Christmas, 1949.

After purchasing the vacant Calvary Baptist Church on Jewett Street, the parish made this location its first home in October of 1950 when Bishop Leo Pursley dedicated the church. The parish quickly outgrew this facility, so beginning in 1953 funds were pledged for a new building. Ground was broken 6 February 1954 at the Highway Avenue location for combination church and school building. The Sisters of Saint Francis of Perpetual Adoration agreed to staff the new school. After daily Mass in the old church on Jewett Street, almost three hundred students together with a faculty of three sisters and three lay teachers walked to class held at the American Legion Hall on Ridge Road and the Presbyterian Church hall on Delaware Street. The new facility was completed at the end of 1954.

In 1955 the worship space was completed in the school building basement to accommodate the

growing number of families. The school enrollment increased to seven hundred students and a second floor was added to the building in October 1956. A Debt Reduction Program was introduced in July of 1958 and parishioners went door to door seeking pledges from their fellow church members. By 1960, the school was educating over one thousand young Catholics, which did not include the children enrolled in the Religious Education Program. The year 1962 brought perhaps the biggest growth in the parish history, and it was clear that a larger church was needed for a parish of now fifteen hundred families.

The parish welcomed Father Albert H. Van Nevel as pastor in 1963.

As Father Van Nevel settled into his new surroundings, he saw the need to look for ways to reduce the parish debt. One of those ways was the creation of the Parish Family Festivals which were designed with two goals in mind: end the parish's debt and bring the people closer together. The festivals, combined with increased parishioner generosity in the collection basket, wiped out the parish debt.

By 1966, ground was broken for the new church. A Mass of dedication was celebrated on Sunday, 10 December 1967.

During this time the Sisters of St. Francis lived on the second floor of the school. During 1974 and 1975, with parishioners volunteering their talents, a convent was erected and used by the sisters until their departure in 1995 after serving for 41 years at the parish. Under the continued generosity of the parishioners in the Sunday collections, the parish financed the school totally until rising costs of the school and parish forced the parish to add tuition in 1992.

Father Edward Moszur succeeded Monsignor Van Nevel as pastor in 1991. Under his leadership and through the pastoral council and parish commissions, the parish emphasizes the journey of faith at all ages and situations of parishioners. Starting with the baptismal program and moving toward senior parishioners who have the opportunity to be together at Ephesus Home. The parish reaches out beyond the local community to a sister parish, St. Louis de Gonzague of Camp-Louise in Haiti, with financial support, visits, and needed supplies.

Jerzy S. Kenar, sculptor

Saint James the Less

Because of the growth in the area of Highland and Griffith, Father Eugene Hoffman was directed by Bishop Grutka to organize a new parish south of Our Lady of Grace. This occurred on 29 June 1967. For almost three years, Father Hoffman canvassed the area and organized the parish. Mass was originally celebrated at Highland Junior High School until 1974. On 3 March 1970 the parish received its second pastor, Father Francis Lazar, who would serve the community until his retirement in 2005. A home was purchased in the Lakeside subdivision to be used as the rectory. In October of 1970, a meeting room was added and a chapel dedicated for daily mass.

In May, 1974, groundbreaking took place for an all purpose building to be used as a church and hall at the northwest corner of Forty-Fifth and Kennedy Avenues. In 1976 the first festival was held on church grounds.

In 1981, the Saint James Food Pantry was established. The parish has been active in its spiritual societies: Saint James Women's Guild organized in 1972, the Holy Name Society in 1976, and the Our Lady of Guadalupe Society in 2001. The parish mission statement reflects the willingness of the parishioners to reach out to others. The Saint James Family Help Service, Counseling and Social Service, and Saint Vincent de Paul Society help hundreds of people throughout the area of all faiths and cultures. The parish also aids a mission in Appalachia, at Olive Hill, Kentucky, where they not only help materially but work side by side with the people. The parish festival gives a percentage of its profits to help some of the poor in the diocese such as the Sisters of Mercy and Sojourner Truth House.

In May of 1988, groundbreaking for a new church took place. The new church was dedicated by Bishop Gaughan on 23 April 1989. The Religious Education Center came after that linking the new church with the old which had then become the Father Eugene Hoffman Social Hall. A new rectory was also added to the parish property.

In 2005, Father Lazar was succeeded by Father Keith Virus as third pastor of the community.

SAINT EDWARD

In 1866 Bishop John Luers traveled to the Lowell area, visiting Catholic families with the purpose of promoting the building of a Catholic Church in the community. The Bishop donated one-hundred dollars toward the project and land was purchased in the northeast section of town. A small, frame building holding 150 people was built and dedicated in 1870. Named after the English king known as a builder of churches, Saint Edward became the seventh parish in Lake County with a population of eight households.

The first few years saw slow but steady growth. In 1883 Mass was held two Sundays per month. Originally serviced by priests from Crown Point, St. Edward became a mission attached to St. Anthony's parish in Klaasville in 1878 and then cared for by the Precious Blood Fathers.

The Catholic community did grow in the Lowell area, purchasing land for a cemetery and building a new church with a fine, tall steeple that was dedicated in 1897. In 1898 the parish was granted its first full-time pastor in the person of Father Frederick Koenig. He was succeeded by

- Father Charles Keyser (1905–1907),
- Father Alphonse Miller C.PP.S. (1907 – 1911),
- Father Hoerstmann (1911-1918),
- Father Charles Scholl (1918-1922),
- Father Simon Ryder (1922-1927),
- Father Anthony Kroeger (1927-1937),
- Father Edward Boney 1937-1968),
- Father Chester Zurawiec (1956-1968),
- Father Matthew Spebar (1968-1979),
- Father Timothy Doody (1979 -1989),
- Father Thomas Mischler (1989-1998),
- and Father Peter Muha 1998 to the present time.

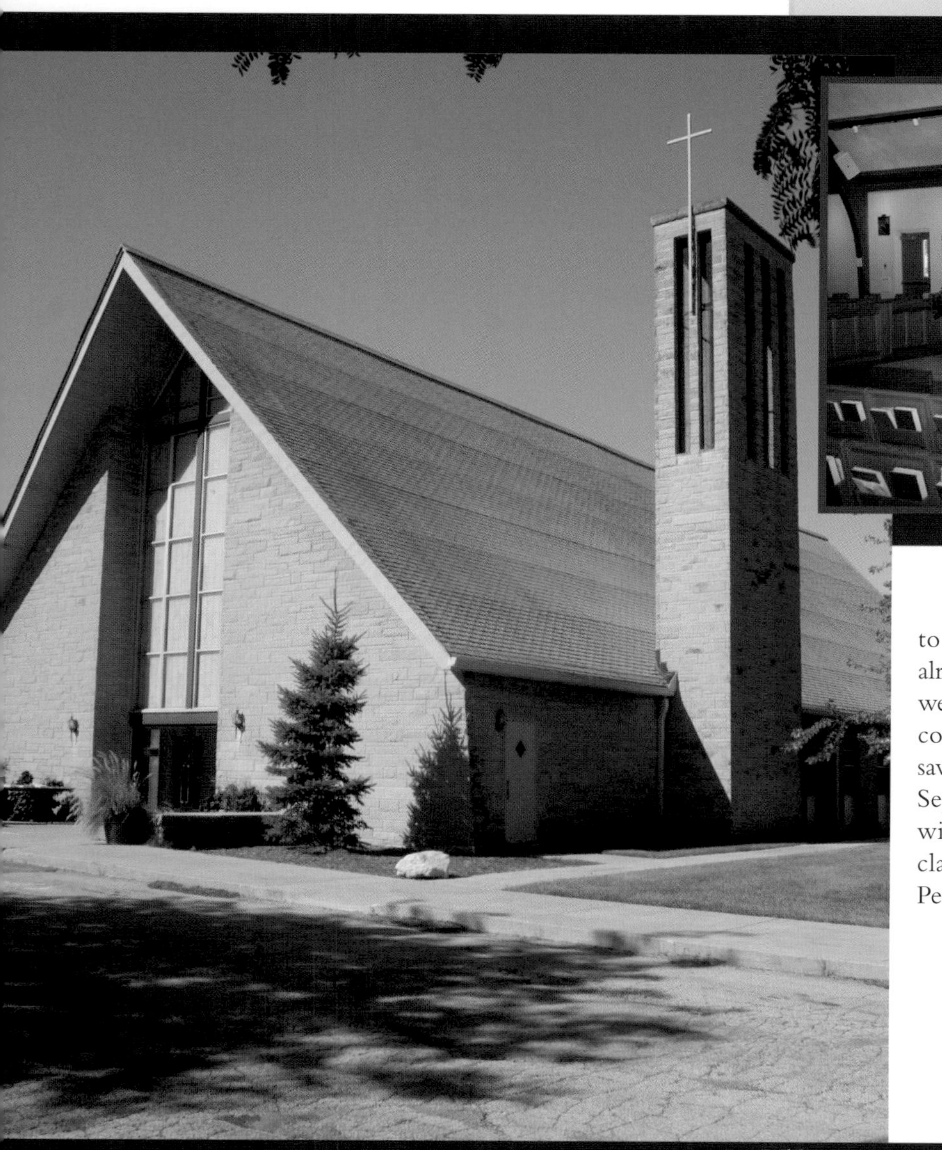

In 1914 the church building was lost to fire. A parish school building was already under construction so modifications were made to convert that structure to a combined church and school. January 1915 saw completion of the structure and in September of that year the school opened with eight grades split between two classrooms. Sisters from St. Francis of Perpetual Adoration provided staffing.

Following World War II, recognizing that the parish was quickly outgrowing both church and school facilities, a building fund was begun. About the time that the Gary Diocese was being formed from the redistricting of the Diocese of Fort Wayne, land was purchased and building commenced for a parish complex on the southwest side of town.

The new church, built from Indiana limestone and seating 450 was dedicated in 1958. Joining the church were a new school building, convent and rectory. In 1970 costs forced the parish school to close.

Unwilling to see the school stay closed, a number of parishioners, along with Sister Virgene Wozniak (Director of Religious Education) worked tirelessly and, in 1978 were able to reopen the school with a kindergarten class. After Sister Virgene's departure, Sister Christine Patrick and Sister Marianne Ridgell, Sisters of Providence joined the parish, serving as principal and pastoral assistant respectively. They were transferred in 1994.

The current pastor and his immediate predecessor have been instrumental in making improvements to the facilities and programs. Additional classrooms and other enhancements to the school have been completed, most accomplished with volunteer labor. The convent building has been converted to a Ministry Center. The church was rededicated in 2003, following renovations that now allow seating on three sides of the altar, improved facilities for choir and musicians and many improvements to the esthetics of the interior. Additional plans are being prepared for a multi-phase project to provide additional worship, meeting and gathering space for the church as well as enlarging the school facilities.

Our Lady of Consolation

Our Lady of Consolation parish was founded in 1947. At that time it was under the title of Immaculate Heart of Mary. The parish was founded after World War II when people in the armed forces returned home, married and started families. It was at that time that development began in the Independence Hill area which today is part of Merrillville. Affordable housing is what brought newlyweds and families to this area.

In 1947, the Catholic population was large enough to look into the possibility to found a parish. It was at that time that Bishop Francis Noll asked Father Alvin Jasinski, a former Army Chaplain, to found a parish in the Independence Hill area. The first Mass was celebrated in a fire station until a store front was purchased on 78th Ave. The people worked together to make the store front into a Church. The original church held at most two hundred persons.

As the population moved south a need was seen to build a larger church. It was in 1959 that the present property was purchased on Taft Street. The new church was built in 1966 under the leadership of Father Herman Schoudel. In 1966 there was another parish in Kingsford Heights near LaPorte, with the title Immaculate Heart of Mary. Bishop Grutka suggested that since there was another parish with the same title that the new church assume the title Our Lady of Consolation. There is a story: Father Joseph Vamos, the present pastor, once asked Bishop Grutka how he named the parish Our Lady of Consolation since Mary as patroness of Luxembourg has that title and there is not a Luxembourg community here in this area. Bishop Grutka told Father Vamos that the reason for the title was that in his former parish Holy Trinity Church in Gary there was a statue of Jesus with the title Jesus the Consoler. He said that Jesus the Consoler should have a Mother of Consolation.

Pastors that have served the parish community have been :

- Father Alvin Jasinski, 1947-1949,
- Father Herman Schoudel, 1949-1970,
- Father Louis Wozniak, 1970-1986,
- Father Lawrence Kew, 1986-1988,
- and the present pastor Father Joseph Vamos since 1988.

Activity at the present location from 1967 to 1988 was difficult since the only structure was the church building. The Faith Formation Programs were held in various areas of the Church, Society meetings were held in the church foyer or children's room and festivals were held in tents set up in the field. After the new Parish Education and Social Center was built there were more opportunities to establish programs and have regular parish activities.

The parish strives to carry out its the mission statement: Worshipping God in word and sacrament, fostering education, instilling family values, promoting peace and social justice and building a community where all are welcome. Reaching out to the community has been a special mission of the present pastor; the parish has broadcast Sunday Mass on WWCA-AM 1270.

Saint Andrew the Apostle

In August of 1964 the first steps in the establishment of the second parish in Merrillville began. Under the guidance of Father John Beckmann, pastor of Saints Peter and Paul Church in Merrillville, land was purchased from Mr. and Mrs. Frank Krieter. This would become the eventual site of a new parish in Merrillville.

Bishop Grutka appointed Father William Vogt as the first pastor of the new parish. The official beginning of the new parish was marked by the first Mass which was celebrated on 7 March 1965. Since, as yet, there were no buildings on the newly acquired farm land, a rented building at 7550 Broadway became the home of the new parish. For some unknown reason, only six months after the founding of the new parish, Father Vogt was transferred to Saint Thomas Aquinas Church in Knox, Indiana.

The second pastor of the new parish was Father Henry Ameling, the uncle of the current pastor, Father Richard Ameling. Under Father Henry Ameling's direction, and with a tremendous outpouring of support from the new church-community, construction on the parish's permanent home at 810 West 73rd Avenue began. The new rectory was completed in March 1966. In the meantime Mass continued to be celebrated in the rented facilities on Broadway. By this time, that storefront had been affectionately named "The Dime Store Cathedral."

Construction continued on the new Eucharistic Hall. The building was designed to be a multi-purpose facility, which would serve as the parish's worship space, work space and social hall. The first Mass was celebrated on 31 July 1966. Bishop Grutka, Father Henry Ameling, the newly ordained Father Richard Ameling, and a host of priests from the Diocese celebrated that Mass. The hall also served as a temporary school while four new classrooms were being completed. In June 1967 Father Henry Ameling was released from the Diocese of Gary to take an assignment with Catholic Relief Services, doing refugee work in Lebanon and Viet Nam.

He was succeeded by Father Matthew Kish who would remain until 1973 when Father James McGrogan became pastor; by this time the congregation of Saint Joan of Arc would share the parish's resources until their own church was completed in 1979. Subsequent pastors, Fathers Emil Bloch, Henry Lazarek, David Gosnell, Terrence Chase, and Richard Ameling have served the parish community. Aquinas school serves all the parishes in Merrillville and adds life to an already vibrant community.

Saint Joan of Arc

Keeping with the attitude of the time, Bishop Grutka formed another small parish community on the east side of Broadway in Merrillville in 1968. The Diocese held donated property on the northeast corner of 78th Avenue and Broadway which the Bishop thought would be an excellent spot for another parish which could also minister to the business community and still growing population.

In 1968, Father Alfred Dettmer was named the first pastor of the new parish named in honor of Saint Joan of Arc. This new congregation celebrated their liturgies in a dime store and also in the public high school auditorium. Subsequent pastors, Father Michael Kenney and Father Clare Hendricks, deemed these inappropriate and the parish was given permission to celebrate with Saint Andrew parish. Father James McGrogan, pastor of Saint Andrew, ministered to both congregations when Father Hendricks was transferred to East Chicago. Father Gerald Sroka was named pastor in November 1976 and began in earnest to provide for a church which was built and dedicated 9 September 1979.

Five stained glass panels over the main altar depict Saint Joan of Arc's life, her calling, mission, imprisonment, capture, and martyrdom.

Through devotion, dedication, and donations, the community had the bare necessities to celebrate their liturgies. There were no pews, just borrowed chairs, no floor coverings, only the concrete slab, and only "hand-me-down" furniture and office equipment and supplies. But the congregation was happy with their own church building. The ladies of the parish were the first group formed to help in gaining all that was needed. Seamstresses of the parish sewed vestments and altar linen, while others in the parish painted, installed tile, varnished and finished yet other projects. Many a fundraiser was organized to purchase needed furnishings and to reduce the debt.

Father Edward Webb, who succeeded Father Sroka, supervised the building of the church hall, which was later enlarged during the pastorate of Father Sammie Maletta.

The present pastor, Father Andrew Corona, is continuing to lead the community as a faith-filled and family oriented parish.

A fire caused serious damage to the sanctuary in 27 April 2005. With the help of neighboring parishes, the community quickly rose to the challenge to re-dedicate the church on 5 October of the same year.

Saints Peter and Paul

In 1841, a group of devout Catholics, many from Bavaria, Germany, gathered in a log cabin to celebrate Mass. This was the first Mass ever held in the area that was to become the town of Merrillville. The area was originally called Turkey Creek and was called thus into the 1950s. It was often referred to as Lottaville. For several years, parishioners shared the faith in their homes, guided by priests visiting from nearby communities. The fledgling congregation grew to forty families.

In 1850, a church building and still-existing cemetery were built on four acres of land by Father B. J. Voors, C.S.C. The rough-hewn log structure was originally named "Saint John the Baptist." The first resident pastor was Father Philip Wegemeyer. A larger church was soon necessary because of added worshippers. In 1863, a stone church was constructed at what is today 5851 Harrison Street. The parish of Saints Peter and Paul was thus established. The name may have been chosen to honor Peter Fox, who donated some of his farm land, and Father H. Paul Wehrle, the pastor responsible for building the church. After Father Wehrle's departure, the parish was served alternately by neighboring parish pastors and resident pastors. Father Francis Baumgartner would take up residence in 1874 while caring for Saint Bridget and founding Saint Joseph in Hammond. He would be succeeded by Father Henry Roth from 1880-1884. Father Charles Stetter was resident pastor from 1888-1903. He built the convent that would house the School Sisters of Notre Dame who arrived in 1905 to staff the new parish school. Under the guidance of

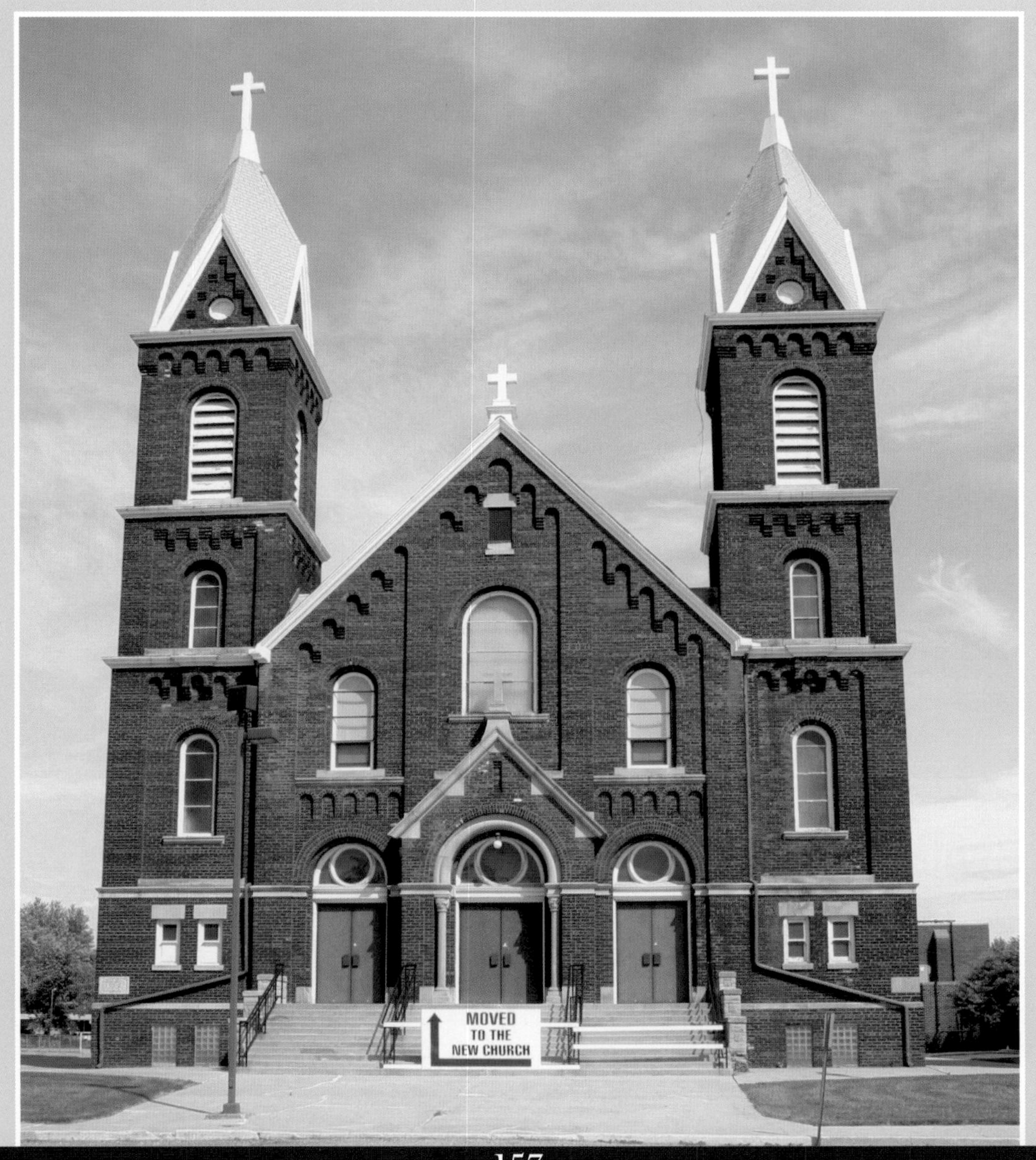

Father F. Thomas Jansen, the pastor of Saint Bridget at Hobart, a two-classroom school was erected that year.

In 1915 the stone church was replaced with a red brick building which still stands. This was accomplished during Father Frederick Koenig's service as pastor (1905-1936). Later beautiful stained glass windows were added. Father Koenig was succeeded by Father Jacob Nickels who served the community from 1936 to 1950. Father Charles Seeberger was pastor from 1950 to 1955.

A new school and gymnasium were built during the 1955-1965 period under the leadership of Father John Beckmann (1955-1972). He was succeeded by Monsignor Casimir Senderak (1972-1977), Father Eugene Hoffman (1977-1980), and Father R. Barry Evers (1980-1984). Since 1984 Father Dennis Teles has led the Saints Peter and Paul community as its pastor. Since 2000 he has also served as the Dean of the Southlake Deanery.

The church building has undergone extensive remodeling in the last number of years but this has not been able to stem the deterioration of the bricks themselves. After studies were made it was decided that it would not be financially feasible to correct the problem. The parish is currently transforming Fidelis Hall (which has been used for Sunday liturgies to accommodate the overflow crowds) into a permanent setting for the community's liturgical celebrations.

For the health of the community and the responsibility of spreading the gospel, one of goals of the parish is to accept and reach out to the people of any new cultures that have chosen to join the parish in worshipping one God.

Saint Stephen the Martyr

In 1968, Bishop Grutka asked Father Lawrence Heeg, an assistant at Saints Peter and Paul parish to organize what would become the fifth Merrillville parish, Saint Stephen the Martyr.

Father Heeg began meeting with the community who envisioned a church built by themselves. Within a year on 18 May 1969 ground would be broken for the new church. A little over a year later it was completed and dedicated by Bishop Grutka on the Solemnity of the Assumption, 15 August 1970. The building would include an apartment for the pastor, as well as parish offices.

Father Heeg formed the backbone of the parish with three basic groups that are still active today: the Men's Club, the Women's Club, and the Youth Group, which has since incorporated with a couple of other parishes in the Merrillville cluster. In 1976, Father Timothy Doody became pastor and was succeeded three years later by Father Bernard Shank in 1979 and would be closely assisted by Deacon Joseph Codespoti who was ordained in the first class of permanent deacons in 1981. Father Shank remained until 1984 when health problems forced him to retire. With the arrival of the new pastor, Father Gerald Schweitzer, the RCIA program was introduced as well as a program of scripture study. He was followed in 1988 by Father John Winterlin who would add a parish hall to the church and build a rectory, thus enlarging the parish offices. When Father David Nowak became pastor in 1996 he was given the added responsibility of care for the patients at Methodist Hospital's south campus. His departure in 2000 left the parish without a resident pastor for a year, and the community was once more under the administration of Saints Peter and Paul in the person of Father Dennis Teles, which brought fears that the parish might be closed. In 2001 however, the parish welcomed Father Michael Maginot, a Merrillville native who was working full time in the Marriage Tribunal of the diocese. This became an ideal situation for both priest and community. With the help of family, he has beautified the grounds with a Marian Shrine dedicated to the Luminous Mysteries of the rosary.

Because the parish has always been small, it has radiated the type of family atmosphere that Bishop Grutka envisioned in the 1960s. The church itself has sometimes been difficult to find as it is tucked away in the western corner of the subdivision. As the area grows to the west, it is the hope of the parish that a new road will give greater access to the church.

Saint Thomas More

The founding of St. Thomas More Parish is a fascinating story. In the 1940s, the pastor of the Ridge area was Father Leo Hildebrandt and his assistant pastor at St. Mary's in Griffith was Father Robert Weis. Both men were convinced of the need for a church in Munster and eventually persuaded Bishop Noll of Fort Wayne to support their vision. From February to September 1945, Father Weis took a survey of the Munster area to solicit requests for a new church from people whom he visited. He was able to obtain the names of 150 Catholic families living in the area. By October of 1945, Father Weis was appointed by Bishop Noll to direct the formation of a new parish in the Munster area while he was still serving as an assistant to Father Hildebrandt. With Father Hildebrandt as a mentor, young Father Weis rolled up his sleeves and set the foundations of this parish, not foreseeing the fact that not only would he be the founder of the parish but would also be its pastor for forty years.

Initially, the Munster area was a sparsely populated Dutch community in the wetlands of the south region. A small group of Catholics raised the money and according to Father Weis, "[built a] shack of a church," and were very proud of their accomplishment. That held them until 1949 when they built the distinctive building that faces Calumet Avenue. The church was growing despite the fact that Munster was a predominantly Protestant community. Today the parish ranks as one of the largest in the diocese.

Since its inception in 1949, Saint Thomas More School has been affiliated with the Sisters of Saint Benedict. In 1968, work was begun to enlarge the school with the addition of more classrooms, a gymnasium, library and offices. The third and present church, with seating for over twelve-hundred, built according to the liturgical norms of the Second Vatican Council, was begun in 1969 and dedicated by Bishop Grutka on 3 May 1970.

After forty years as spiritual leader of the parish community, Monsignor Weis retired in June of 1985 and was succeeded by Monsignor Carl Mengeling who would continue to care for the parish community for ten years. In 1995, he was named the Bishop of Lansing, Michigan. His successor, Father Richard Emerson led the community from 1995 to 2003. During this time he increased the schools capacity by acquiring a building on additional property south of the church. He was succeeded by the present pastor, Father Michael Yadron.

Becoming a parish is a continuing endeavor for each new generation. The agenda today is the same but the situation is different: life in the risen Christ, the celebration of goodness, the commitment to Christian values and collaboration in the mission of Christ.

Saint Michael the Archangel

The development of community began in the late 1800s when Schererville was mostly farmland and rolling prairie. Forced to travel to distant churches over bad roads with only primitive transportation, the German Catholic pioneers of this fledgling town petitioned Bishop Dwenger of Fort Wayne for the establishment of a parish in Schererville in 1873. Permission was granted and a church was constructed on land donated by the town founder, Nicholas Scherer. Father Henry Meissner, the pastor at Crown Point supervised the construction of the church. On 29 September 1874, the feast of St. Michael, the first church was blessed and a parish of eighty families was formed.

Father Gottfried Kueng became the first resident pastor in 1875, he would be succeeded by Father John Bathe (1877), Father Francis Deimel (1877-1881), and Father William Berg who would care for the parish for forty-eight years until his death in 1929. He was to become one of the most remarkable and renowned figures in Schererville's history. During his tenure many improvements to the church were made. A firm believer in Catholic education, in 1890 Father Berg arranged for Franciscan Sisters of Joliet to teach in the town school. On September 10, 1900, Saint Michael School opened as a full time parochial school.

Responding to the vandalizing of the parish cemetery in 1893, two Divine Word Missionary Brothers beautified the cemetery by erecting a Mount Calvary shrine, grottoes, and Stations of the Cross. It is on this mount in the cemetery that some of the former pastors are buried.

By 1920, the parish had outgrown its church and Father Berg began plans for a new building. The building of a new church was begun just before his death in 1929. His successor, Father Peter Biegel would complete the project. He remained as pastor of Saint Michael until his death thirty-one years later. He was followed by Father Timothy Doody (1958-1964), Father Bernard Shank (1964-1979), Father Joseph Vamos (1979-1988), Father Patrick Connolly (1988-2002), and the current pastor since 2002, Father Martin Dobrzynski. The community experienced a population explosion during the late 1970s and the parish has grown to over two-thousand families. The small country church in its picturesque setting was now too small for the congregation. Father Connolly undertook the project of a new church, not without some difficulty. The completed church portion of the building project was dedicated by Bishop Melczek on 3 November 1999.

Father Dobrzynski, a former assistant pastor, returned to care for the parish during Father Connolly's illness and continues to inspire the parish to be a place of prayer, hospitality and charity.

SAINT JOHN THE EVANGELIST

Saint John the Evangelist Parish began in 1837 when John Hack, a German immigrant farmer, his wife Johanna and their family arrived in the area known then as Prairie West. At that time, Indiana had only been a state for twenty-one years and this northwest corner of the state was American wilderness in the truest sense of the word. As more German immigrant settlers arrived in the area, Hack recognized the need for a church to address the spiritual concerns of the community needs and act as the glue to bind them together. Until 1839, Father Francis Fischer would travel to the area twice a month from Chicago to celebrate Mass at the Hack home. From these initial seeds of faith sprung a primitive church building built on the Hack property.

Building materials were hauled from Chicago, an arduous trip that took nearly a week. The resulting new eighteen by twenty-four foot church became the first Catholic Church and, historically, the mother Church of Lake County.

In 1842, the community erected a second, small log cabin church.

From 1843 until 1866 the community would be under the care of the Holy Cross Fathers. In 1846, Bishop de St. Palais presided at the first Confirmation in Lake County in this tiny church. The original log cabin, this priceless piece of St. John history, is now located on the Saint John the Evangelist parish grounds and is home to the Perpetual Adoration Chapel founded by Father Stephen Titko. Under the pastorate of Father Bernard Force, C.S.C., a brick church was constructed in October of 1856 for a congregation of about one-hundred twenty families. His successors include: Father Henry Koenig (1866-1870), Father Anthony Heitman (1870-1906), Father Charles Keyser (1906), Father A. M. Buchheit (1906-1915), Father Anthony Badina (1915-1929), Father John Steger (1929-1939), Father Fred Rothermel (1939-1944), Father Paul Roederer (1944-1963), Father Gilber Wirtz (1963-1966), Father Ambrose McGinnity (1966-1975), Father Joseph Till (1975-1987), Father Gregory Holicky (1987-1991), Father Stephen Titko (1991-2001), and Father Sammie Maletta who has served the community since 2001.

In 1923, the St. John faith community began construction of the present church which was dedicated by Bishop Noll on 27 September 1925. The pastor Father Badina led a congregation of 115 families. Today's parish of 1200 families still meets in this worship space to celebrate the sacraments. To meet the needs of a growing community, the present school was built in the late 1960s. Today it is not only viable but a proud leader in quality Catholic education with an enrollment of 322 students.

The parish grounds include the church and school, the Adoration Chapel, a cemetery, parish office and the former rectory which is now used for meeting space. More importantly, the parish is filled to overflowing with a community that is active in liturgy, spiritual development, devotions, adult faith formation, the religious education of children, social justice activities, support ministries and social events that draw them closer as one family in Christ.

The parish is now planning for the construction of a new church to accommodate its growing community. The current church will remain in all its historic beauty to be used for daily Masses, weddings and funerals. South on U. S. Highway 41, overlooking the Marian Shrine, the new church will continue to stand as the tallest structure in St. John, sitting at the highest elevation.

THE PARISHES OF THE LAPORTE COUNTY DEANERY

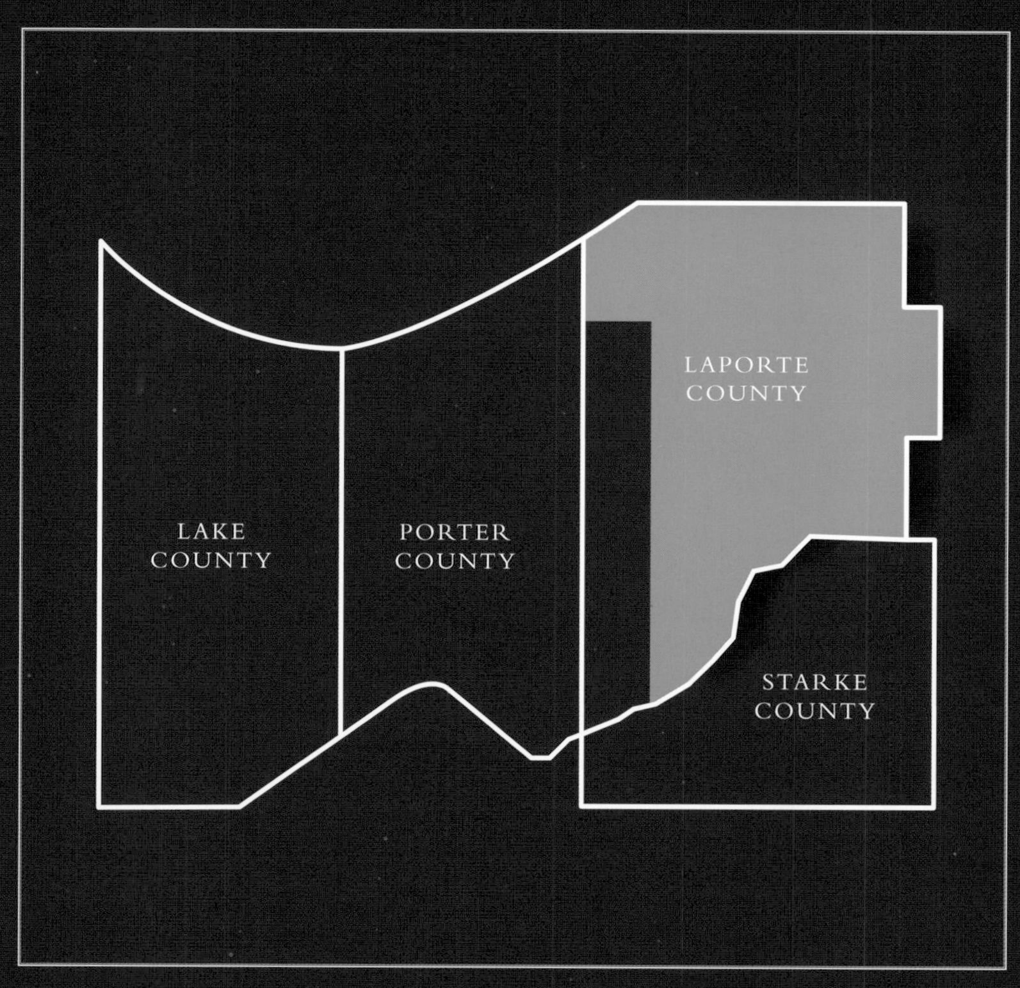

Sacred Heart

The story is told that Polish immigrants in LaPorte County originally would attempt to worship in the city of LaPorte. Members of those parishes at that time suggested they form their own community; they would do that at Otis in 1873. Almost forty years later another generation would make the same attempt, but this time establish a parish in the city north of State Highway 2 and east of the Courthouse in an area referred to as Poletown. In 1912, with the permission of Bishop Alerding, this community was organized under the direction of Father John Osadnik who would come to be the first resident pastor in 1913, celebrating the first mass at the White Eagle Hall. The construction of the new combination church and school building was completed later in that year with the first mass being the Midnight mass of Christmas 1913.

He secured the services of the Franciscan Sisters of Blessed Kunegunda (Franciscan Sisters of Chicago) to staff the parish school which was in operation from 1916 until 1969.

Father Osadnik was succeeded by Father Ignatius Gapczynski (1920-26) who built the rectory and convent and Father Ladislaus Szyzukowski (1926-1931). Father Gapczynski returned in 1931 until 1944 when Father Stanley Zjawinski (1944-1955) replaced him. He was succeeded by Father Walter Pawlicki (1955-1967), Father Joseph Buczyna (1967-1972) who built the present church, Father Dennis Teles (1972-1984), and Father Richard Orlinski (1984-1987). Father Walter Rakoczy, the Principal of Marquette High School was administrator for one year. He was followed by Father Dominic Bertino (1988-1990), Father John Strebig (1990-1997), Father Gerald Sroka (1997-2004), and Father Ian Williams the present pastor. In the late 1980s the community established a very active Saint Vincent DePaul Society. The parish has an annual summer festival that is very popular with the city and surrounding communities.

SAINT JOSEPH

The first Catholics in LaPorte worshipped together in one parish until 1858 when Father Francis Xavier Weninger, S.J., a German Jesuit preacher, convinced the German immigrants of LaPorte that they should have their own parish. And so the parish of Saint Joseph was organized that year. By 1876 there were one-hundred twenty-five German speaking families in the community. The Rev. Martin Scherer was the first resident pastor to serve the community who is said to have ruled with an iron hand from 1858 to 1867. He was succeeded by Father Simon Bartosz until 1870, and Monsignor John Oechtering 1870-1880.

Father Joseph Nussbaum, (1880-1895) purchased and established Saint Joseph Cemetery for the parish. Father Anthony Messman began his duties at the parish in July of 1896 and continued until his death in May of 1912. He is credited with founding Holy Family Hospital which would be in existence until the 1960s. He also built a new school staffed by the Franciscan Sisters of Perpetual Adoration. He was succeeded by Father Ignatius Zircher 1912-1927, and Father Augustine VanRie, 1927-1962.

During his tenure, Father VanRie took advantage of the opportunities to buy more property adjoining the parish. With the addition of more property, it was possible in 1954 to build the present new school and remodel a house for the convent. When Father VanRie arrived at Saint Joseph there were only one hundred families. At his death in 1962, the parish had grown to more than six hundred families.

A Kilgen organ was installed in memory of those in the parish who fought and died in World War II. In 1954 the present school building was erected. Father Albert Zimmerman (1962-1968) succeeded as pastor when Father VanRie died; he is turn was succeeded by Monsignor John Witte. Improvements to the parish property were numerous during his time. He served as pastor from 1968 to 1986. Father Joseph Till served the parish from 1986 to 1994, followed by Father Richard Emerson (1994-1996). In the mid-nineties the parish began celebrating an afternoon mass in Spanish every Sunday for the growing Hispanic community of La Porte County. The parish continues to work hard, supporting the parish school, and various new ministries that have developed over the years. Father Theodore Nordquist, the present pastor has served as Dean of the LaPorte Deanery since 2003.

Saint Peter

On 29 June 2003 Saint Peter parish celebrated her Sesquicentennial Anniversary as a Center of Worship and Religious Practice for the residents of this community. It all began with Holy Cross Fathers from Notre Dame coming here to celebrate the Liturgy for the Irish and German Catholics.

Saint Peter Parish dates its beginning to the work of the Holy Cross Fathers who, from their base at Notre Dame, cared for Catholic settlers moving into the area to either farm or work on the railroads. The original church was given the title Nativity of the Blessed Virgin, but it was later changed to Saint Peter.

The first four Pastors of St. Peter Church were Holy Cross Fathers. After that the Bishop of Fort Wayne assigned Diocesan Priests to serve the Parish and its People. In all, eighteen Pastors have served the parish community: Holy Cross Fathers Michael Rooney, Robert Wallace, Bernard Force, and Edmund Kilroy; and diocesan priests: Fathers Francis Lawler, Timothy O'Sullivan, Matthew Campion, James Twigg, John Crawley, John Grogan, George Schramm, John Wakefer, H. Victor Magsam, Theodore Fettig, Lawrence Grothouse, Eugene Hoffman, George Vrabely, and Joseph Angotti the current pastor.

The first building of the Parish was a Church on the corner of Monroe St. and Osborn Street. Eventually the entire block of properties was purchased by the Parish extending from Noble Street to Osborn Street and Michigan Avenue to Monroe Street.

The Sisters of Holy Cross comprised the staff of teachers for the Parish by first locating at Saint Rose

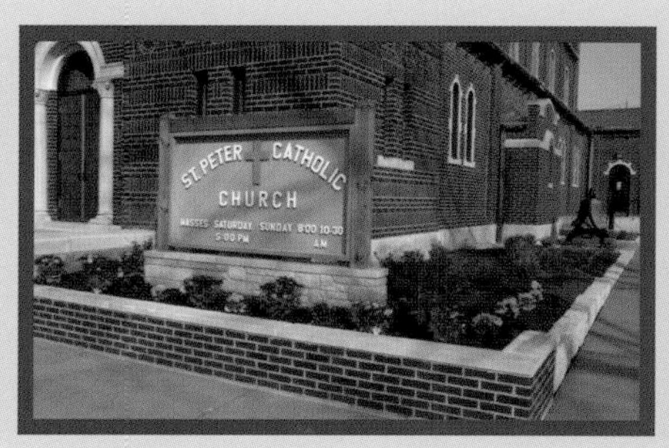

Academy on Ridge Street and later the school was moved in 1923 into a new building next to the Church on Monroe Street and remained in operation until the late 1960s when declining enrollment and increased cost forced the parish to close the school. Since the closing of the school, an extensive Faith Formation or Religious Education Program has been in effect for pre-school children through High School. This extensive curriculum is taught and implemented by volunteer Catechists, Teachers, and Aides.

As the membership grew in numbers, a new Church was built on the corner of Michigan Avenue and Noble Street. This new worship area was dedicated on Thanksgiving Day, 1930.

Currently there are 615 Families enrolled in the Parish with a total of 2,000 individuals: Many have a long history of membership, others have come here because of work assignments, job opportunities, or to retire in this community. More and more people have joined in various activities and ministries as visible witnesses to their faith.

NOTRE DAME

By the end of the Second Word War, the parish of Saint Mary in Michigan City had grown to one of the largest communities in the state. By 1950 its eastern section was established as Queen of All Saints parish but this did not include the town of Long Beach, north of the new parish. A group of citizens from that town met with Monsignor Vurpillat, their pastor, asking that they have a parish and school of their own. Would he kindly meet with the Bishop and see if this were possible? The pastor was reluctant, but knew that his facilities were not adequate for so many people. He was told that property was available on which there was an old barn currently being used as a restaurant. Days later, Bishop Noll gave his assent, funds were provided for the property and the parish was given the name Notre Dame. Monsignor Vurpillat would also give up an assistant in the person of Father James Stapleton, who would become the first resident pastor. The barn turned restaurant, was transformed into a church and the first mass was celebrated on 14 June 1953 with one hundred families on the parish roster. Plans were immediately made for the establishment of a parish school. The building, built in the Georgian style was completed in 1955 and opened that fall under the direction of the Sisters of Holy Cross. In June, 1957 Father Stapleton was succeeded by Father Albert Van Nevel. Full of life, he energized the community and organized it into action. He cared for the community until being transferred to Highland in 1963. Father Leo Armbruster would follow as pastor until 1971. During this time the parish experienced its building phase. The new convent came first, followed by the current church which was dedicated by Bishop Grutka on 18 May 1969. The new rectory was completed in 1970. All buildings are in the Georgian style of architecture. Due to illness, Father Armbruster resigned his pastorate in 1971. The Superintendent of Schools, Monsignor Ferdinand Melevage arrived to care for the parish as its pastor until 1983. Monsignor Edward Litot would become the next pastor. As the Sisters withdrew from the school in 1981, he remodeled the convent into parish offices, meeting rooms and space for kindergarten and preschool programs. When he retired in 1994, he would be succeeded by Father Richard Ameling (1994-2003), Father Richard Emerson (2003-2006), and the current pastor, Father Keith McClellan who would administer the parish at the beginning of 2005 until being named pastor one year later.

Queen of All Saints

In the late 1940s, Michigan City found itself growing on its east side. The only territorial parish was Saint Mary, the Immaculate Conception, (as Saint Stanislaus Kostka was for the Polish and Sacred Heart for the Maronites) and it could not handle the population growth. In 1950, Bishop Noll established the new parish named for the Queen of All Saints. The first pastor was Father John Roesler, who would soon be followed by Father Leonard Cross who arrived in 1951 and would care for the community until 1970.

Groundbreaking for Queen of All Saints Catholic grade school took place in March of 1952 with 160 students in grades 1-4. One year later grades 5-8 were begun, staffed by Sisters of Holy Cross. Father Alfred Dettmer would become the third pastor in March 1970 and would remain for twenty-six years. Under his leadership the church was built in 1966.

In July of 1996 Pastor Father Michael Yadron became the fourth pastor of Queen of All Saints and would be succeeded by Father Terrence Chase, appointed in July 2003. The parish celebrated its golden jubilee in the year 2000. That year also brought the razing of the old rectory and the renovation of the former convent to house parish priests and parish offices with the addition of the Christ the King Adoration Chapel to which all Catholics are welcome to come and pray. During this time major improvements were also made to the school.

Today the parish educates almost seven hundred students in both the parish school and Religious Education Program. It is evident upon entering and exiting the building who the students and faculty are to emulate. Signs prominently posted by the door are: "Enter to learn Christ", and "Exit to teach Christ."

Queen of All Saints church has stained glass windows depicting the Corporal Works of Mercy. A few of the ways in which the community attempts to perform these works of mercy are by collecting food on a monthly basis to be distributed in the community. A favorite project is "Christmas in July" when a decorated Christmas tree is placed in church so that parishioners may place baby gifts under the tree to aid mothers through the organization of Birthright.

Again in December there is a Christmas tree for the same purpose.

The Holy Eucharist is carried to the homebound so that they might receive communion on a regular basis. These are only a few of the endeavors of the parish to bring the love of Jesus to others.

Sacred Heart

The growth of industry affected not only Lake County. At the beginning of the last century, pastors who were accustomed to dealing with German or Irish immigrants found themselves unable to communicate with the vast polyglot community that was entering their parishes. Father Anthony Ellering at Saint Mary in Michigan City was no exception. He put out the word throughout the Midwest that he was in need of a priest who could speak Syrian.

The answer came in the person of Father Michael Abraham who would spend the rest of his life in Michigan City. Born in Syria in 1885, his parents migrated to Canada, but moved to Jerusalem around 1900. He entered the seminary there and was ordained in 1911. While sent on a mission by the Patriarch of Jerusalem to Canada in 1914, Father Abraham found himself unable to return home because of the outbreak of the First World War. He took the opportunity to visit friends in Michigan, and while there heard of the need in Michigan City. With the permission of Bishop Alerding, he arrived in Michigan City in January, 1914.

While staying at Saint Mary Rectory, he was able to build a small church and rectory within eighteen months of his arrival. The property was located on Eighth Street in an area where so many of his parishioners lived working for the Pullman Company.

Father Abraham was so well versed in many European languages that other first generation Americans gravitated to Sacred Heart where there was at least a confessor who understood them.

For forty-five of his forty-nine years as a priest, he worked among the people of Sacred Heart Parish. Nationally known, his funeral was celebrated at Saint Stanislaus Kostka, his own parish church being too small to handle the crowds.

He was succeeded by Father Henry Ameling (1960-1965), Monsignor Edward Sweigart (1966-1970), and Father Vincent Lengerich until 1970 when Father Dennis Blaney arrived and stayed until his retirement in 1998. Father Walter Ciesla cared for the parish until at the beginning of the twenty-first century Sacred Heart had reverted to its original status as a mission of Saint Mary parish and is cared for by the present pastor, Father James McGrogan.

SAINT MARY OF THE IMMACULATE CONCEPTION

The Holy Cross Fathers cared for the Catholics in Michigan City in the middle of the nineteenth century. They first organized the parish of Saint Ambrose in 1849 mostly for the Irish. In 1859 Saint Mary parish was founded for German speaking immigrants. By 1867, as it was deemed unfeasible to support two parishes in the city, both parishes merged to form Saint Mary of the Immaculate Conception on the first of November. Father Julius Becks would become the first resident pastor and care for the parish until 1885.

A new brick church was built on the edge of town where there was also a cemetery. The edge of town at that time was the location of the present church at Tenth and Buffalo Streets.

The parish kept growing and a new two-story brick parish school and convent was built in 1886 and in 1905 a new brick rectory replaced the wooden one. By 1909 the parish had more than 500 families, built a hall and a new convent, remodeling the old one into classrooms so the parish could add a high school. In the early 1920s, the church was enlarged to its present size with the addition of new transepts, sanctuary and sacristies. Exquisite stained glass windows from Germany as well as the renowned Katherine Barker Memorial altar were installed.

By the end of World War II the parish had almost four thousand families and was considered the largest parish in the state of Indiana.

Because of this, the parishes of Queen of All Saints, Notre Dame, and Saint Ann of the Dunes would be formed from the parish community.

A new parish high school was built in 1955 on the parish grounds and Marquette Hall completely renovated. In 1968 the high school would be renamed Marquette High School to reflect its status as an institution for all parishes in the city and the surrounding area.

The first parish council was also established in June of 1968, helping to initiate a new management style for the parish and the schools to assure that the newly independent high school would survive.

During this time of change a food pantry and a clothing center for the needy were established, seeking not only to praise God in worship, but to be active in the daily life of the community.

1984 saw the commissioning of Eucharistic Ministers, and the hiring of a Parish Caregiver Coordinator, a Sister then, but a lay person by the end of the century. As the city aged and its population declined in the 1990s, so did parish membership. On the plus side, though, the parish converted its empty convent into the Angela House Retreat Center. The school reached out to a number of non-Catholic families, but increasing costs forced the school to close in 2003. The building, though, is now being used for Religious Education and also for the services provided by Catholic Charities and Family Services.

After Father Becks the following served the community as pastors:

- Father John Bleckmann (1885-1909),
- Father Anthony Ellering (1909-1924),
- Father George Moorman (1924-1931),
- Father Joseph Lynn (1931-1935),
- Monsignor Edward Vurpillat (1935-1962),
- Monsignor Alfred Reinig (1962-1963),
- Father Timothy Doody (1963-1968),
- Father Albert Zimmermann (1968-1982),
- Father J. Patrick Gaza (1982-1992),
- and the current pastor, Father James McGrogan since 1992.

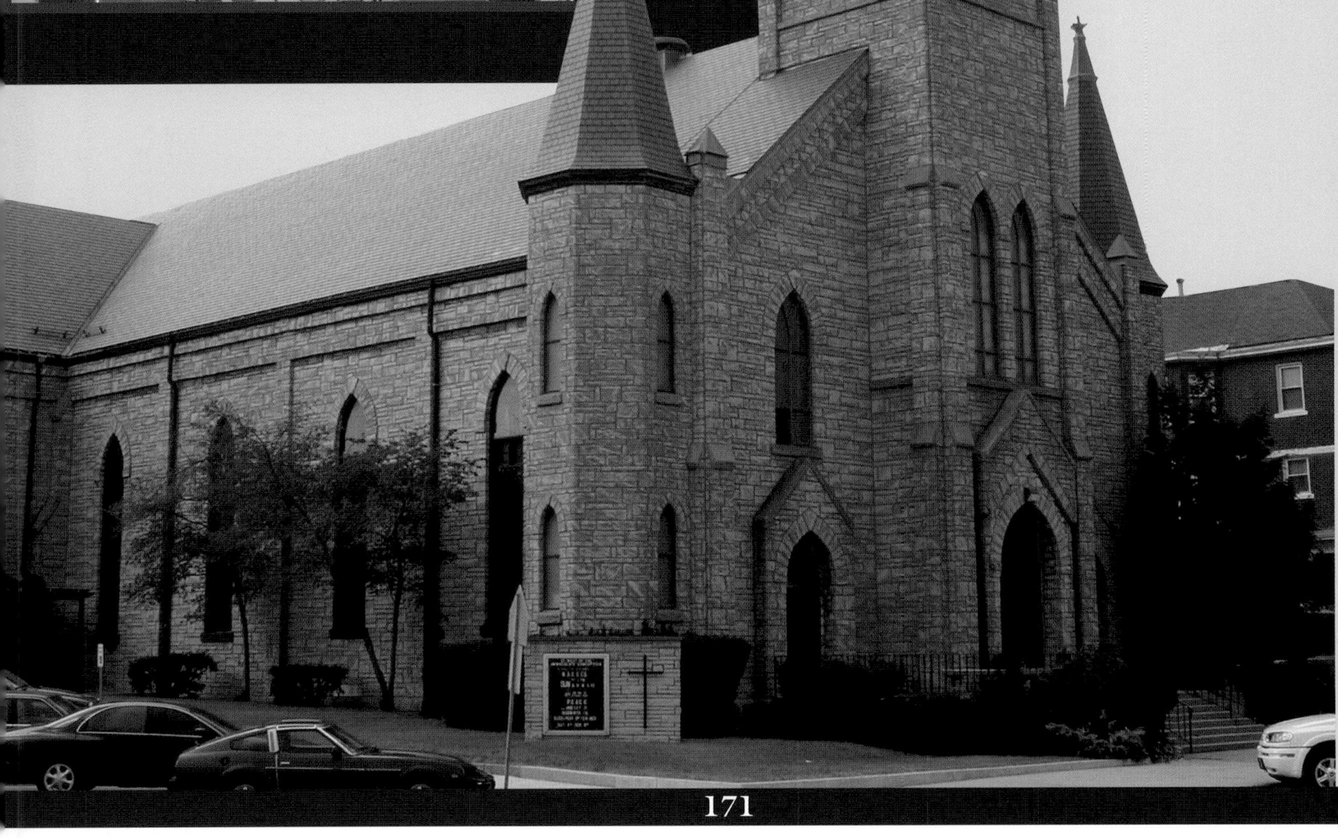

Saint Stanislaus Kostka

The influx of Polish immigrants to northern Indiana continued throughout the last third of the nineteenth century. Assigning Father Emmanuel Wrobel to Saint Mary, the Immaculate Conception Parish in 1890, Bishop Alerding directed him to begin organizing the Polish community in Michigan City into a parish. Temporary quarters were set up for the community to worship on the second floor of the parish grade school.

In 1891 a two storey combination building for use as church and school was built and Father Wrobel was named pastor of the new parish. He was succeeded in 1909 by Father Joseph Bolka who would lead the community for thirty-two years until his death in 1941.

Father Bolka would build the present church in 1926. A new convent would be built for the School Sisters of Notre Dame who had charge of the school from 1897 to 1986. The old school was razed in 1940 and the current school building erected at that time.

The first fifty years of the community were led by two pastors. They would be succeeded by six more:

- Father Julian Doktor (1940-1965),
- Monsignor Louis Michalski (1965-1969),
- Father Stanley Dominik (1969-1988),
- Father Emil Bloch (1988-1990),
- Monsignor Michael Tomaszewski (1990-1999) who would preside over the parish's centennial celebration,
- and the current pastor Father Walter Ciesla from 1999.

The community has centered many of its activities, as many parishes do, around the school. The parish summer festival has always been popular with the citizenry.

The parish, noted as a close-knit community, has accepted new members from other ethnic communities settling in the area, most notably the Hispanic community which has been given the opportunity to worship in their own language.

Saint Mary

The community of Otis comprised of a group of farming families, mostly Polish who attended mass at Saint Joseph in LaPorte. Monsignor John Oechtering, the pastor there, encouraged the community to have their own parish. With his help, the parish would be organized, with the purchase of property in 1873 on a site near the crossing of two railroads. The area at the time was known as Salem Crossing. The frame church was completed and blessed in the spring of 1873. The first resident pastor would be Fathert Peter Koncz (1873-1975) and would be succeeded by Father Lugwig Machzicki (1875-1881), Father Urban Raszkiewicz (1881-1909), Father Alex Buechler (1909-1912), and Father Thomas Jankowski (1912-1914). Father John Wroblewski would arrive in the summer of 1914. The interior and exterior of the church was completely redecorated at that time and three new altars were installed. In February, 1917 fire destroyed the church and rectory, with only the school building left standing. Mass would be celebrated there until the present church would be completed in 1918. Father Wroblewski would be transferred in 1927 and would be succeeded by Father John Biernacki (1927-1932), Father John Hosinski (1932-1938), Father Louis Bozyk (1938-1959), Father Roman Wojcicki (1959-1963), Father John Bargielski (1963-1966), Father Theodore Janicki (1966-1968), Father Julian Jercha (1968-1971), Father Henry Krysinski (1971-1987), Father Matthew Kish (1987-1994), and Father Joseph Pusateri (1994-2005). Since Father Pusateri's retirement, the parish has been in the care of the pastor at Wanatah, Father Gerald Schweitzer.

The school would open in 1914 and be staffed by the Sisters Felician. The Sisters would withdraw in 1965 and the school would close due to declining enrollment.

SAINT JOHN KANTY

Polish immigrants came to the area around Lake Saugnay as early as 1863. They settled working by cutting timber and hauling logs to LaPorte. Working in this way, many earned enough money to buy small farms in the area.

They would usually attend mass at either LaPorte or Terre Coupee, long trips on foot and difficult in bad weather. The priest at Terre Coupee established the parish as his mission in 1888. Father Walter Zborowski would celebrate mass in homes of parishioners until a frame church was built in 1890.

The congregation grew steadily and outgrew the church. A larger building was erected in 1907, while the original building was moved across the road to serve as a school and later, a parish hall. When the rectory was built Father John Hosinski was appointed the first resident pastor.

In 1922, the church was destroyed by fire; a new building was completed in 1924. To help fund the construction, the parish started to serve chicken dinners and have picnics in the wooded area near the church. Word of these events spread and soon people came from South Bend, Michigan City and Chicago on the South Shore to attend. The parishioners donated chickens and all worked very hard to make the events successful. They worked hard not only to raise money for the church but also to enhance their parish community.

Father Aloysius Jarka was pastor from 1925-26, followed by Father Joseph Zielinski who cared for the community until 1937; Father Wencel Karp succeeded him until 1947.

By the late 1940s and early 1950s, many people from Gary and Chicago began moving to the peaceful Saugnay Lake for the summers. Many of these summer residents retired to this area because of its proximity to the church. Because of this continued growth, an addition to the church was built in 1955, adding a new sanctuary and more seating. The basement was also enlarged at this time. The planning for a new parish hall began in 1963 with the purchase of fifty acres of land adjoining the church. Dedication of the new hall with a fully equipped kitchen and classroom space took place in 1977. Today the hall provides a place for religious education, social gatherings and parish events.

Pastors have included:

- Father Theodore Janicki (1947-1960),
- Father Henry Smartz (1960-1967),
- Father Chester Zurawiec (1967-1974),
- Father Vladimir Janeczyk (1974-1977),
- Father Leonard Kronkowski (1977-1997),
- Father James Meade (1997-1998),
- Father Walter Ciesla (1998-1999).

Currently the parish is under the care of Father Michael Heimer, pastor of Saint Anthony in Fish Lake. Saint John Kanty parish celebrated its centenary on 9 October 1988 in the presence of Bishop Grutka.

Saint Anthony of Padua

Saint Anthony of Padua began as a mission parish. In the late 1940s, Father Anthony Letko, the Pastor of St. Patrick Church in nearby Walkerton, Indiana, petitioned and received permission from Bishop Noll to begin a mission parish after realizing the need of a substantially large Catholic community. The first mass was celebrated in 1948 at the Fish Lake Conservation Club, but due to large attendance, services were moved to the lake-front property of the late John Komara. Under the leadership of Father Letko, land was purchased on State Highway 4 and the ground was broken in 1952. Father Letko, his brother Father Louis Letko, local lumber companies running their sawmills to supply the wood, and many of the residents, young and old, literally took hammer and saw in hand and began construction. Every beam in the church was raised by hand, the women stained the exterior wood, supplied meals, and as their parish rose, the people came. The parish, not yet complete, held Mass weekly. St. Anthony of Padua chapel's bells rang for the first time on 4 April 1955. On 10 June 1955, Bishop Leo Pursley dedicated the chapel. In 1957, St. Anthony of Padua found itself severed from its mother parish of St. Patrick's in Walkerton with the establishment of the new Diocese of Gary.

Now an independent parish, Bishop Grutka, named Father Herman Schoudel the first resident pastor in 1958. He was succeeded in 1963 by Father Eric Schaff, Father Leonard Kronkowski in 1969, Father Julian Jercha in 1977 and the current pastor, Father Michael Heimer in 1985.

THE PARISHES OF THE PORTER-STARKE DEANERY

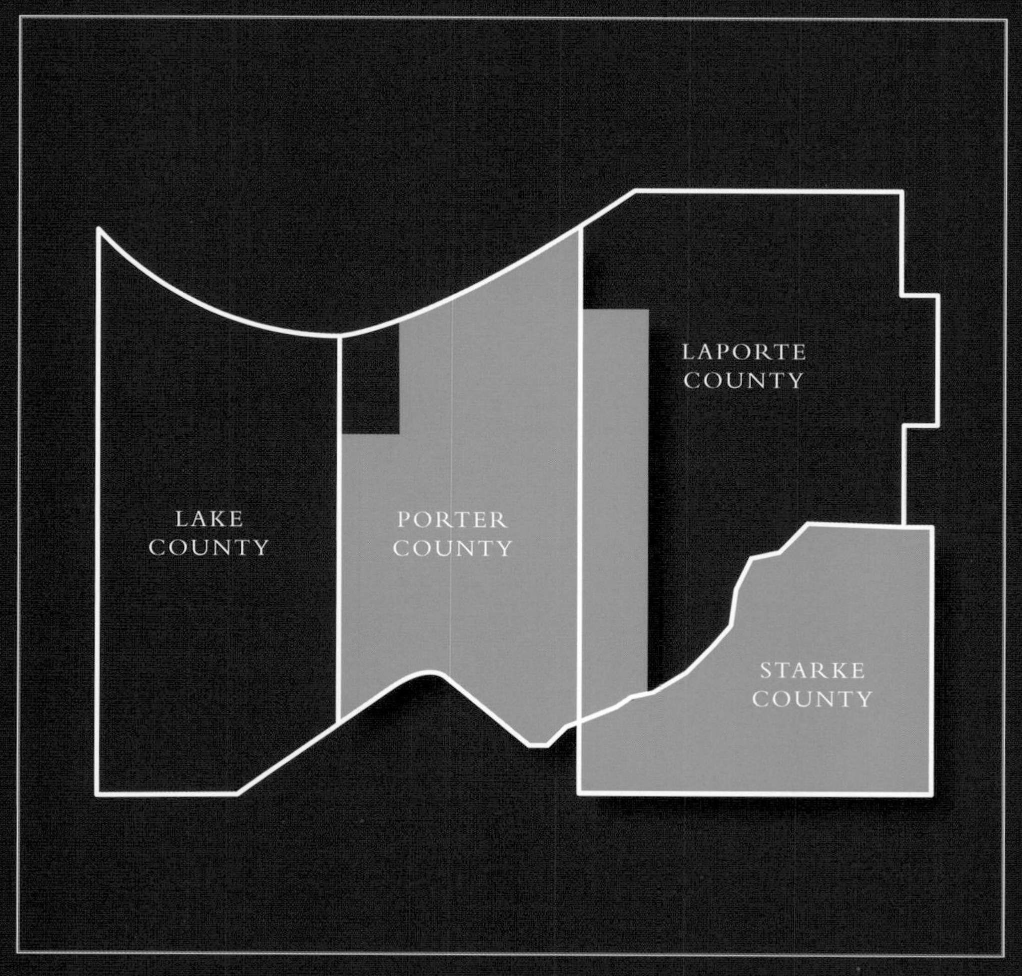

SAINT ANN OF THE DUNES

Bishop Noll established a mission parish in Beverly Shores in September of 1950. A small community of parishioners was served originally by Franciscan priests from Seven Dolors Shrine in Valparaiso. The first mass was celebrated in the Beverly Shores Fire Station. In the first years of the parish the sacraments were celebrated in many places including the Town Hall until the parish began a building fund for a permanent structure.

In 1954 Helen Wood, a friend of the parishioners, donated five acres of land for the location of the church, with the specific understanding that this building also would be available for community gatherings; the church was completed that year.

In 1956 the parish of Saint Ann of the Dunes was officially recognized and Father Joseph Klinker was appointed the first resident pastor. He was succeeded in 1960 by Father Henry Ameling until 1965 when Father Louis Letko replaced him. He would serve the community until 1968.

Father Charles Doyle would arrive in 1968 and serve the parish community for twenty-eight years until his retirement in 1996. Soon after his arrival, the parish desired to remodel and enlarge the church. The new design added two wings to the north and south of the building which became a gathering space and a new sanctuary with large plate glass windows overlooking the dunes and woods as a natural backdrop for the altar. Delays in construction, however, caused some very cold celebrations until Christmas mass. By then most of the work had been completed, including the heating. Another major renovation of the church building took place in 1998. Professional designers and members of the parish volunteered their time and expertise. The interior of the church was painted, carpeted and tiled, blending in with the surrounding landscape of dunes and woodland. The Repository was placed on the west side of the church. The kitchen area was updated with new ranges, more cupboard space, new plumbing fixtures and a window. Additional property was purchased to the north of the church on which a rectory would be built. Under the leadership of Father Doyle the parish community was directed towards an awareness of their social responsibilities to the gospel message.

Father Doyle was succeeded by Father John Barasinski, the current pastor. A competent handyman, he has accomplished many of the physical improvements to the church, rectory and parking lot. A reconciliation room, a parish office, a renovated sacristy and a handicapped-accessible restroom have been added. In addition, a storage shed replaced the old garage which fell into serious disrepair.

The parish now serves approximately 395 permanent families which almost doubles during the summer months.

About 70% of the population is of Lithuanian extraction. Lithuanian liturgies are celebrated regularly on the third Sunday of each month. The Lithuanian influence is present everywhere in the church from the building structure design by E. Masiulis, to the internal artifact such as Baptismal Fount, the road Shrine, the altar, and the Crucifix.

Saint Patrick

Holy Cross missionaries visited the area known as Coffee Creek since the 1840s. In 1858 Father Edmund Kilroy, C.S.C. built a small frame church and dedicated the parish to Saint Patrick.

Father John Flynn became the first resident pastor in 1869, the same year the community came to be known as Chesterton. Father Flynn died in 1870 at the age of twenty-eight and the parish was cared for as a mission again until the arrival of Father John Lange in 1875. Subsequent pastors would be Father C. Hardy (1878-1879) and Father H. F. Kroll (1879-1898), who would build the first parish school in 1887. Father F. von Schwedler (1898-1899) would succeed him for one year and be followed by Father Herman Juraschek (1899-1911) who would build a new school which was staffed by the School Sisters of Notre Dame. He would be succeeded by Father Lawrence Eberle (1911-1920), Father Julius Seimetz (1920-1933), and Father Edmund Eisenhardt (1933-1951), Father Ralph Hoffman (1951-1966), Father John Daniels (1967-1968), Father Patrick Meehan (1968-1969), Father Stephen Vrabely (1969-1976), Father Lawrence Heeg (1976-2001), and Father James Meade since 2001.

Father Eisenhardt would build a new school building on property on the north side of town; eventually the whole parish plant would be relocated there with the building of a new church by the community under the direction of Father Heeg. The present church was dedicated by Bishop Gaughan on 22 October 1989. Currently, the present pastor with the cooperation of the community plans to enlarge the school considerably with the addition of new classrooms and a social hall for the use of the whole community.

Holy Cross

The Catholics at Hamlet were visited during the nineteenth century from various parishes in the area. The original church was built in 1890 by the Precious Blood Missionary Father Dominic Shunk when he was pastor at Wanatah. The parish was attached to Wanatah as a mission until 1899 when the responsibility was given to the pastor at Saint Patrick parish in Walkerton. Subsequent pastors from there would see to the needs of the community when the responsibility was given to the new pastor at Saint Thomas Aquinas in Knox in 1923. Father Charles Malay from Knox would build the present church in 1927.

Since just before the founding of the Gary diocese, there have been resident pastors caring for the parish: Father James Stapleton (1950-1953), Father Herman Schoudel (1953-1958), Father John Frawley (1958-1975), Father Dominic Mrena (1975-1990), Father Emil Bloch (came on tuesday died on thursday in 1990), and the current pastor, Father Anthony Spanley since 1990.

A small, but vibrant community, they are serious in their responsibilities to the faith. Under the direction of Father Mrena they helped with the organization of their daughter parish, Saint Dominic at Koontz Lake.

Saint Helen

Saint Helen Parish in Hebron was organized as a mission of Saint Mary, Kouts in 1932 under the direction of the pastor, Father Augustine Kondziela who bought a building from the Presbyterian Church in 1946 for the use of the fifty-five Catholics who were residents of Hebron. They chose Saint Helen as their patroness. Bishop Noll dedicated the church on 29 September of that year. Father Ambrose Switzer would become the first resident pastor in 1947. The parish would be without a resident pastor being administered from Kouts and various other places until Father Joseph Casey (1967-1975) would arrive to care for the community. He would be succeeded by Father Ambrose McGinnity (1975-1977) and Father Matthew Kish (1977-1987). On ten acres of land that the parish had purchased near the site of the church, he would have a parish hall built, as well as a new rectory. Father Derrick Dudash, the current pastor, would agree with the community that a new church was necessary and began the drive in cooperation with the parish council. The present church was dedicated by Bishop Gaughan on 9 July 1989. The population explosion in south Lake County promises to extend into Hebron as the community is itself experiencing growth recently and will soon be larger than the three hundred fifty families currently enrolled as members. Father Dudash has described the community as one with "a spirit of stewardship… a noteworthy characteristic of the membership is that they continue to volunteer their time to care for the Church, Hall, and parish grounds with the same devotion they would give to their own property. This is mirrored by their willingness to care for one another as well, and to minister to one another in the ways in which Christ has directed us."

Saint Thomas Aquinas

Catholics in Knox had been attended to originally by Father Joseph Stephan who was attached to the Indian School at Rensselaer. Later priests would come from various foundations, such as North Judson at different times of the year.

In 1911 Father Joseph Abel, from Walkerton, purchased the Lutheran church thus enabling the people from Knox to attend Mass more frequently. Father Abel also purchased a house on Washington Street to serve as a rectory which later became the convent. In 1952 Father Conrad A. Stoll bought the house in the rear of the old church intending it to serve as a home for the Sisters who would teach in the Catholic school.

In 1923 the parish was officially organized, given the patronage of Saint Thomas Aquinas, and received its first resident pastor in the person of Father John Lach. He would care for the community until he was transferred to Whiting in 1926.

Father Charles Malay became the second pastor in 1926 and remained until 1932. During his pastorate an addition was built on the rear of the old church in 1927 to form the sanctuary and the sacristies. Father Conrad Stoll was appointed pastor in 1932 and was also given the responsibility of caring for the parish at Hamlet. In 1941, he started a building fund for a new church. As both the community and the economy grew, Father Stoll was able to complete the planned program with the building of the present church in 1954.

In September of 1955 the new school opened with the Dominican Sisters and lay teachers. The following year, 1956, Father Stoll died and was succeeded by Father Herman Schoudel in February of 1957.

Father Schoudel remained only until mid-June, when he was replaced by Father Anthony Suelzer. He served the community until 1960. Father Casimir Senderak was then appointed to his first pastoral assignment at Saint Thomas; he would remain until 1962. The Sisters would withdraw from the school the same year, but the new pastor, Father Stanley Milewski, would be able to keep the school open with the help of a lay faculty. The Sisters of Saint Joseph arrived in 1964. Father Milewski was transferred to Holy Family in Gary in 1965 and would be succeeded temporarily by Father William Vogt and then by Father Emil Bloch. Father Bloch would have the responsibility of guiding the community in the first phases of the renewal of the Church following the Second Vatican Council. Father Anthony Ficko replaced Father Bloch in 1977 and continued some of the changes in the sanctuary and had the sad duty of closing the school for lack of students in 1983.

It was in 1983 that Monsignor Vincent Lengerich was appointed pastor; he converted the baptistery into a room for Reconciliation and the Baptismal font was brought to the sanctuary of the church and a shrines to the Sacred Heart and Saint Thomas were created in the space of the old confessional. Monsignor retired in 1993 and was succeeded by Monsignor Richard Zollinger. Under his leadership several improvements occurred for the parish. A new rectory was built and the old rectory was sold. The entire sanctuary underwent renewal. This entailed a complete cleaning of the bricks in the church, replacing the light fixtures, restorating of the church's statues and repositioning the altar. Monsignor Zollinger retired in 1999 at which time the present pastor, Father John Scott took up his responsibilities toward the community.

Saint Dominic

Just five and one half miles northeast of Hamlet, lay the community of Koontz Lake, which owes its name to Samuel Koontz, who built a dam on an outlet of Woodworth Lake to power a mill there in 1848. The dam formed a larger body of water which bears his name. The small residential community has become a popular resort area for fishing, boating, and water skiing. Father Dominic Mrena, while the pastor of Holy Cross in Hamlet, saw the need for establishing a mission to care for the community whose population increases dramatically in the summer. In 1981, with the permission of the bishop, he was able to obtain a parcel of land to erect a small chapel which was placed under the patronage of Saint Dominic. A small but vibrant community of thirty-five families throughout the year makes up the nucleus of the parish. It would not be surprising to see the area grow in development because of its popularity with sportsmen. Father Anthony Spanley, the current pastor at Hamlet, takes care of the spiritual needs of the parish.

Saint Mary

The community of Kouts was visited from Valparaiso in the middle to late nineteenth century. Father Michael O'Reilly from Saint Paul Parish bought property and built a frame church. The parish was a mission of Saint Paul until 1887 when it was under the care of priests from North Judson and Wanatah consecutively until 1894.

The original church was destroyed by a tornado in 1917; the foundation for the new building was begun in 1918, but the structure would not be completed until 1926 under the direction of Father Joseph Suelzer, who became the first resident pastor in 1921. He would remain at Kouts until 1928 when he would begin to organize the new parish in Griffith. He would be succeeded by Father Jacob Nickels until 1932. Father Augustine Kondziela would then care for the parish until 1951. Other pastors have been Father Ambrose McGinnity (1964-1966), Father John Bargielski (1966-1971), Father George Kashmer (1971-1974), Father Joseph Panavas (1974-1986) and the present pastor Father Thomas Tibbs, since 1986.The parish has undergone improvements in the recent past, including an addition to the church, and the building of a new parish hall in 1994. The community is dedicated to the religious education of their children and is active in liturgical and social ministries. As the population continues to grow in that area of the county, the parish undoubtedly will also.

Saint Martin of Tours

In the current situation, with the anxiety that some parish communities face in the loss of a resident pastor and the fear that they will soon be closed, Saint Martin Parish stands as an example of faith-community cooperation. Since the parish was founded in 1860, there has been only one resident pastor. Father Peter Franzen served the community from October 1878 to August 1881.

The original church was located at Schimmels, about two miles northwest of LaCrosse. In 1856, mass was celebrated for the first time in the small one room home of Joseph Preis by Father Andrew Tusch. The congregation was organized by Father Martin Sherer, the pastor of Saint Joseph in LaPorte who built the first church in 1860. From 1856 to 1878 and again after 1881, the priests who served Saint Martin came from the towns of LaPorte, Michigan City, San Pierre, Lafayette, Logansport and Winamac. After 1887 the history of the parish is closely associated with the neighboring parish at Wanatah.

In 1887, Father Dominic Shunk, C.PP.S., was appointed Administrator. Precious Blood priests served the church from 1887 to 1898, when diocesan priests would take over. A new church was built in LaCrosse in 1914. On Christmas Eve, 1931, the church was completely destroyed by fire; a new brick church would replace it in the summer of 1932. The original bell from the first church building in Schimmels, placed in the second church building, survived the fire and was installed in the present church building. Father Kelner renovated and redecorated the church in 1961.

The pastors who have served the community since 1898: Father A. M. Buchheit, who was appointed by Bishop Rademacher. Father John Rech (1906), Father John Oberholz (1907-1911), Father Edward Werling (1911-1917), Father Theodore Hammes (1917-1922), Father Leo Faurote (1922-1930), Father Paul Anderson (1930-1932), Father Theophilus Chemma (1932-1939), Father John Steger (1939-1948), Father Michael Kelner (1948-1971), Father William Peil (1971-1976, 1978-1983), Father Timothy Benante (1976-1978), Father David Gosnell (1983-1989), Father Robert Tokarz (1989-1992), Father Lawrence Kew (1992-1994), and the present pastor Father Gerald Schweitzer since 1994.

During the fall of 1985, the church was redecorated for the parish's one hundred twenty-fifth anniversary. The celebration took place on Sunday, 3 November 1985 at mass in honor of Saint Martin celebrated by Bishop Gaughan.

SAINTS CYRIL AND METHODIUS

With the coming of the railroads, people began to settle this area in the 1850s. Catholics were not found here until the early 1870s when the Precious Blood Fathers from Rensselaer would cover the surrounding counties caring for the people by celebrating the sacraments in local homes.

In 1881 Precious Blood Father Dominic Schunk, who was responsible for parishes such as All Saints in San Pierre and Precious Blood in Wanatah, would begin to organize the community in North Judson and build a frame church. Father Casimir Kobylinski would become the first resident pastor and care for the community until 1893. He would be followed by Father John Kubacki (1893-1894), Father Peter Kahellek (1896-1899), Father Joseph Bolka (1899-1904), Father Felix Seroczynski (1904-1906) and Father Charles Keyser (1908-1912) who would begin the program to raise the present church in 1910. This was accomplished the next year with the dedication on 11 May 1911 by Bishop Alerding. The school opened that same year with the Franciscan Sisters of Perpetual Adoration taking charge and staffing the parish school until 1970.

Father Augustine VanRie (1912-1927) would succeed Father Keyser and direct the community in liquidating its debt, not before replacing the convent with a larger building. His successor, Father Charles Scholl (1927-1932) in his five year pastorate, spent a good deal of time organizing the young people of the parish as well as looking to the administration of the parish property; Father Felix Seroczynski (1932-1940) and Father Joseph Wonderly (1940-1943) would succeed him.

Father Ladislaus Krause (1943-1967), a much beloved leader of the faithful, would spend the last twenty-four years of his life dedicated to the parish community. He was succeeded briefly by Father Walter Pawlicki (1967-1971). During his tenure the parish school would be closed and a program for Religious Education was developed at that time. Father Leo Armbruster (1971-1986) would become the next pastor and have the delightful responsibility of planning the parish's centennial celebration in 1981. In preparation for the event the church would be remodeled beginning in 1974. Monsignor John Witte (1986-1992) came to North Judson after having served at Saint Joseph in LaPorte for eighteen years. He enjoyed attending to the spiritual needs of this close-knit faith community. Failing health forced him to retire in 1992. He was succeeded by one of his assistants at Saint Joseph, Father Mark Mazza who would care for the community until his departure to work in the Archdiocese of San Francisco in 2002. During his tenure the school building would be razed in 1999; The Knights of Columbus Council was formed as well as a Saint Vincent DePaul Society. Father Mazza would be succeeded by the present pastor Father John Zemelko who has the pleasure of celebrating with the community the one-hundred twenty-fifth anniversary of the parish in 2006.

All Saints

The first parish founded in Starke County, All Saints parish began its development in 1858, in the new diocese of Fort Wayne. Developed in a farming community, Father Joseph Stephan, a German immigrant who had worked in Cincinnati bought an old barrel factory for use as the first church. It was small but adequate for the fledgling congregation. By 1877 an addition was built to increase the seating capacity.

In 1886, a new church was constructed due to the influence of Precious Blood Father Dominic Shunk who was active in both Starke and LaPorte counties. By this time the parish was a mission of Saints Cyril and Methodius in North Judson.

The parish continued in this manner until 1936 when they received Father Louis Bozik as their resident pastor. He remained for two years and was succeeded by Father John Hosinski, who had responsibility for the communities in Medaryville and Francesville both in Pulaski County.

Father Hosinski improved the facilities of the church by adding a basement in 1941 that would serve as a social hall and meeting place for parish societies.

The church building would be given a brick veneer and stained glass windows were installed as well as new Stations of the Cross. He also purchased a house for use as a rectory, but his successor, Father Walter Pawlicki would be its first resident in 1946. He remained pastor until 1950 when he was replaced by Father Louis Jeziorski. The community considered him to be a masterful preacher and appreciated the fact that before the sermon he would reread the gospel in both English and Polish. He remained as pastor through the parish centenary and into the 1960s when he was succeeded by Father John Daniels who cared for the well organized parish community until 1977.

Father Theodore Mens arrived in 1977, a young and energetic man of thirty-six years who would become known as a parish builder in both the physical and spiritual sense. He renovated the rectory, and the parish hall which would be named Father Stephan Memorial Hall in honor of the parish founder. He would also breathe new life in the Religious Education program and spur the parish societies into greater activity. Father Mens supervised the construction of the new All Saints Hall in 1982 with most of the work done by the parishioners.

In 1985, the parish warmly received its present pastor, Father William Spranger, a pious gentleman who would soon assist the community in coping with the tragedy of the devastating fire of their one-hundred two year old church. The fire occurred on 12 August 1988, gutting the sacristy and destroying most of its contents. Parish archives stored in the basement were saved but the building was considered a total loss and would be replaced. Until the new building was completed, the community celebrated mass in the chapel of the Little Company of Mary Health Facility in the north end of the town and later in the parish hall.

The church would soon be replaced due to the energy and hard work of the parish community, which would be able to celebrate the important events of their lives within its walls, and would be happy to add to those occasions the golden jubilee of their pastor, which they celebrated in June of 2006.

SAINT ELIZABETH ANN SETON

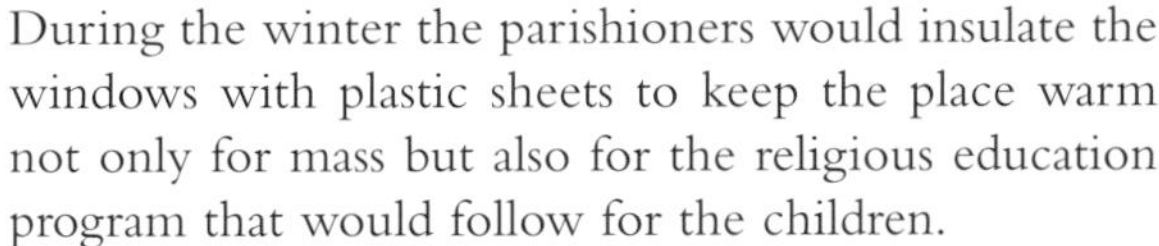

The area southeast of Valparaiso at the edge of Porter County was known as Lake Eliza. It was a farming community but also, with its small lake, became a resort area in the 1940s for Chicagoans. In 1958 Marie Beasly donated twenty acres and a house on her property to the diocese in the hope that one day a parish would be established there. The house would serve as the original rectory, but the parish would eventually be built one mile to the east.

The 1960s and 70s witnessed the development of both Lakes of the Four Seasons and Shorewood Forest, subdivisions that would bring thousands of new residents to the area, with Lake Eliza being the center of the development.

A committee was formed in the seventies and presented a proposal to Bishop Grutka who approved of the plan in 1977. Father John Savio would become the first resident pastor, organizing the community, and with the help of the Fitzgerald family who had provided for a priest to celebrate mass in the summer for the campers who came to their resort at Lake Eliza, the dance hall would be provided the year 'round to the parish until such time that a church would be built. Father Savio celebrated the first mass there in April 1978, for approximately one-hundred families. During the winter the parishioners would insulate the windows with plastic sheets to keep the place warm not only for mass but also for the religious education program that would follow for the children.

The parish grew to approximately four-hundred fifty families by 1979 when a pledge drive began. On 18 July 1982, Bishop Grutka dedicated the completed church. By this time the parish had grown to seven hundred families.

Father Savio was succeeded by Father Gerald Sroka who became pastor in 1983. During his tenure the new rectory was built and a large parish hall that also serves as the Religious Education Center. The parish has developed a fine tradition of religious education for their community. Father Sroka was succeeded in 1997 by the present pastor, Father David Gosnell. During his pastorate the community has continued to take seriously the mission of evangelization. In 1998 the parish witnessed the establishment of the newest parish in the diocese, Holy Spirit.

Our Lady of Sorrows

Monsignor Clement Mlinarovich, the pastor of Assumption Parish in Indiana Harbor, when offered one hundred acres of land in Porter County if a school would be built, contacted the Slovak Franciscans in Pennsylvania to see if they were interested. The Franciscans arrived in 1930 and began their foundation dedicated to the patroness of Slovakia, the Mother of Sorrows. This was the foundation of what would be known as Seven Dolors Shrine. For Slovak immigrants in the area, particularly Lake County, the Shrine became a magnet as a place of pilgrimage. A grotto was built, along with Stations of the Cross and Stations of the Seven Sorrows of the Blessed Virgin. An outdoor altar was erected in honor of Saint Francis. The Shrine was dedicated by Bishop Noll on 10 May 1931, with, according to newspaper reports, fifteen thousand people in attendance. It was not an uncommon site to see hundreds of people on a Sunday afternoon, visiting the shrines with their families and later having a picnic lunch in the grove.

In 1935 the original chapel and friary were completed, and the Friars continued to develop the rest of the property, adding a guest house in 1941, and a retreat house in 1942. The present church was begun in 1958 and dedicated on 4 July 1959.

With the building of the Bethlehem Steel Plant, the area began to develop and as people settled in the once sparsely populated area, Catholics found it convenient to attend mass at the Shrine rather than attend a parish church in Valparaiso or Chesterton.

In 1967 Bishop Grutka approached the Friars and asked if they would be willing to become a parish. With their agreement, the parish was established and named Our Lady of Sorrows, to differentiate it from the Shrine.

The first pastor was the Guardian of the Friary, Father Joseph Portasik. He would be succeeded by Father James Pajkos (1968-1977, and 1988-1989), Father Mark Manczak (1977-1980), Father Damian Cesanek (1980-1985), Father Robert Mancini (1985-1988), Father John Joseph Gonchar (1989-1992) and Father Michael Lenz (1992-1996).

In 1996, because of a decline in vocations, the Franciscans of the Slovak Custody were given a choice of amalgamating with other Franciscan provinces or pulling back and concentrating on the State of Pennsylvania where most of their foundations were. They chose the latter. The buildings and thirteen acres of property were sold to the diocese, and the current and first diocesan pastor, Father Douglas Mayer assumed pastoral responsibilities on 26 December 1996.

The parish is an active community that is dedicated to the religious education of their children, works of charity, prayerful liturgies, and community building. The monthly Fish Fry, popular with the parishioners, also draws a large crowd from surrounding communities.

SAINT PAUL

Valparaiso was visited by Holy Cross priests from Notre Dame almost from the very beginning of their arrival in 1842. By 1858 there were about twenty families that would comprise the congregation of the new parish. Holy Cross Father Paul Gillen would build a frame church not far from the business district and name the parish after his own patron, Saint Paul. For brief periods, Father John Force and Father G. Hamilton would succeed him until 1859. Succeeding pastors would be Father J. Alexis Botti (1859-1862) and Father Michael O'Reilly (1863-1887). Father O'Reilly would build a school in 1867 which would be staffed by Sisters of Holy Cross. He would also build the rectory in 1870, the convent in 1872, and the large gothic church in 1883 that would remain in use until the present church was built some eighty years later. Upon his death in 1887 he would be succeeded by:

- Father John Dempsey (1887-1898),
- Father L. A. Moench (1898-1903),
- Father William Hogan (1903-1915),
- Father Edward Mungovan (1915-1929),
- Father John Sullivan (1929-1942),
- Father Francis Guerre (1942-1947),
- Father Raymond Derrick (1947-1958),
- Monsignor Edward Sweigart (1958-1966),
- Monsignor John Charlebois (1966-1998),
- and Father Joseph M. Pawlowski (1998-).

During his tenure the new church would be built at its present location in the north of the city. The school, rectory and parish offices would remain downtown. The Sisters would withdraw from the school in 1987. Monsignor Charlebois expanded the ministries in the parish, developing a clothing distribution center and day care for the young as well as the elderly. He completely remodeled the parish church in 1991. He added a new wing to the church housing parish offices, a chapel, and meeting rooms. Upon his retirement in 1998, he was succeeded by the current pastor Father Joseph Pawlowski. Currently the parish is building a new Education Center on the present site of the parish.

Sacred Heart

In 1887, German and Irish Catholic families of the Wanatah area established the Church of the Most Precious Blood. Father Dominic Shunk, C.PP.S. was the first resident pastor from 1887-1897. The name of the parish was changed in 1911 to Sacred Heart when diocesan priests were given charge of the community.

In 1888 Father Shunk built a frame church and school. The Sisters of the Precious Blood staffed the school until 1904 when the school was closed due to a reduced enrollment. In its place a church hall was built in 1980 which is presently used for both church and community purposes. Religious education for the parish was continued by the various pastors and in 1950, Missionary Sisters of Our Lady of Victory instructed the youth. Since the 1960s the parish has had a highly successful Religious Education Program staffed by lay persons of the parish.

In 1898, Father A. M. Buchheit was appointed by Bishop Rademacher. He remained at the parish until 1906. Subsequent pastors include:

- Father John Rech (1906),
- Father John Oberholz (1907-1911),
- Father E. G. Werling (1911-1917),
- Father Theodore Hammes (1917-1922),
- Father Leo Faurote (1922-1930),
- Father Paul Anderson (1930-1932),
- Father Theophilus Chemma (1932-1939),
- Father John Steger (1939-1948),
- Father Michael Kelner (1948-1971),
- Father William Peil (1971-1976, 1978-1983),
- Father Timothy Benante (1976-1978),
- Father David Gosnell (1983-1989),
- Father Robert Tokarz (1989-1992),
- Father Lawrence Kew (1992-1994), and the present pastor
- Father Gerald Schweitzer (1994-to present) who also serves as Dean of the Porter-Starke Deanery since 1995.

The original church, built by John L. Conboy, still stands. Renovations to the church itself have been ongoing since 1914 when a flat ceiling was raised to the present arched interior and the stained glass windows were installed. Other changes include everything from the removal of the original altar and communion rail to the commissioning of an oil painting of the Sacred Heart above the tabernacle, to the restoring of the stained glass windows, to new carpeting and padded seats. A new altar was consecrated by Bishop Dale Melczek on 22 December 2002.

Youth groups from junior high through high school are also part of the education program in the parish. In addition, there is an active RCIA program. Adult formation and Bible classes are also offered. Parish Council and Commissions function throughout the year along with the choir, ladies group, the rosary makers, and the Knights of Columbus.

A St. Vincent de Paul building is the newest addition to the parish grounds dedicated by Bishop Melczek on 14 August 2005. A chapter of the organization was begun just seven years earlier on 16 August 1998.

Sacred Heart Parish is a growing community which presently consists of over four hundred families. Father Phillip Gilbert, C.PP.S. from Saint Joseph College in Rensselaer has assisted the parish since 1978.

Holy Spirit

Because of the population explosion that has continued in the south Lake County area, Bishop Melczek directed Father Joseph Murphy to organize a parish in Winfield Township in July of 1996, to relieve the overcrowding at both Saint Elizabeth Seton parish in Valparaiso and Saint Mary in Crown Point. Father Murphy would reside for the time being at Saint Elizabeth, until the daughter parish would be formally organized.

The parish would be situated on thirteen acres at 109th Avenue. Father Murphy envisioned a thriving, enthusiastic community of faith, whose mission would be "to make Christ real in the world" by the way they lived their faith in everyday life.

Father Murphy hosted a meeting in September of 1996, inviting all who were interested in learning more about the new parish. He presented the idea of gathering in small groups that would meet in homes to pray and to discuss the new parish. Ten small groups formed and met at regular intervals. These meetings proved to be the tie that would bind together a new community of faith.

On Sunday, 8 December 1996, one hundred families gathered at the Polish National Alliance Hall on Grand Boulevard to celebrate the first mass. On Pentecost Sunday, 18 May 1997, Bishop Melczek would celebrate mass with the new community, at which time he announced the parish would be placed under the patronage of the Holy Spirit.

As the community grew, a mass on Saturday was added and would be celebrated at the Christ Presbyterian Church on 109th Avenue.

The next Pentecost Sunday, 14 June 1998, Bishop Melczek would again celebrate mass with the community and announce the formal foundation of the parish. There was by this time a community of approximately three hundred fifty families.

The community has worked diligently to raise funds for a permanent church; ground was broken in 1999, and by Pentecost Sunday, 11 June 2000, the six hundred family parish would dedicate their church.

The community continues to grow filled with the Holy Spirit.